909 DAYS

THAT CHANGED THE WORLD

Anne & Jim,

Thank you for your
Support. Enjoy the book.

909 DAYS

THAT CHANGED THE WORLD

ROBERT J. DUNNE III

LEONINE PUBLISHERS
PHOENIX, ARIZONA

Published by Leonine Publishers LLC
P.O. Box 8099
Phoenix, Arizona 85066

ISBN-13: 978-0-9860552-7-0

Library of Congress Control Number: 2014937931

10 9 8 7 6 5 4 3 2 1

Printed in the United States of America

Visit us online at www.leoninepublishers.com
For more information: info@leoninepublishers.com

Dedication

To my wife, Paula,
and our three wonderful children:
Christina, Robb, and Nicole

Table of Contents

Preface

For most of us, what we know about Jesus is shaped by the readings from the gospels we hear at church on a weekly basis, or maybe for the more adventurous among us, from reading the New Testament on our own from time to time. But even for the most devout, doesn't it seem as if we hear the same stories, the same parables over and over again? And doesn't it almost come to the point where we tune out the readings with the excuse, "I know how this one ends"? We hear the same bits and pieces about Jesus' life, but most of us don't know the full context in which these events of his life take place. We don't know the framework or the particular circumstances surrounding the events about which we are hearing or reading. When did this part of Jesus' ministry take place? What took place right before and right after this event in Jesus' life? How could these people react this way? How do the stories and events of Jesus' life as chronicled by Matthew, Mark, Luke, and John all tie together? As a result of not knowing many of these details, much like bits and pieces we hear about current political figures, we don't really think much about Jesus as a flesh-and-blood man—highlights, yes; parables, yes; miracles, yes; God, yes; but man, not so much.

But Jesus was a real man who lived for about thirty-three years some two thousand years ago. He was flesh and blood. He was God, and he was a man, and of those thirty-three years he lived on earth, there were about two and a half years (909 days) when his deeds, actions, and words were, years after he lived and died and resurrected, recorded for all to read. Although there have been many others who have written a "chronological" history of Jesus' life, it seems to me most of them are either too long or too complicated for the "average" Christian to read and follow. It is the goal of this book to provide a chronological timeline of Jesus' public life that will give the reader both a framework of Jesus' ministry as well as help give a better understanding of Jesus as man.

This book very heavily relies upon Rev. Alban Goodier's *The Public Life of Jesus Christ*, printed by P.J. Kennedy and Sons in 1944. Much of the chronology and descriptions have been taken from that book. Other sources include the gospels of the New Testament, *Gospel Parallels* by Burton Throckmorton, *Harper's Bible Commentary*, as well as the personal ruminations of this author. Although it is well established the gospels were not written as strict historical accounts, there seems to be enough internal and external evidence to recreate most of the events of the two and a half years of Jesus' public life in a chronology that is between 75% and 90% accurate. It is not the goal of this book to attempt to fill in the additional 10% to 25%, but rather to use what people more skilled than I generally agree on in order to get to know Jesus Christ as the man he was 2000 years ago.

When reading this book, I would suggest you do so a little at a time. There are seventy-five chapters. Read one chapter a day; take the weekends off. It will take you six months to finish it—a perfect amount of time. This book is not meant to be rushed through over a long weekend but rather one you should ponder as you read. How would you have reacted to these events if you were there with Jesus and the others? What would you have said to Jesus if you were with him? What is this part of the story saying to you about your life? Use your imagination and place yourself in the middle of each event. Read it with as few distractions as possible. I promise this: If you read it slowly and with honesty, it will have a significant impact on your life, not because of the skill of this writer, but because of the power of the man, Jesus.

I would like to thank my children, Christina, Robb, and Nicole, whom I love dearly, for their encouragement and support. A special thanks to Nicole for helping design the cover of the book. The biggest thanks go to my wife, Paula, for all her support, love, devotion, and inspiration. I am a lucky man to be married to her. It is to my wife and children that I dedicate this book. If there is one thing I have personally learned from contemplating the life of Jesus Christ, it is that people are more important than things. Of all the people in my life, my wife and children are the most important to me. I am grateful for my parents, who have gone on to their reward, and for my four siblings, Kevin, Sharon, Patty, and Jeff. It was in our home in

New Jersey where the seeds of this book were first planted. I would also like to thank my good friend, Tom Murphy, who proofread the manuscript and made many helpful suggestions. It would not be as complete a product if it were not for him. I would also like to thank the editor at Leonine Publishers for her careful, thoughtful work. I am sure that reflecting on and striving—albeit imperfectly—to exemplify the life of Jesus Christ will bring us the joy and fulfillment he wants us to have right here, right now.

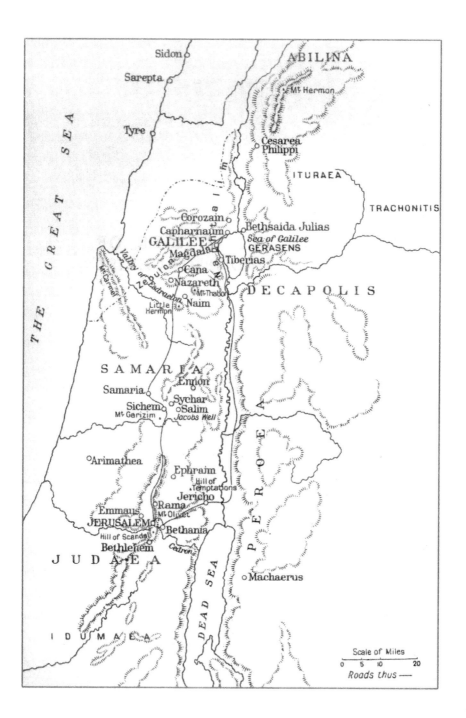

MAP OF PALESTINE CIRCA AD 30

his words, listening carefully and, if they have not done so already, getting in line to be baptized. Jesus is among the latter.

We can only imagine what must be going through Jesus' mind as he listens to John preach. He marvels at the fearlessness and wisdom of this man, his cousin, born of his Uncle Zachariah and his Aunt Elizabeth, the one who "leapt for joy" (Luke 1:44) in Elizabeth's womb when he heard the voice of Jesus' mother, Mary. They had seen much of each other as young boys, but as a young man, John left for the desert, where he lived for many years. Over those same years, Jesus spent his time as a young apprentice to his father and then, as he matured into manhood, as a well-regarded carpenter in Nazareth. While John lived an austere life as a hermit in the desert, Jesus lived an ordinary life in town. Yet the circumstances around John's birth, his father's being struck dumb, John's piercing and insightful words, and his way of life attracted other men, and so, in time, many became his disciples. Meanwhile, Jesus had drawn no attention in the village of Nazareth. For quite a while now, John and his disciples have taken up at this Jordan River crossing, preaching about the kingdom which is to come and the need for repentance. As Jesus watches and listens to John, he smiles with gratitude thinking about his cousin's preparing his way. Jesus knows this man is John, but would John recognize his cousin, Jesus, and more importantly, would he recognize Jesus as the one about whom he was preaching?

After finishing his exhortation to the caravan, John calls for all those who wish to be baptized to step towards him and his disciples—and many do so. Jesus remains at the back of the crowd and is the last one in line to be baptized by John. As Jesus enters the water to be baptized, John instantly recognizes his cousin, even though it has been years—a decade or so—since John has seen him. But what John also recognizes is that Jesus is in no need of baptism. His happiness at seeing his cousin is overcome by the realization that Jesus is much more than his cousin. John says to Jesus, "I need to be baptized by you, yet you are coming to me?" (Matt 3:14). By now, though, the crowd has subsided, they are all moving away, and no one hears Jesus tell John, "Allow it now, for thus it is fitting for us to fulfill all righteousness" (Matt 3:15). No one else sees or hears what happens next as the sky opens up and the "Spirit of God descends like a dove and rests over Jesus, and a voice from heaven states, 'This is my beloved son in whom I am well pleased'" (Matt 4:16-17). John, in a heartbeat, understands it all. Here is the one about whom he has been preaching. John's relentless drive to prepare the way for the Messiah has finally opened to him a revelation no one, other than Jesus' mother Mary, has yet to see. Jesus, his cousin, is the Messiah! Jesus and John look into each others' eyes with understanding. John's eyes overflow with happiness. Jesus puts his hands on John's shoulders and smiles broadly. They stand there and talk for a long time. Jesus waves on the caravan waiting for him on the other side of the Jordan, indicating that they should proceed along with the others. He will be chatting with John for a bit and will catch up with them shortly. And so, for some time, Jesus and John enjoy each others' company on the bank of the Jordan River. It is day one of the 909 days that will change the world forever.

CHAPTER TWO

Temptation in the Desert

As Jesus leaves the river, he rushes to catch up with the rest of the caravan on their way to Jerusalem. He has been recognized as the Messiah by John, but by no one else, so the caravan is not waiting for this one straggler. His mother Mary, traveling with the women of the caravan as is the normal custom, doesn't even realize Jesus has fallen behind. Exiting the water on the Judean side, Jesus breaks into a fast walk—almost a run—on the dry, dusty road trying to catch up. He never will.

A few miles along the road from the Jordan to Jerusalem, on the left, is the ancient, great city of Jericho, the same city surrounded by Aaron's men and taken down by the blast of trumpets well over a thousand years before. Off to the right there are a number of sharp rising hills. From the top of these hills, the terrain quickly turns into a barren desert that stretches for many, many miles into Samaria. The view is breathtaking as the Jordan River is visible back to the east and Jerusalem is visible to the west. Although he has almost caught up with the caravan, for some reason Jesus feels driven to abandon his chase. He stops, watches them begin to disappear in front of him, turns, and begins to climb up one of the hills. Getting to the top, he begins to pray, and feels impelled to spend more time in the desert. Mary, that very night when she can't find Jesus anywhere, realizes Jesus is no longer with the caravan. Someone says they noticed a man they thought might be Jesus climbing up the hills when they had left the Jordan. What is Mary to do? Not surprisingly, she immediately thinks back to the days when he was twelve and lost for three days. Having pondered that event many times over the years, she decides to continue on with the caravan towards Jerusalem for the Feast of Tabernacles. Jesus, as he told her and Joseph some eighteen years ago, "must be about his father's business," so she will trust him to catch up with her when he sees fit.

The caravan arrives in Jerusalem, the feast takes place, and there is still no sign of Jesus. Where can he be? What should she do? Should she wait in Jerusalem or go back with the caravan?

Mary decides to return to the Jordan with the Galilean caravan when the feast is over, but as she arrives there, she changes her mind and decides to wait for Jesus. Perhaps he is still in the desert? Perhaps he did go to Jerusalem but "was about his father's business" there and hasn't finished? She approaches her nephew John, asks him if he has seen Jesus, and when he responds he has not, she asks if there is a place she can stay to see if Jesus will be returning this way. Her heart is heavy, but as she looks into John's eyes and hears his tone of voice, she senses John is aware of the truth about her son. John tells her of a little shack along the Judean side of the riverbank where she can safely stay. This place is nothing more than a hut, one built long ago and now abandoned, consisting of one room, open windows, and a dirt floor—but John and his disciples will see to her safety and comfort. She graciously thanks him and bids farewell to her caravan as it continues to Galilee. Mary waits and, as she does so often, ponders in her heart what all these events can mean.

Jesus meanwhile ends up staying in the desert for forty days, fasting, and constantly in prayer. He is alone. After the forty days are over, he is visited by the devil, who attempts to take advantage of Jesus' hunger: "Command these stones be turned to bread" (Luke 4:3) he says to Jesus. In order to get Jesus to show his true powers, the devil urges him to "Throw yourself off the cliff and have your angels save you" (Luke 4:9); and most insidiously, he tries to get Jesus to take the easy way out: "If you only worship me, I will give you dominion over all the earth" (Luke 4:7). But Jesus will have none of it. He sends the devil on his way, knowing full well that within two and a half short years the devil will, apparently, have his final victory. But this victory will also be the devil's final defeat, and it will happen some thirty miles west of this spot on a hill outside of Jerusalem. For now, though, angels come and refresh him.

Meanwhile, all the time Jesus was in the desert, John is still baptizing at the ford of the Jordan River. Many more people are being baptized, and the chief priests and elders from Jerusalem are hearing so much about John they think it best to go and interview him. So after the feast is over, they send a number of priests, Pharisees—strict interpreters of the law—to question John. When they arrive, they find him and his disciples preaching to all those passing by. Dressed in all their finery as priests and therefore standing out from the others there, they ask to speak to him, and he complies. John's disciples and all those travelers present stop and turn their attention to this meeting between this wild-looking prophet and the well-schooled priests. Surely this will be very interesting....

"Are you a prophet or are you the Christ?" (John 1:21) they ask him, and respectfully he tells them he is neither the Messiah nor a prophet. "Well, then, who are you?" they ask. "I am the voice of one crying out in the desert, but there is one to come after me whose sandal I am not worthy to tie," (John 1:17) he responds. 'Well, the good news is that this man, John, is not declaring himself to be a prophet or the Messiah,' think the Pharisees to themselves. Content with this conviction, they decide to push him no farther, and John also seems content to let them take their leave, still as much in the dark about him as they were before they arrived. For their part, John's disciples and the others listening are a little confused at the abruptness of this meeting. It will get even more confusing for them as time goes on.

CHAPTER THREE

The First Disciples

A month and a half has passed since the day John saw Jesus cross to the Jerusalem side of the Jordan River, climb up the embankment, and then disappear down the road to that city. It is early December, day forty-five of the 909 days that changed the world. Mary is staying in the little shack along the Jordan waiting for Jesus. Many times a day since that afternoon when the Holy Spirit announced Jesus as his beloved son, John has looked over to the other side of the Jordan, waiting, hoping to see Jesus again.

Then one day, the very next day after John's meeting with the Pharisees, it happens. Jesus, coming down from the desert hills, having missed the Feast of Tabernacles in Jerusalem, has turned to the left, away from Jerusalem, and back towards the river. John's heart leaps as he sees Jesus on the embankment on the Judean side. Jesus comes to John and, as they embrace, asks, "Where is my mother?" John smiles and points out the path to the shack where Mary was staying. As Jesus goes to find his mother, John says to all his disciples who are within earshot, "Behold the Lamb of God" (John 1:36). Two of the disciples who are from Bethsaida—John, who will become "the beloved" apostle, and who will write the fourth gospel, and Andrew, Simon Peter's older brother—decide to take action. As the Feast of Tabernacles has long passed and the traffic crossing the Jordan is lighter now, there is plenty of time for these two disciples of John to examine this man, so they begin to follow Jesus down the path.

The path is full of bushes, big trees, and lots of vegetation, all relying on the waters of the river to sustain them. Because of the vegetation, Andrew and John have to hurry in order to catch up with Jesus as he winds his way down this path. But Jesus, slowing down to let them get closer, suddenly turns around, looks them both in the eyes, and says in a warm and inviting voice, "What are you looking for?" (John 1:38). They are both taken aback. It is not just the tone of his voice, but the look in his eyes. Never had these two seen anyone look at them in this way. His attention, his smile, his interest, yes, even his love for them, is evident in his eyes. It is as if the world is standing still and Jesus' only interest is in them. Nothing else seems to matter to him than their presence. And his question is one that immediately resonates in their hearts, as it does in all sincere hearts, not only in Jesus' time but even today. "What are you looking for?" Attempting to gather themselves, John and Andrew, unsure of what to say, respond, "Rabbi, where are you staying?" (John 1:38) and much to their delight, Jesus responds the same way to them as he does to all who seek him with a sincere heart: "Come and you will see" (John 1:39).

As they walk together down the path, their conversation is light and easy, with Jesus asking them questions about themselves. Shortly, they reach the place where Mary is staying. Mary runs out to greet Jesus, her smile as big as the relief she feels in her heart. Jesus hugs his mother, and they draw such joy from looking into each others' eyes; it is as if they were looking straight into the goodness of each others' souls. After that deep drink of love for and from each other, Jesus turns from Mary and focuses his attention back on Andrew and John. Although John doesn't tell us what they speak of, he does tell us "they saw where he lived and stayed with him the whole day" (John 1:39). We can only imagine their conversation, but we can be sure, as they work their way back down the path to cross the Jordan River again before nightfall, that the hearts of John and Andrew are burning inside them. Meeting this man has changed their lives. Little did they realize how much.

Upon returning to their camp on the Perea side of the river, Andrew, his heart on fire, finds his younger brother, Simon, and tells him, "We have found the Messiah" (John 1:41), the one for whom the Jewish people had been waiting and pining for so many centuries. Imagine, after spending just one afternoon with him and only by looking at and talking to him, Andrew is convinced Jesus is the Messiah—no miracles, no special signs, none of that. Simon, his curiosity piqued at the intensity of his brother's conviction, decides to see for himself. He will visit this Jesus tomorrow and make his own judgment about who this man is.

The next morning, Andrew and Simon wind their way down the same path to Jesus' little shack. He is home and hears them coming, and even before Andrew can introduce Simon, Jesus looks at Simon with those loving eyes and says, "You are Simon, son of Jonah. You will be called Peter" (John 1:42). Simon, much like his brother Andrew when he met Jesus yesterday, is taken aback. He came to make a judgment, yet finds himself with this strange sensation that this man, Jesus, not only knows everything about him, but has a profound care and concern for him. After spending some time with Jesus, they both return to their camp. How excited they both feel as they walk back along the path from Jesus' hut!

Right around the same time, a caravan of travelers crosses the Jordan River and, as they stop to rest, a young man from Bethsaida, Philip by name, sees John and Andrew, his fellow town mates from Bethsaida. John and Andrew tell him about Jesus, and Philip is moved to go see for himself. Shyly yet determinedly, he makes his way down the path towards Jesus' hut. Jesus sees him coming, their eyes meet, and those same eyes captivate Philip. Jesus merely says, "Follow me" (John 1:43), and Philip is on his way to becoming one of the beloved twelve apostles. Philip and Jesus then have a long conversation, while Philip marvels at how much Jesus seems to care for him. With his heart bursting with joy, Philip returns to his caravan.

One of the people with whom Philip has become friendly on this trip is Nathaniel, who is in the same caravan but who is from Cana. Philip pours out his heart to Nathaniel about Jesus. Nathaniel, however, being from Cana, a busier, more robust town, is a little more worldly and skeptical. Nathaniel sarcastically asks Philip, "Can anything good come from Nazareth?" Philip, knowing himself not to be a great debater, knowing Nathaniel to be a good man, and having just come to know Jesus, simply responds, "Come and see" (John 1:46). The simplicity of the reply piques Nathaniel's curiosity. So Nathaniel, like Peter before him, goes to see and judge this man Jesus for himself.

As Jesus sees Nathaniel approaching, he cries out. "Behold an Israelite in whom there is no guile" (John 1:47). Nathaniel is confused. "How do you know me?" (John 1:48) responds Nathaniel.

Jesus, looking deeply at him, replies, "I saw you under the fig tree before Philip called you" (John 1:48). Nathaniel is flabbergasted and wonders to himself, 'How did Jesus see me there? And why do I feel as if this man knows everything about me…and loves me just the same?' Nathaniel, like Peter before him, comes to judge but finds himself the one being judged. He comes to see if this man is worth his attention, and now finds Jesus' attention is required for his own happiness. How has this happened so quickly? Overwhelmed, Nathaniel utters these words, making him the first to announce Jesus' role: "Rabbi, thou art the Son of God and the King of Israel" (John 1:49). Those words lie heavily in the air and are not lost on the others standing there. It is a moment of special revelation, and Peter and Andrew, John, Philip, and Nathaniel (who will later come to be called "Bartholomew"), without realizing it, have all taken their first steps towards becoming five of Our Lord's twelve apostles.

CHAPTER FOUR

Wedding Feast at Cana

Having been reunited with her son, Mary watches and ponders as she sees and hears her son interact with these disciples of John the Baptist over the next few days. As she has spent much more time in Judea than she had originally planned, she reminds Jesus of the wedding feast in Cana to which they have been invited. Their original plan had been to return to Nazareth after the Feast of Tabernacles and then go to Cana a few weeks later, but now with time short, it seems best to go directly to Cana via the rougher yet more direct road through Samaria. Jesus agrees and suggests to some of his newfound friends that they return to Galilee with him and his mother via the Samaria route. It is a rugged journey from the Jordan River to Cana, but it passes quickly, as Jesus' new friends very much enjoy traveling with him. They run into no problems with the Samaritans as they pass through the country. When they get to Cana, however, the wedding feast has already begun. The host graciously and warmly greets Mary and Jesus and invites Jesus' friends to join the party. Weddings are indeed a thing of great celebration and the more guests in attendance the better. Being from Cana, perhaps Nathaniel had already been invited to the wedding. In any case, they all enter and enjoy the wedding feast.

As the party progresses, Mary, the delicate woman of details that she is, notices something. She sees a concerned conversation taking place between the bridegroom and the wine steward. She quickly realizes the supply of wine is running low. Knowing how embarrassing it would be for the bridegroom and his family to run out of wine, Mary approaches Jesus, touches him on the shoulder, steps up on her toes to reach his ear, and whispers, "They have no wine" (John 2:3). What is Mary expecting him to do? He obviously takes her comment very seriously. He turns and looks at her as he responds, "Woman, what is that to you and me? Don't you know my hour has not yet come?" (John 2:4). But Mary, making the perfect prayer by just putting the issue in Jesus' hands and allowing him to do what he wills, turns to some of the waiters and tells them, "Do whatever he asks" (John 2:5). Mary has asked, not for something for herself but for others. Her son will grant her wish.

Jesus asks the waiters to fill the jars with water and take the jars to the wine steward. The waiters feel foolish taking jars of water to the wine steward to taste. Likely it is those piercing yet friendly eyes of Jesus that convince them to do so. In any case, if the wine steward spits out the water, they can just say this man Jesus told them to do this. The waiters react in amazement when the wine steward tastes the wine, instantly calls for the bridegroom, and tells him, "Everyone at first serves the good wine and then, after all are well served, offers the lesser wine, but you have saved the choicest wine until now" (John 2:10).

This news of Jesus' somehow turning the water into wine, an obvious foreshadowing of his turning wine into his own blood at his last supper some two years from now, spreads like wildfire among the wait staff. They all come by to surreptitiously catch a glimpse of this man. When the bridegroom realizes the wine supply is holding out, he approaches the wine steward to ask how he obtained the additional wine. Amazed at the story he hears from the wine steward, the bridegroom quietly pulls Jesus aside, saying, "I have no idea how you did this, but thank you for providing more wine for our wedding feast." Word begins to make way among the guests that something extraordinary has happened with the wine. Jesus' friends, his new disciples, noticing too what has just happened are also amazed and "believe in him" (John 2:11). As the focus of the party begins to shift more towards Jesus and what he has done, he gathers his new friends and his mother, bids good-bye to the family and the happy newly-wed couple, and leaves the celebration. He does not want to take any attention away from the bride and groom on their big day. It is mid-December—day fifty-four of the 909 days that will change the world, and this is the first recorded miracle. Taking place as it does during a wedding feast, it speaks volumes about Jesus' concern for the importance and sanctity of marriage.

Although the gospel of John states that Jesus and his mother depart for Capernaum, on leaving the wedding feast they likely first turn west and go back to Nazareth, at least for a short while. Nathaniel stays in Cana, and Andrew, Peter, John, Philip, and the others go back east to their homes surrounding the Sea of Galilee. It is early winter, and the rainy season has begun. Jesus tells his disciples he will see them again in Capernaum in a few months when he will make the trip to Jerusalem once again for the solemn feast of Passover. For now, though, it is time for everyone to return to their homes, their families, and their normal work activity. We can only imagine how the hearts of these new disciples are burning within them as they say good-bye to Jesus. What thoughts about Jesus will they have in the months ahead? They will not be able to get him out of their minds and heart. Is Jesus indeed the Messiah they were all waiting for? Did he really turn water into wine?

Jesus, for his part, returns to Nazareth, takes up his carpentry tools, and continues his trade as he had been doing for the last fifteen years or so of his life. He has been away for a while, and there are now some stories circulating about his doing something extraordinary at a wedding in Cana, but Jesus just smiles and appears to be the same friendly, honest, competent carpenter he has always been. There are many people who are looking for him to do carpentry jobs for them—after all, he has been away for some time. The stories die down, and life in Nazareth continues on as it has for years.

CHAPTER FIVE

The First Paschal Visit to Jerusalem

As the rainy season subsides and winter turns into spring, the flowers and plants begin to grow again, nourished by the winter water. The solemn feast of Passover is approaching. It is mid-March. Jesus and Mary make plans with their family members to go to Tiberias, on the west side of the Sea of Galilee, which serves as a meeting place for Galileans traveling to Judea for the Paschal celebration. The path of the pilgrims will take them down the west side of the Sea of Galilee, crossing the Jordan River into Decapolis just below the point where the Sea ends. They will then travel along the western back of the Jordan through the rest of Decapolis and into Perea, crossing back into Judea just south of Jericho on the east side of the river. When Jesus and his family arrive at Tiberias, they make camp, looking to add others to their caravan for safety and convenience' sake. Although not specifically mentioned in the gospels but implied by the actions that later take place, it is likely Jesus meets up with some (maybe all) of his early disciples (John, Andrew, Peter, Philip, Nathaniel). Not having seen Jesus in about three months, their joy in seeing him knows no bounds, and they jump at his suggestion to travel in his caravan to Jerusalem.

It is day 153 of the 909 days that changed the world, and as the caravan begins its journey, crossing the Jordan River into Decapolis, they are greeted by John the Baptist and his disciples. Since the time John met Jesus some five months ago, he and his disciples have moved up the Jordan River to this crossing. John the Evangelist in his gospel reports, "John was…baptizing in Aenon near Salim" (John 3:23), a place that no longer exists but that many believe was up the Jordan River at this crossing. Once again, John points out Jesus to his disciples and any others within earshot as Jesus and his caravan pass them by. John's endorsement of Jesus stirs the interest of those traveling in Jesus' caravan. Who is this man? Why is John acting this way towards him? As the caravan passes John and moves on down the east side of the Jordan, Jesus' early disciples also eagerly point him out to many of their own friends. Echoing Philip's words to Nathaniel, they tell their friends in the caravan to come and see. "This is the one we have been telling you about." Many do come to meet him, and most are impressed with how he speaks, how he interprets things, but above all, how his eyes seem to speak an unconditional concern for each. They hear it in his voice and see it in his actions, but they are mostly taken by the concern for each of them individually, which seems so evident in his eyes.

The three days' journey down the Perea side of the Jordan River seems to go quickly for all those who have met Jesus. The caravan is abuzz. There are no miracles, yet he speaks with such authority, and his eyes are so riveting. Then there is talk of what he did at a wedding in Cana a few months ago. By the time they are ready to cross back again into Judea, many more people are asking themselves if this man Jesus is actually more than just a carpenter from Nazareth. When the caravan gets near Jerusalem, some continue on into the city to stay with family or friends but most pitch camp in and around Mt. Olivet, which lies a short walk from the Golden Gate entrance of the city. Jesus, Mary, and other members of their extended family make their camp and, as is the custom, as soon as they are set up, leave to enter the city and visit the temple.

Making the short walk to the Golden Gate entrance, Jesus, with many others in tow, surveys the scene he has witnessed countless times before. Many follow him because they are curious to see how he is going to act when he gets into the city. His early disciples and a number of people he has met on the caravan are right behind and beside him as he goes under the arch of the Golden Gate. On immediately entering the city, there is a big, open courtyard before one gets to the temple. As always is the case during festivals, this space is disorganized, filled with festival mercantile activity. There are those who are selling all kinds of animals to be used as a sacrifice at the temple. The courtyard is filled with the bleating of goats and sheep, the groaning of oxen, the shouts of their owners driving them here and there and offering them to the newly-arrived pilgrims. Filth and noise are everywhere. Back in the corners, for those who could not afford larger animals, there are others who are offering turtle doves, rows of the birds crowded in cages. Amidst all this confusion and cacophony, sitting behind tables close to the gates, are the money changers, coldly calculating and watching the goings on. Not only are they there to change money for foreigners but also to keep an eye on all transactions to make sure the temple is getting its fair share of the profits. Today, however, they are going to see something very different.

Suddenly, as if he is on a mission, Jesus bends down and picks up one of the small whips used by oxen owners, stretches out his arms, cracks the whip to get the attention of those merchants closest to him, and with a look of authority never seen by these people before, begins to drive them back away from him towards the temple. Jesus, before pressing forward more, turns around and kicks over the tables of the money changers, spilling their coins all over the place in the muck and mud of the courtyard. Turning back towards the other merchants, eyes flashing, he presses forward. Many attempting to gather their wares and animals run into others who see the same look in Jesus' eyes. A near-panic fills the courtyard. Jesus comes up to some of those selling turtle doves and, with his glance somewhat softened towards these people who, unlike the coldhearted money changers and other unscrupulous merchants, are not the major violators, says, "Take these things out of here, and stop making my Father's house a marketplace" (John 2:16). They rush to obey him, grabbing as many cages as they can, and rush away from him towards the temple. This is truly the most amazing scene: one man, with a small whip, by the sheer force of his presence has emptied the courtyard of all the merchants. Imagine the thoughts of those recent followers of Jesus as they stand behind him and watch this scene unfold. Indeed, we do get insight from St. John as to what they were thinking: "His disciples recalled the words of scripture; zeal for your house will consume me" (John 2:17). We can imagine these followers looking at one another and saying once again that perhaps this man is indeed destined for great things.

At the other side of the courtyard on the steps of the temple, the chief priests and leaders are indignant, hearing the noise of the panic and seeing the merchants fleeing. Who is this man driving these people out? On what authority is he doing this? Some of the more worldly of them become quite angry as they realize this panic will hurt the finances of the temple. But as Jesus approaches them, they too see the look of authority in his eyes, so, rather than attacking him, they ask, "What sign can you show us for doing this?" (John 2:18). Jesus, lowering his hands to his side, looks at them with a combination of respect and disdain—respect because they are the religious leaders of his people whom he has come to save; disdain because he knows the hardness of their hearts. He decides to answer them in a way they will not now understand but will come to understand later. "Destroy this temple and in three days I will raise it up" (John 2:19). The leaders are baffled. What could he mean? One Pharisee, voicing the thoughts of them all, mockingly replies, "This temple was under construction for forty-six years, and you will raise it up in three days?" (John 2:20). The sarcasm is thick in his voice. These leaders of the Jews dismiss Jesus and turn away, but, for those of good heart, the scene that has just taken place and that look of authority in Jesus' eyes make them wonder. Indeed, some of them who have made eye contact with him feel a strange yearning in their hearts. One of those leaders is Nicodemus.

Nicodemus, a Pharisee and a member of the Sanhedrin, is one of those rare men who, although in a position of power and authority, is not content to champion the status quo. Lover and interpreter of the law as he is, he yet feels the need to go deeper than the externals of the law. He is looking for more than rituals and customs. Nicodemus has been out to see John baptizing in the Jordan, and John's words have captivated him. He has heard John say the kingdom of God is at hand, and he has wondered not only when, but how and through whom this would take place. Watching the goings on in the temple area this day, and having met Jesus' eyes with his own, he has been stirred to the core. Could this be the man through whom the kingdom of God will come? He decides to make inquiries about this man among the people. He goes into the city streets, abuzz with the goings on of the day, and looks for someone who can tell him more about this man. Seeing a group of Galileans, he approaches them and, with a certain air of disinterest so as to not give himself away, asks what they know about Jesus. He hears nothing but gushing reports. "Never has one spoken with such authority." "Did you see his power over all the people in the courtyard?" "His eyes shine with such intensity of interest when he is speaking with me." "Did you hear what he did at a wedding feast in Cana a few months ago?"

'Yes,' Nicodemus thinks to himself, 'never has one spoken with such authority, and yes, I did see his power today, and yes, there is something so unique about the way he looked at me.' So when he is told about Jesus' turning water into wine at the wedding feast in Cana, he resolves to go meet the man himself.

Saint John makes note that Nicodemus comes to meet Jesus "at night" (John 3:1). Although stirred to know more about Jesus, Nicodemus is careful not to appear as if he is fully sold on this man, as many of these Galileans seem to be. No, better to go at night; better to be a little cautious. So having inquired as to where Jesus is camped outside of the city, Nicodemus does not dress in his Pharisee finery but dons ordinary clothes to draw no special attention to himself and slips out of the city to make the short trip to see him.

After walking out the Golden Gate, across the bridge spanning the Kidron, and ascending up the west side of Mt. Olivet, Nicodemus finds Jesus with only a few people around his small campfire. Nicodemus is immediately taken aback as Jesus looks him in the eyes and invites him to sit down. Nicodemus can almost sense his belief in this man growing stronger at that moment. "Rabbi," he says, "we know that you are a teacher who has come from God, for no one can do these signs you are doing unless God is with him" (John 3:2). Jesus, acknowledging Nicodemus' budding faith, but realizing he is dealing with a learned Pharisee and wanting to impress upon him the importance of faith in Jesus, the God/Man, and not in laws, rituals or even intelligence, decides to challenge him further. "Amen, Amen, I say to you, no one can see the kingdom of God without being born again" (John 3:3). Interestingly, the word used for "again" in the ancient Greek is "anothen" which also can mean "from above." Nicodemus has chosen to interpret Jesus' "anothen" as meaning "again" and so, learned scholar that he is, finds himself confused. What can this man mean? What kind of nonsense is he talking about? With these questions rattling around in his head, his faith held in check for the moment, Nicodemus asks, "How can a person grown old be born again? Surely he cannot re-enter his mother's womb and be born again, can he?" (John 3:4). It is a question from a man who wants to believe, but finds there are some apparent intellectual contradictions that shake his faith. Jesus responds by showing Nicodemus how he is using the word "anothen." He is not referring to being born again of the flesh, but being born from above: "You must be born from above" (John 3:7). You must be "born of the Spirit" (John 3:8). Although still not fully comprehending what Jesus is saying, at least now Nicodemus feels some relief, for, like many will do over the ensuing centuries down to our day, he realizes that his faith in this man and his reason are not opposed to each other. Still, he wants to know more and so asks, "How can this happen?" (John 3:9). Knowing Nicodemus has made great strides in his faith, Jesus decides to challenge his faith even more. It is he, Jesus, who gives testimony to the truth and to eternal life, with the implication being that truth and eternal life are not found in man-made rituals and laws. And in words Nicodemus will wistfully recall one day, Jesus says, "And just as Moses lifted up the serpent in the desert, so must the Son of Man be lifted up so that everyone who believes in him may have eternal life" (John 3:14-15). No one responds as Jesus looks to be in deep thought. For a moment all that can be heard is the normal conversational noise coming from near-by campsites. Finally though, Jesus focuses back on Nicodemus and asks him about his wife and family. Nicodemus is touched all the more by his apparent genuine concern for his family members.

After fifteen minutes or so, Nicodemus takes his leave of Jesus and slowly, in deep thought, walks back into the city. We can only imagine how this meeting has stirred his heart, his mind, and his soul—so much to ponder and think about. Nicodemus knows one thing, though: he will never be the same for having met this man. Exactly what that means, he is not yet sure, but he and his wife stay up late into the night discussing what Nicodemus feels stirring in his heart.

CHAPTER SIX

Jesus in Judea;
Cure of the Beggar at the Pool;
John Arrested

As the Paschal feast ends, caravans organize themselves to begin the journey back home. As we know, John the Baptist and his disciples have abandoned baptizing at the ford of the Jordan River just east of Jericho and have moved up the river below the Sea of Galilee. As Jesus' caravan makes its way east from Mt. Olivet and towards the Jordan River, Jesus tells his mother first, and then his followers later, that he is going to stay at the Jordan crossing, taking up the preaching and baptizing that John had been performing there. He invites many of those who have become his followers to stay with him. Many want to stay, and some do, but most, with heavy hearts, have to return to Galilee as work and other duties call them home. Jesus and those who remain with him stay there a long time: from late March into the summer month of July, as the gospel says he "spent some time with them baptizing" (John 3:22). However, what draws more attention to Jesus is a trip from the Jordon to Jerusalem during the Feast of Pentecost in May.

In the northeast part of the city outside of its walls is a pool called Bethsaida. This pool is known to have magical powers, and there are many ill people who congregate there. When the water of the pool is stirred up, the first one in the water is cured of his ailment. Jesus happens by the pool on a Sabbath during the Feast of Pentecost and engages in conversation with a man who has been there for thirty-eight years. Jesus looks at him and, moved by his condition, asks, "Do you want to be well?" (John 5:6). The man looks with sadness at Jesus and replies, "Sir, I have no one to put me into the pool when the water is stirred up; while I am on my way, someone else gets there before me" (John 5:7). Jesus gives him a concerned look and says, "Rise, take up your mat, and walk" (John 5:8). Immediately the man feels a huge difference in his body, his muscles responding in a way he cannot remember. He stands up, lets out a cry of happiness, bows towards Jesus while thanking him, picks up his mat, and runs to show his family this miracle.

As the man is running home, some Pharisees nearby stop him and admonish him for carrying his mat on a Sabbath. The man looks at them with puzzlement—they are making a stupid point; what difference does it make? He has been cured—but decides not to challenge them. He responds, "The man who made me well told me 'Take up your mat and walk'" (John 5:12). When they ask him who the man is who cured him, the cured man realizes he doesn't even know the miracle worker's name, so he turns back towards the pool, but Jesus is nowhere to be found. He has slipped away in all the excitement. Later that afternoon, however, Jesus finds the healed man in the temple courtyard. He approaches the man, who stands up and beams at Jesus. Jesus tells him his name and then continues, "Look, you are well; do not sin anymore, so that nothing worse will happen to you" (John 5:14). It is an interesting comment. Does Jesus really mean this man's poor condition was because of a sin he committed? Perhaps the sin he committed was the cause of his malady, but either way Jesus' comment is certainly meant to stir the man on to be more virtuous. From other things he will say later in his ministry, however, it is clear that illnesses and bad luck are not always the direct result of personal sin. As Jesus continues walking on, the healed man runs over to the temple steps and points out Jesus to the Pharisees standing there. They, of course, recognize Jesus instantly and call him over, criticizing him for telling the man to carry his mat on the Sabbath. Turning around and walking slowly back towards the temple steps, Jesus says to them in a loud voice, "My Father is at work until now, so I am at work" (John 5:17). Then waving his arms as if letting everyone know he wants them to hear these words, he faces the Pharisees and launches into a long challenge against these Jewish leaders.

"Amen, amen, I say to you, a son cannot do anything on his own, but only what he sees his father doing; for what he does, his son will also do. For the Father loves the Son and shows him greater works than these, so that you may be amazed. For just as the Father raises the dead and gives life, so also does the Son give life to whomever he wishes. Nor does the Father judge anyone, but he has given all judgment to his Son, so that all may honor the Son just as they honor the Father. Whoever does not honor the Son does not honor the Father who sent him. Amen, amen, I say to you, whoever hears my word and believes in the one who sent me has eternal life and will not come to condemnation, but has passed from death to life. Amen, amen, I say to you, the hour is coming and is now here when the dead will hear the voice of the Son of God, and those who hear will live. For just as the Father has life in himself, so also he gave to his Son the possession of life in himself. And he gave him power to exercise judgment, because he is the Son of Man. Do not be amazed at this, because the hour is coming in which all who are in the tombs will hear his voice and will come out, those who have done good deeds to the resurrection of the life, but those who have done wicked deeds to the resurrection of condemnation.

"I cannot do anything on my own; I judge as I hear, and my judgment is just, because I do not seek my own will but the will of the one who sent me.

"If I testify on my own behalf, my testimony cannot be verified. But there is another who testifies on my behalf, and I know that the testimony he gives on my behalf is true. You sent emissaries to John, and he testified to the truth. I do not accept testimony from a human being, but I say this so that you may be saved. He was like a burning and shining lamp, and for a while you were content to rejoice in his light. But I have testimony greater than John's. The works that the Father gave me to accomplish, these works that I perform testify on my behalf that the Father has sent me. Moreover, the Father who sent me has testified on my behalf. But you have never heard his voice nor seen his form, and you do not have his word remaining in you, because you do not believe in the One whom he has sent. You search the scriptures, because you think you have eternal life through them; even they testify on my behalf. But you do not want to come to me to have life.

"I do not accept human praise; moreover, I know that you do not have the love of God in you. I came in the name of my Father, but you do not accept me; yet if another comes in his own name, you will accept him. How can you believe, when you accept praise from one another and do not seek the praise that comes from the only God? Do not think that I will accuse you before the Father; the one who will accuse you is Moses, in whom you have placed your hope. For if you believed Moses, you would have believed me, because he wrote about me. But if you do not believe his writings, how will you believe my words?" (John 5:19-47).

It is a blistering challenge, and the Pharisees shake with anger. How dare this man compare himself to God! How dare he attempt to pass judgment on them! They are the leaders, not he. But Jesus' voice and command is so strong they are unable to respond, and so they say nothing, and turn their backs on him. Walking back into the temple, they talk among themselves about the need to get rid of, even kill this Jesus, not only because he has broken the Sabbath, but also because he is calling God his Father and therefore making himself equal to God (John 5:19), not to mention the way he challenges their authority. Jesus watches them walk away, turns around, and works his way back out the Golden Gate, returning to the Jordan River, where he and his disciples will continue to baptize. It has been a momentous day, and the Jewish leaders will be all the more intent now on finding a way to eliminate Jesus.

Meanwhile up the river, John and his disciples continue to baptize also, but as word of the number of people being baptized by Jesus and his disciples comes to John's camp, his disciples "come to John and say, 'Rabbi, the one who was with you across the Jordan, to whom you testified—here he is baptizing, and everyone is coming to him'" (John 3:26). The tone of their voices indicate a genuine concern for their leader, and a questioning as to what this means for them individually, and perhaps just a tinge of jealousy about Jesus' success. John's response, however, is one of total humility. "You yourselves can testify that I said I am not the Messiah, but that I was sent before him…. He must increase; I must decrease" (John 3:28-30). Yes, his listeners all agree to themselves, John has told us all along he is not the Messiah, and, yes, he has even pointed Jesus out as a special man, but these last words of his—"He must increase; I must decrease"— leave little doubt in their minds, with some sadness attached to the conclusion, that John's ministry is on the wane. Nevertheless, John continues to preach boldly, unafraid of the consequences. For this, he will pay the ultimate price.

Where John is baptizing and preaching is a favorite spot for the tetrarch, Herod, to cross the Jordan from Machaerus, his mountain castle just east of the Dead Sea, to Magdala, a busy and worldly seaport, where he, his wife, and entourage like to spend a good part of the cooler times of the year. When the weather gets warm again, they cross the river at the same spot and return to Machaerus. Herod, although a Jew, is a political and moral abomination to all Jews, for not only is he a puppet of the Roman government, but he had married Herodias, the daughter of an older half-brother of his who had also been the wife of another one of his half-brothers. John the Baptist would leave the political issues to others, but seeing Herod and Herodias as they cross the Jordan in late June on their way back to Machaerus, John says to them that it is not lawful for them to be husband and wife. John has accosted Herod and Herodias about this more than once. He, who is not afraid to call the Pharisees a "brood of vipers," is not shy in speaking the truth about Herod. Herodias is infuriated at John, but much to her chagrin, Herod will do nothing now while they are crossing the river because of John's popularity. So, with his wife nagging at him to silence John's tongue, Herod bides his time.

On returning to Machaerus, after some time has passed, Herod—feeling more secure from popular outcry and tiring of his wife's constant bitterness about John—sends guards to bind and arrest him and bring him back to Machaerus. His plan is to put him in prison and hope that by the time he and Herodias come back to Magdela in four months or so, the people will have forgotten all about John. 'Who knows?' he thinks to himself, 'Maybe I can even persuade John to change his opinion of me.' For as much as John's words sting him, and as much as his wife's bitterness goads him to be vengeful, Herod feels a strange attraction to John—as do all men towards those who speak the truth, even if the truth is an inconvenient one.

Herod's guards quietly march to the spot where John and his disciples are baptizing. They wait until early morning so that they will not be observed by many. The guards approach John and stiffly and formally tell him he is under arrest for treason and is ordered by Herod to go with them to Machaerus. John's disciples are crestfallen, and some move forward to protect him. John holds up his hand to keep them back and offers his wrists to the guards to be bound. He has known this day would come. Seeing John offering no resistance, most of his disciples also offer to be arrested, but the guards refuse to do so. Before he is led away, John asks to be able to speak to his disciples. John tells them to persevere and to make sure that they go down the river to tell Jesus the news about his arrest. One by one he bids them farewell with a look of gratitude none of them will ever forget. When he finishes talking to the last of his disciples, he signals to the guards that he is ready to go. Just like that, he is marched off, leaving his disciples gazing after him in silence as John slowly disappears from sight.

CHAPTER SEVEN

Jesus Meets a Woman in Samaria

As Jesus and his disciples continue to preach and baptize at the spot where John had been before he moved up river, the leaders of the Jews in Jerusalem dramatically increase their surveillance of Jesus. They intensely desire to get rid of him. John now having been arrested, they begin to worry all the more that his followers might also turn to Jesus—they can see Jesus' popularity with the people is rising. The Pharisees do not like it at all that Jesus has bested them twice: once at the Paschal feast two months ago and just recently at Pentecost. They are angry and determined, so they begin to harass him and his disciples.

Jesus and his disciples of course notice they are being more closely watched by the authorities. It is clear there is a lot of bitterness towards Jesus. They can't quite trick him into doing or saying anything they can use to arrest him, but they do not tire of trying. This uncomfortable situation goes on for over a month until shortly after Jesus gets the news of John's arrest. Knowing that this is not yet the time for his full confrontation with the Jewish leaders, Jesus, "When [he] hears that John has been arrested, withdraws to Galilee" (Matt 4:12). Jesus' heart grows heavy with the news of John's arrest, and the hatred of the Jewish leaders drives him to move his ministry to the northern province of Galilee. The Galileans, a rural and simple people, will not question him with the affected sophistication of those in Jerusalem. Only a few of his disciples make the trip back to Galilee with him as the newer disciples from Judea return to their homes and responsibilities just as many of his Galilean disciples already have. It is mid-July and day 270 of the 909 days that changed the world when Jesus leaves Judea, deciding to take the more difficult Samaria route back to Galilee.

Having left in the morning, a day and a half later, Jesus and the few disciples with him are half-way though Samaria. At one point, the road swerves around the foot of a range of mountains running alongside them down towards an open valley until the road slips westward through a narrow opening into Sichem. As this high road glides into the valley, there is Mount Gerizim on the left, which is the sacred Samaritan mountain on which is built the rival temple to the one in Jerusalem. On the right down the road several hundred yards is the well of Jacob, which he had given to his son Joseph. Higher up the valley on the right is the village of Sychar, about a half mile from the well. The village of Sichem is not yet visible up the road on the left, as it is hidden by the mountains. This area is full of Old Testament memories: this is where Jacob had settled after moving from Mesopotamia and where Joseph was buried after Joshua had conquered the land, bringing back with him Joseph's bones from Egypt.

It is late in the afternoon, and Jesus sends his disciples into the village to try to get some food. Weary from the travel and his heart still heavy from John's arrest and the Jewish leaders' harassment, Jesus sits and waits for them by the Well of Jacob. Presently a Samaritan woman comes to fetch some water. Usually the women of the village get the water in the morning and early evening, but this woman is somewhat of an outcast in the village for reasons we learn as Jesus talks to her. He surprises her by asking for a drink of water. Stunned by his words but seeing that he is tired and thirsty, she honors his request, draws some water, and offers him a cup. Instantly Jesus seems energized, and his eyes shine with that look that has captured so many already. The Samaritan woman, still taken aback and not being shy, asks the question foremost on her mind: "How do you, a Jew, ask me, a Samaritan woman, for a drink?" (John 4:9). Jesus knows who this woman is and what her life has been like, but he responds to her generosity by trying to draw her deeper, saying, "If you knew who it is who is saying to you 'Give me a drink,' you would ask, and he would give you living water. Whoever drinks the water I shall give shall never thirst; the water I shall give will become in him a spring of water welling up to eternal life" (John 4:10). This poor woman has no idea what Jesus is talking about, but, drawn to this man, she makes her first act of faith, albeit for worldly reasons, saying, "Sir, give me this water so I may not be thirsty or have to keep coming here to draw water" (John 4:15). Things really get interesting from here. In response, Jesus makes a request that causes her to stop. "Go call your husband and come back" (John 4:16). She wonders how she will respond to this request, because she doesn't want this man she has come to like knowing about her personal failings. 'I know,' she thinks to herself, 'I will tell him a half-truth that he will likely interpret differently from my intent.' Like most of us, she doesn't want her serious faults laid bare, so she coyly replies, "I do not have a husband" (John 4:17). With eyes still bright fixed on hers, Jesus smiles slightly and nodding says, "You are right to say you have no husband for you have had five husbands and the one you have now is not your husband. What you have said is true" (John 4:17-18). With those words, Jesus fully captures her, as she thinks to herself, 'He knows the full truth about me, yet he does not seem to condemn.' Her heart is suddenly lightened. They talk some more, and reflecting if this man could be he, she asks him, "I know the Messiah is coming, the one called the Christ" (John 4:25). The anticipation in her voice is palpable. How will he respond? Jesus then, for the first time in his ministry, to a poor Samaritan female sinner no less, speaks the powerful truth about his mission. "I am he who is speaking with you" (John 4:26). There, by the Well of Jacob, on a hot day, Jesus reveals himself to this woman. He has not proclaimed it to the masses, nor shouted it from the mountain top of nearby Gerizim; he has spoken it softly to one woman. Such will be the way of this Jesus. He will speak to individual hearts. Those who want to hear will do so; those who do not want to hear, or are too busy to hear, will not. Such is his respect, even to this day, for the freedom of his human creations.

Just then, Jesus' disciples return with food from the village and are scandalized to see him talking with this Samaritan woman. She, for her part, takes one last, long look into Jesus' eyes and runs off, forgetting her water jar, back to her village of Sychar. She cannot wait to tell everyone about the man she has met. "Come see a man who told me everything I have done. Could he possibly be the Messiah?" (John 4:29). She believes so in her heart, but knows the men will have to judge for themselves. She runs home and tells her husband, but he is unimpressed and scoffs at her enthusiasm. Ignoring his coldness, she goes into the village and tells everyone she meets the same thing. Regardless of her reputation, her enthusiasm is so great that the men of Sychar indeed go out to visit Jesus. Even her husband decides to join the men, although he hangs towards the back. Jesus' disciples see this group coming down the hillside road and turn towards them. What can this mean? Are they, as Jews, safe with all these Samaritan men approaching them? Could it be that Jesus has insulted the woman, and these men are coming to avenge her? Perhaps they should gather themselves and go back the other way? All these questions stir in the disciples' minds, but as they look at Jesus, he appears calm and even has a small smile on his face anticipating the arrival of these Samaritan men.

When they do arrive, Jesus greets them warmly. Being men of good will, they are impressed and inspired by his words and demeanor. The disciples let out a sigh of relief to see these men have come to learn more about Jesus and not to attack them. As Jesus speaks with the men from Sychar, and the hour grows late, the Samaritan men invite him and his disciples to stay with them overnight. Samaritan men asking Jewish men to stay overnight as guests in the village? This is unheard of; clearly something unprecedented is taking place here—and so unique that Jesus ends up staying there for two days. He has so captivated the town of Sychar that, on his leaving, the people of the town say to the Samaritan woman, "We no longer believe because of your word; for we have heard ourselves, and we know that this is truly the savior of the world" (John 4:42). We can only imagine the scene as Jesus leaves while the whole town, all of them standing together, wish him good-bye. Even the husband of the woman at the well is there inspired after his encounter with Jesus. We must also ask ourselves why these people, non-Jews, embrace him so quickly, while so many others have pushed him away. Jesus asks none of them, "Follow me," but is content to let them live the words he has spoken to them in their own village. Although no one follows him now, many will get to see him again in a little over a year, when Jesus takes the Samarian route to the Feast of Tabernacles. We can only imagine what these people will think a year and three quarters from now when they learn Jesus has been put to death by his fellow Jews.

CHAPTER EIGHT

Second Miracle at Cana

Jesus, on his way back to Galilee, continues on the road through Samaria and, when he gets into Galilee, slows down his pace, taking time to meet and speak to the people as he proceeds north. Word of Jesus' arrival in Galilee spreads like wildfire as travelers take the news to different parts of the province. Jesus seems to be in no rush to get back to Nazareth; indeed, he doesn't turn west off the main trail to his hometown, but continues north to Cana, the scene less than a year ago where he changed the water into wine.

The common-folk Galileans are happy to see him. Arriving in Cana, Jesus seems to meander, almost as if he were waiting for something or someone. They have all heard about what he did in Jerusalem at the Passover, how he had cleared the temple area of merchants and silenced the Jewish leaders. They know he has been baptizing in the very spot John had been at the Jordan River. They have heard the story of the man he cured at the pool during Pentecost. Many even know John himself has deferred to Jesus...and then there is the incident about his turning water into wine at a wedding right here in town.

Meanwhile, news of Jesus' return comes to one of the Roman officials in the town of Capernaum. He is in charge of overseeing the town but is in the midst of a great family crisis. His only son, eleven years old, is gravely sick with a high fever threatening his life. The doctors have tried everything, and nothing is working. It appears only a matter of time before his beloved son will be dead. Being the kind of man who keeps his ear to the ground, he knows the stories about this Jesus. After asking the doctors yet again if there is any hope for his son and receiving the same negative response, he decides to go see this Jesus himself. There are stories that he turned water into wine, and, although they may be fabrications, as he looks at his son he decides he has nothing to lose. When he tells his wife his plan, she shakes her head in disbelief. With their son on his death bed, how can he go chasing after some Jewish folk hero? Has he no sense of how ridiculous he will look? For the love of his son, however, the official tells his wife he will swallow his pride and go to this man to see if he can help.

Taking one of his guards with him, he saddles up the horses and makes the twenty-five mile trip in about half a day, arriving at Cana in the early afternoon. Inquiring as to Jesus' whereabouts, he is led to him by the local townsfolk who recognize this man as one of the Roman authorities. The townsfolk wonder what this meeting could possibly entail. Is Jesus, like John the Baptist, in trouble with the Romans? The Roman doesn't seem to have enough guards to arrest him, so perhaps the official will just be questioning Jesus. In any event, curiosities run high; a large crowd draws near as Jesus is introduced to the man. This is the one for whom Jesus has been waiting.

The Roman official bows respectfully to Jesus and, with a tone of voice that tries to be commanding yet betrays his heavy heart, asks him to come to Capernaum and heal his son. Although the official is trying to address Jesus as his superior, Jesus looks on him with love for the faith he is showing by making the trip and this request. True, he is here as a last resort, but he is a Gentile, and this request he makes of a Jew is remarkable. To further deepen his faith, Jesus will challenge him to see if the Roman will believe in *him*, Jesus, and not simply in the miracle. We will see time and time again that Jesus is interested in alleviating suffering, but he is most interested in their faith in him and not in the signs. Most, unlike this Roman, will not be able to do so.

When Jesus says, "Unless you see signs and wonders, you believe not" (John 4:48), the Roman official immediately gets the point; it is not about signs and wonders, but about believing in Jesus Christ. Somehow, in a way hard to explain, he knows Jesus has the power to do this and just about anything he wants to do. His response to Jesus shows his change of heart. Acknowledging Jesus as his superior now, he says, "Lord, come down before my son dies" (John 4:49). Jesus answers him by giving him one final test of faith. "Go on your way; your son will live" (John 4:50). The official, convinced so thoroughly in his heart about Jesus, easily passes the test, and without protest, turns, gets back on his horse, gives Jesus one last long look, and rides off towards home. The crowd watching all this, yet missing the point, is stunned at the Roman official's leaving so quietly.

It gets late in the day as the official makes his way home and, as the roadway back to Capernaum is not an easy one to travel in darkness, he decides to spend the night camped out with his guard in a safe spot along the road. Although his desire to return home to confirm his son's recovery is powerful, he feels an even more powerfully profound peace and security in believing his son will live. He has never felt so sure of something in his life. He tells his guard how confident he is his son will live, but the guard says little, not sharing his leader's faith. The guard nods his head in agreement, because he does not want to offend his boss, but in his own heart, he thinks his superior crazy for being so sure his son is cured. Time will tell.

The next morning the official and his guard get up early, make themselves a quick breakfast, and resume the trip back home. They are only a short distance from Capernaum when they see a group of men riding towards them with arms and voices raised. The guard recognizes the riders as some of the other guards assigned to the official. The official's heart begins to race now with excitement. The riders arrive and, bursting with joy and shouting over one another, say that the official's son is healed. "It is a miracle!" they say. "He got better in an instant." The official, subdued with humility, asks one question. "At what time did the fever leave him?" The reply from the guards is as he expects: "Yesterday at about one in the afternoon" (John 4:52). His faith, confirmed, grows even stronger. The guard who accompanied him to Cana stands with his mouth open in disbelief. Could this be?

Upon arriving home, the official's son and wife run out to greet him. He embraces his son with tears in his eyes as his wife, crying, watches them. After a brief second, she also approaches her husband, apologizing, thanking, and asking for his forgiveness all at the same time. The official gathers her in his arms and gently tells her all is fine. The three of them together walk arm in arm back inside the house. Immediately the official painstakingly relates to his entire family and household the events of the last day. His faith is contagious, and his whole household comes to believe in Jesus. As the news of this miraculous cure spreads all over Capernaum, talk about Jesus heightens to a feverish pitch.

Chapter Nine

Jesus Returns Home to Nazareth

Jesus lingers a few more days in Cana but then decides to return to Nazareth. The route from Cana to Nazareth is winding and undulating. As it approaches the town, the road rises over a ridge and drops into a large amphitheatre, around the sides of which clings the town of Nazareth. Beyond Nazareth to the south, the hills slope gently upward again; beyond these there is a steep drop into the beautiful Valley of Esdraelon. Nazareth, however, is a backwater kind of town. It is far off the beaten path and not a place anyone who likes action and excitement lives. The people here are provincial, yet they are his neighbors, and Jesus loves them for the thirty-odd years he has lived with them.

Things are much different now as he returns. The last time he had come home, after turning the water to wine at the wedding feast in Cana a little less than a year ago, there was some talk about him, but it had died down as Jesus had gone about his normal work. The town is abuzz now with stories offered by firsthand witnesses about what he did six months ago at the last Paschal feast in Jerusalem and how he had both tamed the crowd and stood down the Jewish leaders. Many have heard of or seen him and his disciples taking up John the Baptist's old spot on the Jordan River. There is the story of his cure of a lame man in Jerusalem on the Feast of Pentecost. Fresh on everyone's mind came the news the other day of this miraculous cure in Capernaum of a Roman official's son. Yes, the people of Nazareth are eager to hear more from their neighbor. They are anxious to judge for themselves who and what their townsman, Jesus, has become. They will do so in a few Sabbaths' time.

On one of the Sabbath mornings after his arrival back home, Jesus and his mother make their way to the temple for the services. Jesus and Mary sit together towards the back of the temple and greet their neighbors sitting around them. As it is the custom to have someone in the congregation read and expound on the scriptures, the elders, eager to hear him, ask Jesus to do so today. Jesus accepts the invitation and rises from his seat next to his mother. The whole assembly is quiet and follows him with their eyes as he walks to the front and is handed the scroll from which to read. He makes his way to the side of the temple altar from which the readings are proclaimed. The anticipation of his reading is so thick it is palpable.

Jesus unfolds the scroll from the Book of the Prophet Isaiah and finds the passage he wants to read: the beginning of the sixty-first chapter. To say he reads the chapter is not entirely accurate. With the scroll open in his hands, he looks directly at the congregation, meets many of them eye-to-eye, as he speaks more from memory than from words, "The spirit of the Lord is upon me, because the Lord has appointed me to bring glad tidings to the poor. He has sent me to proclaim liberty to the captives and recovery of sight to the blind, to let the oppressed go free, and to proclaim a year acceptable to the Lord" (Luke 4:18-19). His tone is both meek and commanding, spoken with such sincerity that all who hear him are touched deeply. They all sense he is speaking about himself. He finishes the passage, pauses a long moment as he looks at the congregation in silence, rolls up the scroll, hands it to the attendant, and sits down. There is not a pin drop to be heard in the synagogue when, after another pregnant pause, he raises his voice and loudly proclaims, "This day is this scripture fulfilled in your hearing" (Luke 4:21).

The people, at first, are mesmerized; they are captivated by the way he has spoken this passage from Isaiah. They have each heard this same passage read aloud numerous times before, but never has anyone read it and made them feel the passage was about the reader, as Jesus has just done. They all look at one another and nod in agreement as to the wisdom and the wonder of their fellow townsman, Jesus. Something special indeed is going on here and they all begin to speak very highly of him—but not for long.

After a few minutes of these nodding accolades, some of the elders begin to rethink their initial response. 'Wait a minute,' they say to themselves, 'how can this young man insinuate that he is the one the great prophet speaks of?' The crowd begins to question how such words could come out of Jesus' mouth, and so they say to each other, "Isn't this the son of Joseph?" (Luke 4:22). They go from being awed by his words and sincerity to doubting someone they have known for so long could be thus destined. Many, thinking about this news of the miraculous healing of a Roman official's son just a few days ago in Capernaum, wonder to themselves why he is not doing the same kind of miraculous works here in his hometown of Nazareth. Surely there are enough gravely ill here he could help. If he is genuine, shouldn't he take care of his own first? Jesus, however, is reading their minds and readies himself to make a response he knows will not be received kindly.

"Surely you will quote me this proverb," he begins, "'Physician cure yourself,' and say, 'Do here in your native place the things we have heard were done in Capernaum.' But amen, I say to you, no prophet is accepted in his own native place. Indeed I tell you…there were many lepers in Israel during the time of Elisha the prophet, yet not one of them was cleansed, but only Naaman the Syrian" (Luke 4:23-27). The implication of his words is obvious to all. Not only is he unapologetic for not doing any special deeds here in Nazareth, he uses the scripture to explain why. He sets himself up as a prophet who has come to help the Gentiles as much as the Jews. Cries of blasphemy go up from parts of the congregation; complaints of insult go up from other parts of the congregation. Within five minutes, the mood has changed, and the scene turns ugly.

Some from the congregation get up and angrily storm Jesus' seat. They force him to get up and, amidst all the noise and shouting, drive him out of the temple. Jesus is calm, though, permitting them to proceed, and says nothing as the crowd hurries him through the town. As the crowd pushes him along, they all become louder and bolder as Jesus offers no resistance. Some in the crowd yell to the others to drive him up the hill on the south side of the town that overlooks the Valley of Esdraelon. They encourage one another as they move up the hill, thinking they will do away with this blasphemer by pushing him over the steep drop to his death in the valley below. This is an ugly crowd: no one listens to the few cautioning them to think clearly. The mob has taken on a life of its own and they are determined to see him through to his death.

Meanwhile, following behind the crowd is Mary, at first one of the voices admonishing the crowd for what they are doing, but now in tears. She can hardly believe what is happening. How can things have turned so quickly? Will her son's life be ended here? For what purpose would his death now serve? Is this the sword that Simon years ago had said would pierce her own soul also? As the crowd reaches the summit of the mountain and readies to push Jesus off, Mary weeps bitterly and watches from a small garden area near the top of the hill, a spot where even today there is a chapel in her honor. It is called the Chapel of Mary Weeping.

Suddenly the noise of the crowd changes; no longer are there shouts of anger, but now the voices sound puzzled and surprised. Mary notices. What can be happening? They are asking where Jesus is. They have somehow or other lost him. He has disappeared from their midst. Many in the crowd are incredulous that those in the front did not hurl him off the hill yet don't know where he is. The realization that Jesus has somehow escaped them drains the mob of its energy in an instant. Baffled, they all walk back down the hill, each left to reflect on what has just happened. When they see each other in the street the next day, they will not dare to bring up this embarrassing event. Mary, for her part, although unsure where he is but relieved that her son appears to be safe, wanders back down the hill, gives thanks to God, and ponders what this could mean.

CHAPTER TEN

Jesus Settles in Capernaum

When Mary gets back to their home Jesus is there. She hugs him tightly as he does her. Jesus looks deeply into her eyes and tells her they must leave Nazareth; they will move to Capernaum and make it their home. Tears begin to pool in Mary's eyes, more for her rejected son than for herself, yet she knows she will follow him to Capernaum and to wherever else he leads her. They pack their things quietly and quickly, say good-bye to their neighbors, offering them the furniture and things they will not be able to take with them, and leave town. News of Jesus' leaving spreads quickly, but few approach him, ashamed by their actions on the Sabbath and confused as to how he got away from them. Both Jesus and Mary are silent as they turn their backs on the town they have called home for the last thirty years. With the exception of some extra clothes, they leave Nazareth with nothing. It is mid August—day 306 of the 909 days that changed the world.

The journey to Capernaum from Nazareth on foot takes a full day to complete. Jesus and Mary arrive just before dark and make arrangements to stay with a distant relative who has a home in the village. The news of Jesus' arrival spreads quickly, and by mid-morning, many stop by the house to see him. The recent cure of the Roman official's son has excited much of the town, and they are all eager to see him. Shaking off any sadness, Jesus greets them lovingly. They are all anxious to see him and hopeful they will see more miracles, similar to the few already attributed to him. James and John, Peter and Andrew also come to see Jesus. He greets them even more warmly than the others, but gives them no special charge or any indication he expects anything from them. Indeed, he encourages them all to go about their normal daily routine. Jesus, for the moment anyway, seems content simply to blend in.

He and his mother go to the temple every Sabbath, and he is frequently asked to read and comment on the scriptures. He preaches repentance, and his voice and piercing eyes strike the congregation to the very core. They hang on his every word, but upon leaving the temple, Jesus always returns home, while the others do likewise. When it is not the Sabbath and others are working at their various professions, Jesus too finds employment working as a carpenter for one of the local tradesmen. With the exception of the Sabbath service addresses, though, there are no other miracles or even confrontations with the Pharisees, as Jesus avoids the religious leaders. All eyes are on him, and he continues to be friendly, but he stays mostly to himself, frequently going up into the hills on the west side of Capernaum to pray. Many weeks, and then months, pass like this as Jesus works, prays, and prepares himself for the beginning of the most active part of his public life. But there are no miracles, so by the time the rainy season arrives in early December, much of the buzz about Jesus has died down. It will all change over the course of a few days.

Chapter Eleven

Jesus Calls the First Four;
A Day of Miracles

One day, after so many months of quietly living in Capernaum, Jesus gets up early and walks along the shore of the Sea of Galilee from Capernaum to Bethsaida. As he nears Bethsaida, he watches from the shore as Andrew and Simon fish. After a long night of fishing, the fishermen begin sailing back towards the shore. Simon and Andrew see Jesus looking at them as they cast their nets one last time. They are close enough to shore to hear Jesus when he calls out, "Come follow me, and I will make you fishers of men" (Luke 1:16).

Andrew and Simon look at each other. They have seen and talked to him a number of times since he has moved to Capernaum, but never has he indicated he wanted them to drop everything and follow him. Both of them now interpret Jesus' call as an invitation to do so, and without hesitation pull in their nets and bring their boat to shore. While they sort out the day's catch and sell it to the local retailers, Jesus tells them he will be back shortly and walks further down the shore towards Bethsaida. He sees James and John mending their nets and calls them to follow him also. Like Andrew and Simon, they both immediately stop what they are doing, leave the boat, say good-bye to their father Zebedee, and follow Jesus. Zebedee calls out to his boys to wait, but they only turn back and smile, so all he can do is shake his head from side to side as he watches his boys go back up the shore towards Capernaum. Zebedee is not entirely surprised; his boys have spoken much about this man, and he knows they believe something great will happen with him. Although his wife very much agrees with the boys and welcomes the idea of her sons following Jesus, Zebedee is more skeptical. 'Besides,' he thinks to himself, 'who is going to help me run this successful fishing business?' How to react to a call one's child receives from Jesus to follow him was as much an issue for parents then as it is today.

Jesus, John, and James walk up the shore to where Andrew and Simon are wrapping up their business transactions, and the five of them proceed up the beach towards Capernaum. Jesus, smiling and clearly happy to be with these men, at first asks them questions about the day's catch and then asks if they have a place to stay. Simon's mother-in-law lives here, so he and Andrew tell Jesus they can stay with her. Simon's wife, as it turns out, is already in Capernaum as her mother is ill, and she is taking care of her. John and James also have relatives in Capernaum. No one asks Jesus, though, and he doesn't say how long he expects them to remain in Capernaum. A day or two from now, though, the four will have a much clearer picture of what is in store.

The next Sabbath, Jesus takes the four, along with his mother, to the temple for services. As has become the custom, Jesus is asked to read and interpret the scriptures for the congregation. This morning, however, after Jesus has read the scriptures and is seated explaining the words, a man, with wild eyes and looking disheveled, and not a normal Sabbath attendee, cries out in a loud voice from the back of the temple, "What have you come to do with us, Jesus of Nazareth? Have you come to destroy us?" (Mark 1:24). The crowd turns to look at him and then immediately turns back to Jesus to see how he will respond. They all know this crazy man and wonder what he is saying and how Jesus will react. Jesus, standing up slowly, with eyes of intensity and power, rebukes the man sternly. "Quiet! Come out of him" (Mark 1:25).

The man throws himself on the floor and starts screaming wildly. It only lasts a few seconds, but the sight and sound are horrifying. As quickly as it began, it ends. The man calmly gets up, sits back down, and looks at Jesus and at the congregation as if he has no idea what happened. Jesus walks down the aisle to the back of the temple, whispers something to the man, who smiles and leaves the temple. The rest of the crowd is left aghast. They ask themselves who this man is who both teaches with authority and "commands even the unclean spirits and they obey him" (Mark 1:27). This is the kind of miracle many have been waiting to see. Little do they know it is only a preview of what will be performed this day.

As they all file out of the synagogue, the people chatter among themselves about Jesus' power. When they return to their homes, they share the news with their neighbors not lucky enough to be at the temple. "This Jesus is indeed a miracle worker, and he lives here in our village," many exclaim. The excitement in the town is unlike anything before. Some even begin to think to themselves that, just perhaps, Jesus might be able to heal their mother who is not thinking clearly, their son who cannot walk because of a diseased leg, or their daughter who is unable to see.

Jesus, meanwhile, on leaving the temple, makes his way with his four disciples to the house of Simon's mother-in-law. Some of the temple congregation follow behind them, anxious to see where he is going and what he might do next. As they enter the house, Simon tells Jesus about his mother-in-law's illness. She has been in bed for days with a severe fever and seems to be getting weaker and weaker. Jesus goes directly to the bed on which she is lying. Sitting on the bed with the sick woman is Simon's wife, gently stroking her mother's hair. The sick woman is unconscious. When Jesus and the others enter the room, Simon's wife turns first to Jesus and then to her husband, her burdened eyes pleading for help. Jesus steps forward and sits down on the bed. As he gently picks up the hand of Simon's mother-in-law, the sick woman opens her eyes. Looking into Jesus' eyes, hers brighten and, with an audible sigh, a smile comes across her face. She feels the illness leaving her body and begins to feel like her old self. Jesus smiles back at her and helps her to her feet. She thanks him profusely and insists that he and the others sit down while she prepares something for them to eat. Simon's wife cannot contain her joy. She thanks Jesus and then runs over to her husband. As she embraces him, she can only say, "Oh Simon, I love you. This is a miracle!" A few of Simon's other relatives, marveling at this scene, walk outside to the small crowd of people at their door and breathlessly announce that Jesus has rebuked the woman's fever, and she is now cured. The people say to themselves, 'What he has done for the Roman official's son, he has now done to one of us, his fellow Jews. What more might he do…?'

Jesus and the others enjoy the modest but well-prepared meal offered by Simon's mother-in-law. Afterwards, they spend the next few hours talking and enjoying one another's company. The four disciples and the others in the household hang on Jesus' every word as they wonder what will happen next. They will soon find out.

As the sun sets and the Sabbath ends, Jesus and the others begin to hear the sounds of a large movement of people coming towards the house. There is a lot of commotion. As they look outside, they see many bringing their ill or those possessed by demons to Jesus. Some are even carrying their sick on their backs or in cots. They lay them all around the house and down the street. Jesus, looking back at his four disciples, walks outside. He puts his hand on a boy who cannot speak and instantly the boy talks, thanking Jesus for his favor while his parents weep for joy. He bends down to a woman on a cot who cannot walk and with a gentle smile touches her, and she immediately gets up, praising God in a loud voice at the joy of her cure. One by one, he cures all the people who have been brought to him. The noise level reaches a feverish pitch as the miracles are performed. On hearing the noise, many others bring their sick to Jesus for a cure. It starts at sunset and lasts long into the night, but he cures every last one of them. At long last, there are no more sick outside the door; the day of miracles has ended. The whole town is alive with what has just happened, and every household on returning home stays up late into the night discussing the day's events. Jesus takes his mother back to the house where they are staying. Mary too stays up late and, as she lies in her bed, ponders deeply about the day. John and James also go back to their relatives' house, and Simon and Andrew stay with Simon's mother-in-law. The four new disciples and their families now believe they are on the "ground floor" of what is going to be a world-changing enterprise. John and James even discuss how proud of them their dad, Zebedee, will be because they have clearly made the right decision in following Jesus. Little do the four of them know how right they are, but how wrong their expectations will turn out to be. In any event, this day in mid-December, day 423 of the 909 days that changed the world, will be a memorable one indeed. Prior to day 423, there have only been three recorded miracles: the Cana wedding feast, the healing of the cripple at the pool in Jerusalem, and the healing of the Roman official's son. On day 423, the miracles are too numerous to count.

CHAPTER TWELVE

Jesus Takes his First Tour of Galilee

E arly the next morning Jesus gets up and without waking anyone goes out the door and makes his way into the hills on the west side of town. As the sun begins to rise in the east, he finds a little indented spot in those hills, out of view from the town below, and begins to enter into intense prayer with his Father. Yesterday was a big day, his public life taken up a level by all the miracles. He knows that is the turning point in his ministry. We leave Jesus in deep, loving communication with his Father and return to the town below.

Some time after Jesus leaves the house, Mary is awakened by the sound of people gathering outside the door. It is early dawn, and the people are clamoring for Jesus. Mary, noticing he is not there, tells them that perhaps he is at the house of Simon's mother-in-law. When they get there, Simon and Andrew say they do not know where he is. The crowd is growing bigger by the minute as more and more people wake up and, with thoughts of yesterday's events fresh in their minds, come to look for Jesus. Perhaps he is at the house where John and James are staying? A quick run over there is not rewarded with his presence. Where can he be? The townspeople begin searching around to see if they can find him.

The four disciples, having observed Jesus' predilection for praying in the mountain hills since they moved to Capernaum, slip away and move up the hillside to see if Jesus is there. After a short search, they find him. He is sitting down, eyes closed, with such a look of peace on his face. They do not want to disturb him, but with the noise of the crowd in the background, Simon calls his name softly and Jesus opens his eyes. "Everyone is looking for you" (Mark 1:37), says Simon. Jesus smiles softly at Simon and the others and tells them that he will greet them all but he cannot stay in Capernaum and adds, "Let us go to the nearby villages that I may preach there also. For this purpose I have come" (Mark 1:38).

Others have also been coming up into the hills looking for Jesus, especially after they notice Simon doing so. Just as Jesus is finishing talking with his four disciples, a few of them reach the spot where Jesus and the four are standing. The cry of having found him goes up, and many others hurry to see. They are gushing over him, thanking him for yesterday's cure of their loved ones, offering to have him stay at their houses, asking if there is anything they can do for him. Jesus smiles and thanks all of them but tells them as he did the four, "To the other towns also I must proclaim the good news of the kingdom of God, because for this purpose I have been sent" (Luke 4:43).

The crowd lets out a collective gasp and begs him to stay with them a bit longer. When they see he is resolute, many offer to go with him, but Jesus tells them all to go back to their homes and their work. They have responsibilities and should tend to them. He promises he will return, but for now he will only be taking Simon, Andrew, James, and John. The crowd begins to break up and return to their homes, but two linger on. One is Philip, who, having heard the news of Jesus' miracles yesterday, has made the short trip to Capernaum from Bethsaida. Jesus walks up to him and with that same look that captivated him back at the Jordan riverbank over a year ago asks him to join them on the trip. Without any regard for what he might be missing back home, Philip says "yes" and is ready to go.

Finally the crowd has totally dispersed, and there remain only Jesus, Simon, Andrew, John, James, Philip, and one other person standing there. It is Mary, and she looks at him with inquiring eyes, wondering if she will be going with him. He walks up to her and puts his hands atop her shoulders. He asks her to wait here in Capernaum for his return. Mary longs to be with him but she agrees without hesitation. She thinks to herself that her son will now more publicly be about his Father's business. Mary walks back down the hill towards the town, and Jesus and the other five head over the hills into the other parts of Galilee.

During this "first tour" of Galilee, Jesus preaches in the synagogues, heals all manner of sickness, and casts out many devils. We don't get much detail from the gospels about specific miracles, but there is one that stands out. As Jesus is passing from one town to another, a leper comes out of hiding from the side of the road. The crowd gasps as the leper, in violation of every law, runs towards Jesus. The crowd scatters in all directions, but Jesus does not move. This poor man "full of leprosy" (Luke 5:12) kneels at Jesus' feet and begs, "If you wish, you can make me clean" (Luke 5:12). Jesus looks at him and sees not just a man in search of someone to lift his misery, but more. This is a man who has genuine faith in Jesus as his words "if you wish" clearly indicate. He wants to be cured, true, but he asks it to be Jesus' will and not his own. Jesus is touched to the core of his heart, and the crowd, far enough away so as not to catch the leprosy from the contaminated man, but close enough to observe the interaction between the two, notice the intense look of affection and concern on the face of Jesus. Even so they are not prepared for what comes next. Jesus stretches out his hand and touches the leper. Imagine the horror and confusion of those watching. Touching someone with leprosy is anathema. Doesn't Jesus know he is risking getting this ugly disease himself? Jesus does not care at all. "I do will it. Be made clean" (Luke 5:13), and the leper is immediately cured. The man's joy knows no bounds. He gets up, embraces Jesus, and runs off "to show himself to the priest and offer what Moses prescribed for his cleansing" (Luke 5:14). Nothing moves Jesus to action as does faith; it remains still true today.

In every town he visits on this tour, the pattern is usually the same. He preaches, he heals, and the people beg him to stay longer. Everyone wants to be with him; no one wants him to leave. He frequently goes out to the deserted places to pray and gather strength, but the people keep coming to him (Luke 5:15-16). We can imagine the enthusiasm Jesus generates as he goes from town to town. Never have the people seen such miracles, and brought about by such a meek, humble, and loving man. Who is this man? The idea of Jesus being the "Messiah," the one to save the Jewish people from Roman rule, begins to build up steam. Although his demeanor does seem meek, perhaps he is the one who will lead the people to a new era of power and success. Truly, no one has ever worked as many wonders as he has in these towns and villages.

There are a group of people, however, who are more skeptical—or, rather, jealous of Jesus. The chief priests of these towns see the people flocking to him and hanging on his every word. Inevitably some of these chief priests begin to fear he is usurping their power. Some try to throw cold water on the people's enthusiasm, but mostly to no avail, and as Jesus leaves each town or village to go to the next one, these chief priests are left pondering what they are to do about him. After numerous weeks on this tour of Galilee, Jesus and his five disciples make their way back to Capernaum. He has won over large numbers of the people of Galilee, but it is now time for him and his disciples to get back home to their respective jobs and families. It is early January, day 441 of the 909 days that changed the world. Simon Peter is about to make a startling insight, and Jesus is about to make a proclamation that will scandalize many and steel the chief priests even more against him.

CHAPTER THIRTEEN

Jesus Returns to Capernaum

On returning to Capernaum, Jesus tells the five to go back to their homes in Bethsaida for a few days to see their families. Peter's wife is thrilled to see him and excited because everyone has been telling her how Peter seems to be one of Jesus' favorites. John and Andrew's mother is also beside herself with happiness; she knows in her heart this is all going to mean something great for her boys and her family. Even Zebedee begrudgingly agrees the boys' connection with Jesus could turn out to be a great portent. Philip's family is full of approving questions as they inquire about all that took place while he was away. Meanwhile, it doesn't take long for the town of Capernaum to realize Jesus is back. There is constantly a crowd around him as they are all waiting to see what is next. A week or so later, Jesus, early one morning, begins walking along the shore towards Bethsaida, a large crowd, as usual, in tow, swelling even more as he walks along the shore. Jesus approaches Bethsaida, gets to where Peter's boat is anchored, and stops to speak to the crowd, but they have a difficult time hearing him. They press in on him to hear better and get closer to him. Jesus, seeing Simon Peter cleaning up after a hard night's work, gets in his boat and asks Peter to put out in the water a bit so he can speak for all to hear. The crowd is silent as they watch Jesus move away from the shore in Peter's boat, but they are overjoyed when they see the boat anchor and hear him speak to them. He speaks so eloquently, with such authority, and with a message that touches most of their hearts. The only audible sounds are Jesus' strong voice carried in by a slight breeze and the gentle lapping of the water on the seashore. The sky is bright blue, and there is a faint coolness in the air. Most will remember this moment for the rest of their lives.

After Jesus finishes his sermon, he tells Simon, "Put out into the deep water and lower your nets for a catch" (Luke 5:4). Simon is exhausted from the previous night and early morning fishing, which netted him little and he doubts anything will come of it, "but at your command, I will lower the nets" (Luke 5:5). The result is so overwhelming Simon needs to call for another boat, the one belonging to James and John, to help bring up the catch. The boats are so full they are in danger of sinking. They work feverishly to secure the catch and immediately afterwards Peter falls on his knees in front of Jesus and humbly acknowledges his lack of faith by saying, "Depart from me, Lord, for I am a sinful man" (Luke 5:8). Jesus looks at him with love for he knows here is a contrite and humble man who is learning to love Jesus for who he is and not just for what he can do. As Jesus raises his eyes, he speaks loudly so James and John in the other overloaded boat can also hear him. "Do not be afraid; from now on you will be catching men" (Luke 5:10).

Meanwhile, many of the chief priests of Capernaum and of the other towns and villages in Galilee are looking for ways to diminish his popularity. Even as far away as Jerusalem, there are leaders who vividly remember Jesus' purging of the temple almost one and a half years ago and his baptizing at the place where John first baptized. They too have been following the news of the crowds Jesus has been drawing during his first tour of Galilee, and they too are anxious of his growing popularity. To observe Jesus more closely, a number of these leaders come to Capernaum. All of them, however, look for ways to trap him in speech or actions to dampen the popular enthusiasm for this man and to re-establish their own primacy over the people.

One day, Jesus is engaged in conversation with these chief priests and leaders. He is in a small house, and many gather to see him, but the crowd becomes even bigger as news quickly spreads of this dialogue between the traditional leaders of the Jewish faith and this man. The townspeople are all the more interested because they hear some of the high priests from Jerusalem are talking with him. Shortly, the house is full of people inside and outside; people are craning their necks and pressing up against one another in order to hear the conversation. This battle of words and wits between the chief priests and

Jesus is not to be missed, but day 450 in mid-January of the 909 days that changed the world will also see Jesus make a bold claim.

Elsewhere in town, a group of men, knowing that Jesus is back, decide to take their severely palsied neighbor to him. The man's body is racked with the disease, and his limbs twitch and shudder. His appearance is difficult to bear. These men, however, and many more of his neighbors have been kind to him and his family in the midst of his misery. They lift him by his stretcher and walk to the house where they have heard Jesus is in a discussion with the chief priests. Getting near the house, their hearts sink as they see how many people are crowded around it. There will be no way to work through the crowd. They attempt to get people to move aside, but they are greeted with "Be quiet; Jesus is in a deep discussion with the Scribes, which we can barely here from out here, and it must not be disturbed. Listen yourselves how he is besting the chief priests." But these four men are not interested in this religious debate; they know Jesus can heal their neighbor, and they regroup to figure out a solution.

One of them offers the creative solution of carrying him up the steps that lead to the top of the roof. Most homes in Capernaum have these steps to the roof, as they allow the men to sleep outside on the roof on warm summer nights. In addition, the roof tiles were laid over one another in such a way that they could be peeled aside, creating a hole in the roof. Families would regularly peel back these tiles to increase the ventilation in the house. They decide to carry him up the steps to the roof, peel back some of the tiles (surely those below will think it is being done just to increase the air flow in the packed home), and lower their neighbor down through the opening. They believe with confidence that when Jesus sees this poor man he will heal him. What Jesus will say, though, will be more impressive than even what he does.

As the cot is lowered through the hole in the roof, everyone in the house realizes there is something strange going on. The conversations stop. At first it is a bit difficult to make out what is on the cot, but as he gets closer to the floor, everyone can see it is a man, albeit a pity of a man, as he is shaking and convulsing with his illness. Those who have lowered him down say nothing, content that they have brought him close to the feet of Jesus. They will now leave it up to Jesus, for their neighbor's need is obvious and requires no explanation. Everyone in the room quiets down even more, ready for the miracle they are sure will follow. The chief priests eye Jesus suspiciously, not quite sure what to expect, but looking for some way to criticize Jesus.

Jesus looks for a long moment with tenderness at this poor man. With affection in his voice, he says, "Courage, child" (Matt 9:2), and then pauses, the whole crowd waiting for Jesus to cure this poor man. But instead of curing the man of his physical ailments, knowing full well the controversy these words will generate, he completes his sentence: "your sins are forgiven" (Matt 9:2).

The effect is immediate. Your sins are forgiven? Everyone in the room is stunned. The chief priests, in particular, are scandalized and apoplectic. Why, only God can forgive sins! They say to themselves, 'This man is blaspheming' (Matt 9:3). How dare he put himself on equal footing with God? Their disdain for Jesus grows even greater.

Jesus, knowing full well what lies in the hearts of the chief priests, turns his gaze from the sick man back towards them. With a hard and sharp voice, he chastises them. "Why do you harbor such evil thoughts? What is easier to say, 'Your sins are forgiven' or to say 'Rise up and walk'? But that you may know that the Son of Man has the authority on earth to forgive sins," he turns back to the paralytic and with kindness says, "Rise, take up your mat, and go home" (Matt 9:4-6). The man does so at once. The people in the room let out a cry of surprise as the man stands and rolls up his mat. He looks over his now-functioning body with amazement and thanks Jesus sincerely. The crowd opens up a path to the door so the man, beaming from ear to ear, may leave. His friends on the roof let out a big cheer and call down their thanks to Jesus. The bewilderment of the crowd knows no limit and most excitedly talk with one another about it. Some, however, are thinking to themselves, 'Another miracle, and a wonderful one at that, yes, but saying he has the authority on earth to forgive sins? Who is this Jesus? Can he really mean those words?' Jesus, looking at the chief priests and shaking his head from side to side to indicate the end of this discussion and his disappointment at their hardheartedness, follows the paralytic out the door. He's had enough of these leaders for the moment. Besides, in a day or two, it will be time to gather up another follower, one who will cause even more scandal to the chief priests and other upright Jews.

CHAPTER FOURTEEN

Jesus Chooses Another Unlikely Disciple

T he talk of the town about both the miracle cure of the paralytic
and the words Jesus said about forgiving sins spreads like wildfire. Almost two weeks afterwards, Jesus, as is his custom (Mark 2:13)
is walking along the beach early in the morning. It is a cloudy and
cool day but with little wind, and it is easy to hear the water quietly
lapping against the shore. As has been happening daily, many people
rise early in the morning to follow him as he goes on his seashore
walks. He talks to them about many things, asks them about their
families, and frequently stops to raise his voice and make a point to
the crowd. But as the early morning passes, he bids them all good-
bye, knowing they all must be about their daily responsibilities.

As the crowd dissipates, Jesus retraces his steps and begins his
walk back into town. As he and the few remaining disciples who
have not left for their daily work get to the city, they walk along the
main road parallel to the lake. On the right is the water with many
boats and a few shops, and on the left are a plethora of shops, offering fresh fish, fruits, vegetables, clothes, and other wares. In one of
those shops opposite the water, there is a man, Levi-Bar-Alpheus,
who is a tax collector. He is a meek man, as tax collectors go, and
is "liked," as much as any Jew who both collects taxes and works
for the dreaded Romans can be liked. He has a reputation as being
"fair" in a profession where fairness is usually not included in the
same paragraph, let alone sentence. Most tax collectors try to get
as much as possible from the taxpayer, pay the minimum required
amount to the Romans, and keep the balance of the money as their
profit. Levi is considered one of the least greedy tax collectors of the
bunch. Moreover, Levi has listened to Jesus, heard and seen some of

his miracles, and has a longing in his heart to know him better. As Jesus makes his way up the street, Levi notices him but casts his eyes downward, thinking surely he will have nothing to do with him, a hated tax collector. How wrong he is!

Jesus suddenly moves away from the center of the street and walks towards Levi's little office. His disciples are surprised, not quite sure where he is going. As it becomes clear he is making his way to Levi's, his disciples all stop. What does Jesus have to do with this man? Does Jesus owe taxes? Although Levi is a good man as tax collectors go, surely Jesus is not going to befriend him, is he? Levi, who has snuck a peek and has seen Jesus walking towards his shop, has his eyes downcast again as Jesus enters. His mind is racing. He isn't looking but can this person entering be Jesus? No, it can't be, but maybe, maybe, maybe…. This is quite the scene. The disciples, somewhat in shock, are outside the shop looking in. Jesus is standing in front of Levi's desk with a friendly smile, and Levi is looking down at his paperwork almost as if he doesn't know Jesus is there at all.

After a few seconds, which feels like an eternity to all watching, almost haltingly, Levi raises his eyes and meets the smiling gaze of Jesus. He is overwhelmed by the look in his eyes. They are warm and inviting, yes, but never has Levi seen anyone look at him like this. Not even his wife or children have ever looked at him like this. It is as if love is pouring out of those eyes. Those eyes tell Levi that Jesus knows him as he is, the bad and the good, and yet loves him unconditionally. Levi is held speechless. With the smile disappearing from his face but with affection in his eyes, Jesus says, "'Follow me.' And leaving everything behind, Levi gets up and follows him" (Luke 5:27-28). To do so seems so right to Levi. Walking out the door with Levi, Jesus introduces him to his disciples, some of whom he already knows. Although stunned at Jesus' affection for this man, they welcome him as part of the group, some a little bitterly, some with open arms, most with surprise. Levi, with great enthusiasm and lightness of heart, asks Jesus if he can have a dinner that very evening in Jesus' honor. Levi is excited to introduce him to all of his friends, and Jesus accepts, knowing full well the tongue-wagging it will cause.

The dinner crowd that evening is not exactly the "Who's Who" of Capernaum. Because of his profession, most of Levi's friends are tax collectors themselves or other people with professions or personal lives frowned upon by the Jews. When Jesus arrives at the dinner, Levi proudly introduces him to everyone. Jesus is smiling and appears to be very much at home and happy to be with these people. Some of his disciples who have accompanied him to the dinner feel uncomfortable. They don't enjoy these dinner guests, so they pull away and fade into the background.

Meanwhile, the news of this dinner party has reached the ears of some of the chief priests, so they decide to walk by Levi's house to see what it is all about. Some of them are excited, because they believe Jesus' association with despised people like Levi will drive many of his followers away. Indeed, they have heard word that some of his closer disciples are scandalized by his befriending Levi at this dinner. What a good time to put a big dent in Jesus' popularity! Walking on the other side of the street from Levi's home to show their disapproval, the chief priests stop and glare at the goings on inside the house. A few of them notice that some of his disciples are standing off by themselves in the corner. It is time to strike. Crossing the street, they engage those disciples, saying, "Why do you eat and drink with tax collectors and sinners?" (Luke 5:30). The disciples do not know what to say, for they themselves are asking the same question. The chief priests can see the doubt and confusion in the eyes of those disciples and gloat in their likely victory in driving a wedge between Jesus and his disciples.

From across the room and clearly out of earshot of the discussion between the chief priests and his disciples, Jesus politely excuses himself from the conversation and walks towards the chief priests. The entire room falls quiet, and all eyes are on Jesus as he approaches the chief priests. His look is severe and reveals his disdain for the chief priests' motives. His tone is stern as he says in a voice loud enough to be heard by the whole dinner party, "Those who are healthy do not need a physician, but the sick do. I have not come to call the righteous to repentance but sinners" (Luke 5:31-32). The disciples are relieved to see Jesus, using that authoritative tone of voice of his which demands respect, rebuke the Jewish leaders. The leaders, too, hear the command and power in his voice and are taken aback. 'How did he hear what we were talking about when he was on the other side of the room?' they wonder to themselves. Everyone in the room is now looking at them. Jesus' disciples are clearly encouraged by his power over these men and no longer look confused. Somehow, someway, what the chief priests thought was going to be a victory a moment ago has turned into defeat. Their hardness of heart and bitterness ratchet up another level. Turning his gaze from these chief priests as they leave, Jesus once again engages himself with the people at the dinner party, and his disciples walk back into the thick of the room to socialize with Levi and his friends. Levi, for his part, will become known as Matthew and will be counted among Jesus' twelve apostles, and some of these guests at the dinner party will change the way they live their lives as a result of this encounter with Jesus.

CHAPTER FIFTEEN

Jesus Teaches About Fasting and Breaks the Sabbath Rules

It has been months since John was arrested, and although many of his disciples, at the suggestion of John himself, are followers of Jesus, some remain loyal to John. On top of their affection for John, however, they have a general distaste for the way Jesus and his disciples carry themselves. Whereas John and his disciples fast and wear rough clothing, Jesus and his disciples wear normal clothes and never seem to fast at all. John had frequently pointed out to them the importance of fasting and not being vain about their appearance. Jesus seems to pay no attention to fasting and takes care of his appearance much like everyone else. When they hear the news of Jesus' dinner at Levi's house, some of them decide to ask Jesus about this.

The next day they approach him. They do so respectfully, as they know the tremendous esteem their beloved John has for him. Jesus sees them approaching. These are good men, and his smile acknowledges that fact. Unlike the Pharisees and chief priests, they do not have a malicious agenda. They are confused and looking for some clarification and so ask, "Why do we and the Pharisees fast so much, but your disciples do not fast?" (Mark 2:18). Jesus' reply is full of affection. "Can the wedding guests fast while the bridegroom is with them? As long as they have the bridegroom with them they cannot fast. But the days will come when the bridegroom is taken away from them, and then they will fast on that day" (Mark 2:19-20). Jesus is not denigrating fasting but symbolically pointing out that his presence represents a very special time. There will be plenty of time for his disciples to fast; indeed, many of them will give their very lives for him, but for now fasting is not the key issue. Paying attention to the message and the person of the "bridegroom" is the important point. John's disciples realize Jesus is referring to himself as the bridegroom but aren't quite sure what the symbolism means. However, they are men of faith. Thus, as they take their leave from Jesus, they reflect and talk among themselves about these words. None of them become Jesus' disciples this day but eventually they will come to see him for who he is. But for now, these are men of good will and Jesus is content to let them progress in their understanding of him at their own pace.

Weeks pass. One Sabbath, Jesus and his disciples walk together enjoying each other's company after the services. As usual, people are following. With their hatred for Jesus increasing, the Pharisees, Scribes, and chief priests keep an eye on him to see if they can catch him in some fault. It is towards the end of the rainy season, late February, and day 504 of the 909 days that changed the world.

The day is clear, and the sun is shining. The grain is beginning to grow. As they make their way through a field, Jesus' disciples start picking some of the immature heads, rub them in their hands, and eat them. The Pharisees seize on this apparent violation of the Sabbath and immediately call to Jesus and his disciples from behind. "Why are your disciples doing what is unlawful on the Sabbath?" (Luke 6:2). The disciples pause. Jesus stops, turns back, and looks at the Pharisees with sharpness in his eyes. Their hardness of heart is wearisome, yet he will use their question to make an important point. "Have you not read what David did when he and those who were with him were hungry? How he went into the house of God, took the bread of offering, which only the priests could lawfully eat, ate of it, and shared it with his companions?" (Luke 6:3-4). Oh yes, Jesus knows he is making himself at least the equal of David and knows it will increase their ire, but he is not finished. Jesus is greater than David, and all their man-made rules miss the point, so before turning his back to these Pharisees, he looks them in the eyes and slowly, with his voice rising, says, "The Sabbath was made for man, not man for the Sabbath. That is why the Son of Man is Lord even of the Sabbath" (Mark 2:27-28). The Pharisees, unable to respond, stand apart and look at one another. The disciples continue with their Sabbath snack. There will be many more events when Jesus shows that the Sabbath is much more than mere burdensome ritual. Another occurs the very next Sabbath.

On that day, Jesus as usual reads from the scriptures, sits down, and expounds on what he has just read. As usual, everyone in the gathering is glued to his words. He speaks eloquently and profoundly but in a way that makes each person believe he is speaking directly to him. When the other readers, usually Pharisees, finish their reading, sit down, and start making comments, the intensity of the listeners has dropped dramatically. Everyone notices it each week, and it is making the leaders more and more furious. Today they have another plan in their callous hearts.

The Pharisees bring a man with a withered hand close to Jesus. If he cures the man, they can accuse Jesus of violating the Sabbath; if he doesn't cure the man, they can hope the tide of public opinion will turn against him. Having been bested already last Sabbath, the Pharisees try another route of attack. They are confident this will work. Jesus, knowing full well their malice but filled with pity for this poor man, says, "Come up and stand here before us" (Luke 6:8). The man gets up hesitantly to stand before Jesus. He too has heard and seen what Jesus has done for men like him. Jesus angrily turns his gaze to the Pharisees, saying, "I ask you: is it lawful to do good on the Sabbath rather than evil, to save life rather than destroy it?" (Luke 6:9). "Which one of you who has a sheep that falls into a pit on the Sabbath will not take hold of it and pull it out? How much more valuable a person is than a sheep?" (Matt 12:11-12).

He pauses for an answer…but none comes. Jesus, his eyes softening, turns to the man with the withered hand and cures him. The whole congregation lets out a great cry as the man waves his hand for all to see. Thanking Jesus, the man takes his seat again as does Jesus, but the miracle has changed the tone of the assembly and, after the last one or two readings are done, everyone pours out into the street to talk. Even the humiliated Pharisees walk out of the temple talking, but not about the merits of the miracle but rather ways to get rid of this Jesus. They hastily decide to make plans with the Jewish supporters of King Herod, who also happened to be in Capernaum observing Jesus, for ways to turn Jesus over to him. So later on the same day, the Pharisees meet with them and begin to strike up an unholy alliance. It will take them about thirteen months from now to do so, but ultimately they will succeed.

CHAPTER SIXTEEN

Jesus Chooses His Apostles

Jesus had felt the heat from the leaders in Judea while he was baptizing in the Jordan upon John's arrest some six months ago, and had moved back to Galilee. Now he is feeling the heat increasing from them here also. He is becoming more and more weary of them, so for the time being, Jesus takes his preaching outside the city of Capernaum and moves north. He also does this because, as noted in the gospel of Mark (3:7ff), many people from districts far and wide, including places outside of Judea and Galilee, are coming to see him. They come with their infirm and ill, pitch tents, and press Jesus to work his miracles. The crowds become so intense that Jesus frequently "tells his disciples to have a boat ready for him because of the crowds, so they will not crush him. He cures many, and as a result, those who have diseases are pressing upon him to touch him. And whenever unclean spirits see him they fall down before him and shout out, 'You are the Son of God.' He warns them sternly not to make him known" (Mark 3:9-11). It is a scene the likes of which have never been seen before: massive numbers of people coming to see Jesus. As far as the eye can see are tents and people. Jesus, seemingly tireless, looks each person in the eye and makes him feel as if he alone has his attention. Even when he is on a boat talking to them, he makes each person feel as if he is addressing him alone.

But he is not tireless, and frequently, if not every night, he disappears into the mountains opposite the shore line. There he prays intensely. His closest disciples, knowing he does this, marvel at how he seems re-energized after a night in the mountains. On daybreak of one morning, however, Jesus has not returned from the mountains. The throngs of people are looking for him and press the disciples to know where he is. After some attempt to hold the crowd, they finally tell them he is likely in the mountains. The disciples and most of the crowd, reminiscent of the morning after that day of great miracles in Capernaum, which began with the healing of Peter's mother-in-law a few months ago, begin the trek to find Jesus.

As they work their way up the mountain, they come to a large plateau-like plain, and from there they can see Jesus coming down from the higher parts of the mountain. The sun behind them now is a little higher up on the horizon, and the sunlight seems almost to be pointing directly at Jesus. As they get closer, Jesus motions for them all to stop. It takes a minute, but the crowd quiets down; they are anxious to hear what he has to say. In a loud voice—one so loud it has each member of the crowd looking at one another—Jesus calls out the names of twelve people. He calls for Simon, who will become Peter, and his brother Andrew; John and his brother James who will be called the Sons of Thunder; Philip and his friend Nathaniel, who will come to be known as Bartholomew. Five of these six have known Jesus from the days John pointed him out at the Jordan River almost a year and a half ago. He calls Levi, the tax-collector he has just met a few weeks ago and who will be known as Matthew. He also calls five others who, like Levi, have not known Jesus as long as the original five. He calls Thomas, a hard-headed, stubborn man, James Bar-Alpheus, and his brother Jude, who is also known as Thaddeus, and Simon, who is also called the Zealot to differentiate him from Simon Peter. The latter three (James, Jude, and Simon) are kinsmen of Jesus, and, appearance-wise, the least impressive of the lot. His final call is the one man who most people regard as the brightest of the twelve, Judas Iscariot. Judas is a successful man in his own right and is well respected by those who know him for his prudence, calm demeanor, and leadership. He, of course, the seemingly best of the lot, will turn out to be the worst. As these twelve approach him almost at the point where the mountain meets the plateau, Jesus bids the crowd to sit down on the plain.

The twelve make their way up the mountain to meet Jesus. His smile is as warm as they have ever seen. His eyes are on fire. He tells them to sit down and says that, after an intense night of prayer with his Father, he has chosen these "twelve (whom he also names apostles) that they might be with him and he might send them forth to preach and to have authority to drive out demons" (Mark 3:14-15). Not one of his new apostles really understands. Most of them are thrilled, because they believe the time of when Jesus will reveal himself as the Messiah is close at hand. Soon, they believe, he will free the Jews from the bondage of the Romans, and the Promised Land will be theirs once again with Jesus as the new ruler. They are all proud Jesus has picked them to be of special importance in this new kingdom on earth. They, of course, have no understanding of the real nature of this new kingdom, and Jesus will let time, and the Holy Spirit, gradually reveal it to them.

CHAPTER SEVENTEEN

The Sermon on the Mount

Jesus and his twelve apostles make their way down the mountain and walk towards the people waiting for them on the plain. It is mid-March—day 522 of the 909 days that changed our world. As Jesus, with his apostles following him, makes his way to the center, the crowd remains seated and quiet, waiting to hear what he will say about these twelve men. But he says nothing about them. Instead, he looks up to heaven before he begins a talk that will forever change the way people think about the law.

The Sermon on the Mount, so called in Matthew's gospel because Jesus was coming down from the mountain, is called the Sermon of the Plain in Luke's gospel, because it was actually delivered on the plateau of the mountain. Both gospel writers emphasize different points, as Matthew is writing primarily for a Jewish Christian audience and Luke for a Gentile Christian audience. Moreover, Matthew, as he is inclined to do throughout his gospel, tends to lump topics and speeches together rather than sticking to chronological order. Luke, like all the evangelists, is not following strict chronological order, either, but is more attuned to it than Matthew. This likely explains why the Sermon is so much longer in Matthew; it likely includes parts of sermons given at other times. What is key here is that Jesus will change the whole understanding of the law.

Although some of this as recorded by Matthew was likely spoken at a different time, let us sit down with the crowd on the plain and listen intently to Jesus. He brings his gaze back down from the sky, and those who are close can see that look of love and authority in his eyes. His voice is strong and clear as he begins to speak. "Blessed are the poor in spirit...." Everyone, no matter how far away, can hear him. "...for theirs is the kingdom of heaven. Blessed are they who mourn, for they will be comforted. Blessed are the meek, for they will inherit the land. Blessed are they who hunger and thirst for righteousness, for they will be satisfied. Blessed are the merciful, for they will be shown mercy. Blessed are the clean of heart, for they will see God. Blessed are the peacemakers, for they will be called children of God. Blessed are they who are persecuted for the sake of righteousness, for theirs is the kingdom of heaven. Blessed are you when they insult you and persecute you and utter every kind of evil against you because of me. Rejoice and be glad, for your reward will be great in heaven. Thus they persecuted the prophets who were before you.

"You are the salt of the earth. But if salt loses its taste, with what can it be seasoned? It is no longer good for anything but to be thrown out and trampled underfoot. You are the light of the world. A city set on a mountain cannot be hidden. Nor do they light a lamp and then put it under a bushel basket; it is set on a lamp stand where it gives light to all in the house. Just so, your light must shine before others, that they may see your good deeds and glorify your heavenly Father.

"Do not think I have come to abolish the law or the prophets. I have come not to abolish but to fulfill. Amen, I say to you, until heaven and earth pass away, not the smallest letter or the smallest part of a letter will pass from the law, until all things have taken place. Therefore, whoever breaks one of the least of these commandments and teaches others to do so will be called least in the kingdom of heaven. But whoever obeys and teaches these commandments will be called greatest in the kingdom of heaven. I tell you, unless your righteousness surpasses that of the scribes and Pharisees, you will not enter into the kingdom of heaven.

"You have heard that it was said to your ancestors, 'You shall not kill, and whoever kills will be liable to judgment.' But I say to you, whoever is angry with his brother will be liable to judgment, and whoever says to his brother, 'Raqa' (which means imbecile), will be answerable to the Sanhedrin, and whoever says, 'You fool,' will be liable to fiery Gehenna. Therefore, if you bring your gift to the altar, and there recall that your brother has anything against you, leave your gift there at the altar, go first and be reconciled with your brother, and then come and offer your gift. Settle with your opponent quickly while on the way to court with him. Otherwise, your opponent will hand you over to the judge, and the judge will hand you over to the guard, and you will be thrown into prison. Amen, I say to you, you will not be released until you have paid the last penny.

"You have heard that it was said, 'You shall not commit adultery.' But I say to you, everyone who looks at a woman with lust has already committed adultery with her in his heart. If your right eye causes you to sin, tear it out and throw it away. It is better for you to lose one of your members than to have your whole body thrown into Gehenna. And if your right hand causes you to sin, cut it off and throw it away. It is better for you to lose one of your members than to have your whole body go into Gehenna.

"Again, you have heard that it was said to your ancestors, 'Do not take a false oath, but make good to the Lord all that you vow.' But I say to you, do not swear at all; not by heaven, for it is God's throne; nor by the earth, for it is his footstool; nor by Jerusalem, for it is the city of the great King. Do not swear by your head, for you cannot make a single hair white or black. Let your 'Yes' mean 'Yes,' and your 'No' mean 'No.' Anything more is from the evil one.

"You have heard that it was said, 'An eye for an eye and a tooth for a tooth.' But I say to you, offer no resistance to one who is evil. When someone strikes you on your right cheek, turn the other one to him as well. If anyone wants to go to law with you over your tunic, hand him your cloak as well. Should anyone press you into service for one mile, go with him for two miles. Give to the one who asks of you, and do not turn your back on one who wants to borrow.

"You have heard that it was said, 'You shall love your neighbor and hate your enemy.' But I say to you, love your enemies and pray for those who persecute you, that you may be children of your heavenly Father, for he makes the sun rise on the bad and the good, and causes the rain to fall on the just and the unjust. For if you love those who love you, what recompense will you have? Do not the tax collectors do the same? And if you greet your brothers only, what is unusual about that? Do not the pagans do the same? So be perfect as your heavenly Father is perfect.

"Take care not to perform righteous deeds in order that people may see them; otherwise you will have no recompense from your heavenly Father. When you give alms, do not blow a trumpet before you, as the hypocrites do in the synagogues and in the streets to win the praise of others. Amen, I say to you, they have received their reward. But when you give alms, do not let your left hand know what your right hand is doing so that your almsgiving may be secret. And your Father who sees in secret will repay you.

"When you pray do not be like the hypocrites, who love to stand and pray in the synagogues and on street corners so that others may see them. Amen, I say to you, they have received their reward. But when you pray, go to your inner room, close the door, and pray to your Father in secret. And your Father who sees in secret will repay you. In praying do not babble like the pagans, who think they will be heard because of their many words. Do not be like them. Your Father knows what you need before you ask him.

"This is how you are to pray: Our Father in heaven, hallowed be your name, your kingdom come, your will be done on earth as in heaven. Give us this day our daily bread; and forgive us our debts, as we forgive our debtors; and do not subject us to the final test, but deliver us from the evil one. If you forgive others their transgressions, your heavenly Father will forgive you. But if you do not forgive others, neither will your Father forgive your transgressions.

"When you fast, do not look gloomy like the hypocrites. They neglect their appearance, so that they may appear to others to be fasting. Amen, I say to you, they have received their reward. But when you fast, anoint your head and wash you face so that you may not appear to be fasting, except to your Father who is hidden. And your Father who sees what is hidden will repay you.

"Do not store up for yourselves treasures on earth, where moth and decay destroy, and thieves break in and steal. But store up treasures in heaven, where neither moth nor decay destroy, nor thieves break in and steal. For wherever your treasure is, there also will your heart be.

"The lamp of the body is the eye. If your eye is sound, your whole body will be filled with light, but if your eye is bad, your whole body will be in darkness. And if the light in you is darkness, how great will the darkness be.

"No one can serve two masters. He will either hate the one and love the other, or be devoted to one and despise the other. You cannot serve God and mammon.

"Therefore, I tell you, do not worry about your life, what you will eat or drink, or about your body, what you will wear. Is not life more than food and the body more than clothing? Look at the birds in the sky; they do not sow or reap, they gather nothing into barns, yet your heavenly Father feeds them. Are you not more important than they? Can any of you by worrying add a single moment to your life span? Why are you anxious about your clothes? Learn from the way the wildflowers grow. They do not work or spin. But I tell you that not even Solomon in all his splendor was clothed like one of them. If God so clothes the grass of the field, which grows today and is thrown into the oven tomorrow, will he not much more provide for you, O you of little faith? So do not worry and say, 'What are we to eat?' or 'What are we to drink?' or 'What are we to wear?' All these things the pagans seek. Your heavenly Father knows that you need them all. But seek first the kingdom of God and his righteousness, and all these things will be given you besides. Do not worry about tomorrow; tomorrow will take care of itself. Sufficient for the day is its own evil.

"Stop judging, that you may not be judged. For as you judge, so will you be judged, and the measure with which you measure will be measured out to you. Why do you notice the splinter in your brother's eye but do not perceive the wooden beam in your own eye? How can you say to your brother, 'Let me remove that splinter from your eye,' while the wooden beam is in your eye? You hypocrite, remove the wooden beam from your eye first; then you will see clearly to remove the splinter from your brother's eye.

"Do not give what is holy to dogs, or throw your pearls before swine, lest they trample them underfoot, and turn and tear you to pieces.

"Ask and it will be given to you; seek and you will find; knock and the door will be opened to you. For everyone who asks receives; and the one who seeks finds; and to the one who knocks, the door will be opened. Which one of you would hand his son a stone when he asks for a loaf of bread, or a snake when he asks for a fish? If you, then, who are wicked, know how to give good gifts to your children, how much more will your heavenly Father give good things to those who ask him?

"Do to others whatever you would have them do to you. This is the law and the prophets.

"Enter through the narrow gate; for the gate is wide and the road broad that leads to destruction, and those who enter through it are many. How narrow the gate and constricted the road that leads to life! And those who find it are few.

"Beware of false prophets, who come to you in sheep's clothing, but underneath are ravenous wolves. By their fruits you will know them. Do people pick grapes from thorn bushes, or figs from thistles? Just so, every good tree bears good fruit, and a rotten tree bears bad fruit. A good tree cannot bear bad fruit, nor can a rotten tree bear good fruit. Every tree that does not bear good fruit will be cut down and thrown into the fire. So by their fruits you will know them.

"Not everyone who says to me, 'Lord, Lord,' will enter the kingdom of heaven, but only the one who does the will of my Father in heaven. Many will say to me on that day, 'Lord, Lord, did we not prophesy in your name? Did we not drive out demons in your name? Did we not do mighty deeds in your name?' Then I will declare to them solemnly, 'I never knew you. Depart from me, you evildoers.'

"Everyone who listens to these words of mine and acts on them will be like a wise man who built his house on rock. The rain fell, the floods came, and the winds blew and buffeted the house. But it did not collapse; it had been set solidly on rock. And everyone who listens to these words of mine but does not act on them will be like a fool who built his house on sand. The rain fell, the floods came, and the winds blew and buffeted the house. And it collapsed and was completely ruined" (Matt 5:2-7:27).

When Jesus finishes his discourse, the crowd remains silent for a long time. There is so much meat in this sermon! His words have touched each person, who ponders them in his heart. Even the Scribes and Pharisees in the crowd contemplate what he has said. Some in the crowd understand more deeply than others, but all know that his teaching is radically different from what they have heard before. They were accustomed to hearing what they should not do, but now, without negating the law, he is emphasizing what they should do. They were accustomed to hearing how they should follow the rules and rituals exactly, but now, without eliminating the rules and rituals, he is emphasizing understanding the spirit behind them. No longer is it the simple justice of "an eye for an eye and a tooth for a tooth" but now it is forgiving everyone. No longer is it "show everyone how much you are fasting," but now it is fasting without others knowing. Most importantly, Jesus is now emphasizing a fundamental but often overlooked point of the law: the primacy of people over things, relations over possessions, others over self. This emphasis is radical. Never have these people heard someone speak about the law like this, but his words burn with truth in the hearts and minds of those who hear him with good will.

Jesus' eyes and voice soften as he finishes his discourse. It is getting to be mid-morning, and many of these people have had nothing to eat, so he walks through the crowd towards the end of the plateau, motioning for all to get up. He makes his way back down the hill towards the shore and the camps, and everyone follows, each returning to his own campsite or home. The day and night are filled with deep conversations as people share their reflections on this Sermon on the Mount.

CHAPTER EIGHTEEN

The Centurion's Servant

A few days after the Sermon on the Mount, Jesus decides to leave the outskirts of the city and return to Capernaum as the influx of new people arriving has slowed. He tells those remaining to return to their homes, their families, and their jobs. They do not want to go, but he is firm in his request, so over the course of a day or so most people take their leave. Some have to travel only a short distance to a town in Galilee and some longer distances to Judea and other countries. But they all go wondering what great things will come from Jesus. Their hearts burn with admiration and anticipation. Jesus has chosen his special twelve and delivered his gospel, the good news, about how people ought to live their lives. It is now time for Jesus to return to town. Because he has been away and because of his immense popularity, he has not been bothered recently by the chief priests, Pharisees or Scribes. It is getting close to the Pasch, and many of the leaders and townspeople have already begun the pilgrimage to Jerusalem. As Jesus re-enters Capernaum, there are less Pharisees with whom to contend. It is late March—day 531 of the 909 days that changed the world. Jesus will not go to the Paschal celebration this year, as he is not ready yet for his final confrontation with the Jewish leaders in Jerusalem, which will take place about one year from now. Instead he will use the time to perform more miracles and take another tour of Galilee.

Back in town, the Roman centurion in charge of a small band of Roman soldiers patrolling Capernaum has heard about Jesus and his miracles. He has heard the report from his men whom he sent to observe the influx of people north of the city to see Jesus. His slave, a young Jewish man who is his personal assistant, is ill and dying. This centurion, however, is not like most of the occupiers of the

Galilean towns. He is sensitive to the Jews and their beliefs; indeed, he has even helped them in various endeavors, including building the local temple. He is also friends with the Roman royal official from Cana whose son had been healed by Jesus last summer, some seven months ago. He thinks to himself that maybe Jesus will work the same miracle for his beloved slave. Hearing Jesus is back in town, he decides to ask some of the Jewish elders if they will go to Jesus on his behalf and ask him to come and cure his slave. Aware of the controversy, he chooses elders he knows are favorably disposed towards Jesus. These elders, having genuine concern for this man, willingly agree to approach Jesus. They greet Jesus and urge him to come to the centurion's house, saying, "He deserves to have you do this for him, for he loves our nation and built our synagogue for us" (Luke 7:4-5).

Jesus can see these elders have the beginnings of faith in him, and they are sincere in their concern for this Roman centurion, and so he agrees to go to the man's home. Those walking along grow excited as they see him making his way towards the centurion's house. They can sense another miracle about to happen. A few people run ahead and, getting to the house first, tell the centurion's guards that Jesus is on the way. When the news is passed along to the centurion, he is deeply moved. Remembering the story of his friend's son, he is filled with humility thinking a similar miracle is about to happen. Sensitive to the Jewish law that Jews should not enter the homes of pagans, and not wanting to offend Jesus by asking him to cross his portal, in his own act of faith the centurion writes a quick message and sends servants to meet Jesus along the way.

When they meet Jesus, he is only a few minutes from the house. On seeing them approach, he stops and so does the crowd with him. The messengers are nervous, but Jesus' countenance reassures them. One of them gives him the message: "Lord, do not trouble yourself, for I am not worthy to have you come under my roof. Therefore, I did not consider myself worthy to come to you, but say the word and my servant will be healed. For I, too, am a person subject to authority, with soldiers subject to me. And I say to one 'Go' and he goes; and to another 'Come here' and he comes; and to my slave 'Do this' and he does it" (Luke 7:7-8).

Jesus turns to the crowd and, with a look of astonishment, says, "I tell you, not even in Israel have I found such faith" (Luke 7:9). This

Roman is expressing exactly what Jesus is looking for: faith in him and not merely faith in the miracles he performs. Jesus' comment is not only a compliment to the faith of the centurion, it is also a sign that his salvation is meant for the whole world and not only for Jews. Jesus turns back to the messengers with a smile on his face as he tells them to go back home; the boy is healed because of the great faith of their master. The messengers return home and find the slave fully healed and their master, the centurion, pondering the events of the last hour. Even though Jesus does not, the Jewish elders also return to the centurion's house. They do not enter, but when they see the centurion and his slave come out to greet them, they too are struck deeply. One of them even makes the point to the others about Jesus' performing miracles not only for the Jewish people but also for the Romans. What can that mean? They take their leave contemplating this question. Although we never hear about the centurion again, can there be any doubt that he and his family become faithful followers of Jesus? Indeed, it is hard not to imagine the man making his way to see Jesus, likely that very day, and thanking him for his mercy and compassion.

Chapter Nineteen

The Widow's Son

This is the time when Jesus' popularity with the people is growing exponentially. He has been in Capernaum about seven and a half months, has performed many miracles, and has attracted a large number of followers from all parts of Galilee, Judea, and even foreign places. It is early spring, the rains have stopped, and the mountainsides are teeming with new growth. It has been about one year since Jesus was in Jerusalem for the Pasch and cleared out the temple. One day, shortly after healing the Centurion's slave, Jesus, his disciples, and a large crowd make their way over the mountains towards the little town of Naim.

From Capernaum to Naim is about one day's journey. The road leads over the hills that skirt the western side of the Sea of Galilee, then cuts south to the foot of Mt. Tabor. The road then passes around Mt. Tabor and enters the upper end of the Valley of Esdraelon. From there they can look behind them and to the west where hidden up in the mountains is Jesus' hometown of Nazareth. Looking forward, which is south, they can see the mountain range of Little Hermon, which divides the valley from Samaria. There, a little above the level of the valley, stands Naim, a village with a white wall surrounding it. Jesus will spend the night there.

As Jesus and the crowd approach the town gate, they hear the loud wailing of a funeral procession from inside the city, which gets louder as Jesus and the procession draw nearer to each other. Just before Jesus and the followers enter the gate, the funeral procession exits. It is a man, the only son of a widow, who has died. His mother is bitterly weeping next to the four men carrying the corpse on a bier. Behind her are the customary mourners who also are loudly wailing. It would be customary for Jesus and his companions to step aside, bow their heads, and let the funeral procession pass. Instead of moving off to the side of the road however, Jesus turns and signals for his followers to stop. His followers are miffed—his actions appear disrespectful. Jesus alone approaches the funeral procession, puts up his hand to indicate they should stop, and "moved with pity, he says to the mother 'Do not weep'" (Luke 7:13). Many in the procession wonder who this man is. Is he some relative of the family no one knows? Surely he can't be a stranger to act like this! One or two, however, do recognize Jesus, and a murmur begins to rise from the people.

Jesus has looked deeply into the eyes of this grieving mother, and his look has consoled her. She stops crying. He then turns to the bier and touching it, says, "Young man, I say to you arise (and immediately) the dead man then sits up and begins to speak" (Luke 7:14-15). The man looks around, startled and dazed. The crowd is in an uproar. How has this happened? Surely this young man was dead. How is he now alive?

Jesus smiles at the young man, helps him off the bier, and walks him the few steps over to his mother and puts her hand into her son's. Her tears return in gushes as she feels the warmth of her son's hand and the full reality hits her that he is back from the dead. As she embraces him, she looks at Jesus through her tears of gratitude and tries to say something, but cannot. The crowd remains aghast by what they have witnessed. Fear seizes many of them as they reflect on the power of this man to raise the dead back to life.

As the crowd presses in on the mother and boy to see more closely for themselves, Jesus and his followers continue into the city where they will spend the night. We can only wonder how many people from the village of Naim will walk by the house where Jesus is staying to try to get a glimpse of him. More notably, the news of this miracle, different from other miracles Jesus has performed in his ministry, spreads like wildfire "through the whole of Judea and in all the surrounding regions" (Luke 7:17). Jesus has healed many sick people, some of whom seemed destined to die—but this time he has brought someone back from the dead! All the more, people want to see this man who now shows power over death itself. And all the more, the Pharisees and leaders want to do away with this Jesus, who clearly is challenging their authority in the hearts and minds of the Jewish people.

Chapter Twenty

The Messengers from John the Baptist

Meanwhile, in Perea in the town of Machaerus, on a lonely mountainside overlooking the Dead Sea, John the Baptist is languishing away in Herod's fortress prison. Because he respects John, Herod periodically allows John's disciples to visit him and they update him on news about Jesus. John addresses "two of his disciples and sends them to the Lord to ask, 'Are you the one to come or are we to look for another?'" (Luke 7:19). At first blush, this seems an odd question for John to ask, since he has already many times indicated that Jesus is the one he has been preaching about. Indeed, he has urged his disciples to follow Jesus. Why would he ask this question now? It is possible that John, in the darkness of Herod's prison, might be experiencing doubts about Jesus; but it is more likely John is using this as an opportunity to gently convince his remaining disciples to see Jesus the way John sees him. He hopes Jesus' answer to this question will convince these disciples what John knows to be true: Jesus is the Messiah.

In any case, these two, probably accompanied by others of John's remaining disciples, make their way towards Galilee from Machaerus. They walk along the east bank of the Dead Sea and up along the same side of the Jordan River. They pass the spot where they had spent many a day baptizing, where the path from Galilee crosses from the Perean side of the Jordan to the Judean side. Further up the path, as they cross from Decapolis into Galilee, they pass the place where they baptized people after John had moved from his original location. And they pass the very spot—and they all stop and ponder for a long moment—where Herod's men had arrested John some seven months ago. As they cross into Galilee, the region is abuzz with talk about Jesus. They hear that he has recently been in the little town of Naim, where he raised a young man from the dead. They hear of healings and miracles, and, by talking to people along the way, figure out Jesus' apparent route as he is going from village to village. By moving quickly, they are able to catch up with him as he is curing people in a village in Galilee.

Arriving into town and seeing all that is occurring, John's disciples stay in the background at first. They do not want to interrupt him, for "at that time he is curing many of their diseases, sufferings, and evil spirits; he also is granting sight to many who are blind" (Luke 7:21). Indeed, if it weren't for their clothing, John's disciples might even be confused with the Pharisees and Scribes, who are also standing on the sidelines. Presently, as Jesus has healed the people brought to his attention and all are sharing their stories with one another, John's disciples hesitantly approach him. Seeing them, Jesus smiles and welcomes them, indicating how pleased he is to see John's closest friends. They ask Jesus the question, "Are you the one who is to come or should we look for another?" (Luke 7:20). They are really asking if they should be following him as the Messiah, as John suggests.

Jesus, seeming oblivious to the rest of the crowd, gets that look in his eyes that his apostles have so clearly come to recognize. It is a look of both great love for the person to whom he is speaking as well as a look of authority that leaves no doubt about the importance of the words being spoken. "Go and tell John what you have seen and heard: the blind regain their sight, the lame walk, lepers are cleansed, the deaf hear, the dead are raised, the poor have the good news proclaimed to them. And blessed is the one who takes no offense at me" (Luke 7:22-23). In other words, Jesus means to say: "I am the Messiah; look at all of these signs. I do not fast and dress as austerely as you do, but, yes, I am the Messiah—so blessed are you if you do not take offense at the differences between John's ways and my ways." He then asks them how John is doing in prison, speaks of his admiration for him, and tells them to bring his greetings to him. It becomes clear to these disciples of John that Jesus is the Messiah; they quickly take leave to make the nearly three-day journey back to John. John will be pleased by their enthusiasm when he sees them. He will feel he has done his job and that the end of his own time on earth is near.

Jesus watches John's disciples depart and, as soon as they are out of earshot, raises his voice in a manner that silences the crowd. "What did you go out to the desert to see? A reed swayed by the wind? Then what did you go out to see? Someone dressed in fine clothing? Those who wear fine clothing are in royal palaces. Then why did you go out? To see a prophet? Yes, I tell you, and more than a prophet. This is the one about whom it is written, 'Behold, I am sending my messenger ahead of you; he will prepare your way before you.' Amen, I say to you, among those born of women there has been none greater than John the Baptist, yet the least in the kingdom of heaven is greater than he. From the days of John the Baptist until now, the kingdom of heaven suffers violence, and the violent are taking it by force. All the prophets and the law prophesied up to the time of John. And if you are willing to accept it, he is Elijah, the one who is to come. Whoever has ears ought to hear" (Matt 11:7-15). It is a ringing endorsement of John.

As Jesus says these words, he notices some Pharisees and others standing off to the side, still with their disdainful looks. Down the road, he also sees a group of children playing a popular imitation game, and he booms, addressing the Pharisees, "To what shall I compare this generation? It is like children who sit in the market-places and call to one another, 'We played the flute for you, but you did not dance; we sang a dirge, but you did not mourn.' For John came neither eating nor drinking, and they said, 'He is possessed by a demon.' The Son of Man comes eating and drinking, and they say, 'Look—he is a glutton and a drunkard, a friend of tax collectors and sinners.' But wisdom is vindicated by her works" (Matt 11:16-19).

Jesus' words hang over the crowd. The Pharisees snicker and walk away. The rest of the crowd disperses discussing the miracles which have taken place today. We are close to the high-water mark of Jesus' popularity. Nevertheless, his opponents' hardness of heart is increasing, and their resolve to undo Jesus strengthens.

CHAPTER TWENTY-ONE

Jesus Meets the Woman of Magdala

As Jesus is working his way back to Capernaum from Naim, he cuts back east to the shore of the Sea of Galilee and passes through the city of Magdala. The city is located almost equidistant from Capernaum to the north, from which it receives many of its supplies, and Tiberias to the south, from which come much of the leisured class to spend a few days at this sophisticated city. It is a vacation city, with nice villas along the sea for the visitors. Immediately to the west of the city the mountain range rises very quickly and offers a beautiful view with the rising morning sun. This is the same Magdala which is a favorite summer dwelling place of Herod and his entourage, and the place from which he was returning to his castle in Machaerus seven months ago when he arrested John the Baptist.

Jesus is no stranger to this town, and as he approaches it, one of the local Pharisees, Simon, who has met Jesus before, sends a messenger to ask him to have dinner with him and his friends. Simon is a Pharisee, yes, but being from the more culturally eclectic Magdala has a much more open mind toward Jesus than many of his fellow Judean and Galilean Pharisees. Although Simon has not seen any miracles himself, he has heard of the growing wave of them and has seen the enthusiasm they are generating in all of Galilee and beyond. It will be interesting for him and impressive to his friends to have dinner with Jesus. Maybe he will perform some miracle for them. Besides these thoughts, there is something more: when Simon met him, he had sensed something unique about him. It was his eyes; no one had ever looked at him with such intensity of interest. Since then, Simon has been unable to shake that feeling.

Jesus accepts the dinner invitation, and when he arrives into the town goes directly to Simon's house. With him are only a few of his closest disciples, his apostles. On entering the house, Simon, as if to show Jesus off, immediately starts introducing him around. In his excitement at having this miracle worker in his home, he forgets to offer him the usual and customary greeting rituals. Jesus is quite gracious as he meets all of these people. He can tell most of them are only interested to see if he will perform a miracle, but there are a few who want to learn more about him. He lingers longer with these few and leaves an unforgettable impression on them.

As the introductions end and the guests are all seated on their couches for the meal, everyone's eyes are suddenly drawn to the front of the home. Like many homes, there is a large and open veranda separating the dining area from the street. Standing there is a woman. She seems to have appeared out of thin air. Some, however, recognize the woman. Her dress is multicolored and brilliant; the skirt has multiple attractive folds. There are rings on her fingers, silver bands on her wrists and ankles, golden bracelets on her bare arms, and a stunning necklace of gold coins. Her hair is long and black, her face is strong yet feminine, and her striking eyes are artfully made up. She is holding a small container in her hand and has no smile on her face. Instead, she is peering over the crowd looking for someone in particular. Whom can she be looking for? She looks back and forth to see all the guests until her eyes fall on Jesus. Instantly, she rushes towards him. Stunned, the diners remain still as this woman makes her way to the couch where Jesus is reclining.

When she gets to him she immediately kneels on the side of the couch where his feet are resting. She gently cups his feet in her hands and begins caressing them. Almost instantly tears from her eyes wet Jesus' feet as she continues to rub them. Her cries turn into sobs, and then, after what seems like an eternity but is actually only a minute or so, her sobbing subsides, and she begins to use her hair to wipe his feet dry. Nothing does she say to Jesus; not once does she lift her eyes to look at him. As the others in the dining room stare in amazement, Jesus, with a look of concentration, gazes on the woman. He says nothing. The woman says nothing. The dinner guests say nothing. Finally, the woman opens up the small container. The room is immediately filled with the rich aroma of the ointment—it is clearly expensive—and all watch as she pours it on his feet, massages them with it, and then dries his feet yet again with her hair. Still she says nothing; still she does not raise her eyes to meet his; still Jesus says nothing but only stares at her; and still no one in the room knows what to say.

Simon, the dinner host, echoing the thoughts of many in the room, wonders to himself, "If this man is a prophet, he would know who and what sort of woman this is who is touching him, that she is a sinner" (Luke 7:39). Jesus turns his gaze from the woman and looks directly at Simon. In a tone that invites Simon to respond, Jesus says, "Simon, I have something to say to you" (Luke 7:40). Simon responds, "Tell me, teacher" (Luke 7:40). In a quiet voice, almost as if speaking only to Simon, Jesus says, "Two people were in debt to a certain creditor; one owed five hundred days' wages and the other owed fifty. Since they were unable to pay the debt, he forgave it for both. Which of these will love him more?" (Luke 7:41-42). It is an easy answer, but Simon, perhaps even guessing where Jesus is going with this story, hedges. "The one, I suppose, whose larger debt was forgiven" (Luke 7:43). Jesus hops right away on his response, saying "You have judged rightly" (Luke 7:43).

Jesus now turns towards the woman, still addressing Simon with his words, but doing so in a louder voice now so all in the room can hear. "Do you see this woman? When I entered your house, you did not give me water for my feet, but she has bathed them with her tears and wiped them with her hair. You did not give me a kiss, but she has not ceased kissing my feet since the time I entered. You did not anoint my head with oil, but she anointed my feet with ointment" (Luke 7:44-46). In a louder voice still, Jesus continues, "So I tell you, her many sins have been forgiven; hence she has shown great love" (Luke 7:47). In a gentle rebuke aimed at Simon, he continues, "But the one of whom little is forgiven, loves little" (Luke 7:47).

On hearing these words, the woman slowly raises her eyes. Her heart feels light; she feels refreshed, renewed, and restored. Her eyes shine with gratitude as she hears Jesus say, "Your sins are forgiven. Your faith has saved you; go in peace" (Luke 7:48, 50). She can barely speak her thanks, gets up off her knees, and departs from the room as quickly as she had entered it. After a brief silence during which all are lost in their own thoughts, Simon breaks the spell by calling for the servants to serve the meal, but just like the Pharisees in the house where Jesus had healed the paralytic a few weeks ago in Capernaum, these men are thinking, "Who is this one who even forgives sins?" (Luke 7:49). Jesus lets them stew in their thoughts as the dinner is being served, but then, without further discussion about the woman, speaks to them about the importance of forgiveness. His words are received critically by most, but there are a few guests taken by the wisdom of his words and they go home reflecting on them.

CHAPTER TWENTY-TWO

Jesus' Female Followers

Jesus spends the next few days slowly passing through towns and villages as he works his way north to Capernaum (Luke 8:1). Along with his twelve apostles and other disciples, a number of woman have also been making this "tour" of Galilee with Jesus. Three of them are "Mary, called Magdalene, from whom seven demons had gone out, Joanna, the wife of Herod's steward Chuza, Susanna, and many others who are providing for them out of their resources" (Luke 8:2-3). Jesus had touched these women's lives in some way in his travels, whether it be curing them or a loved one of an infirmity, or captivating and rejuvenating their souls with his words and actions, or asking them to help him in his work.

In any event, in a culture that generally relegates women to second place, every woman who meets Jesus sees and feels the difference. He looks and speaks to each of them with utmost respect and attention. They have seen how he was so concerned for the widow who had lost her son in Naim. Why, just the other day, they heard how he treated the sinful woman who crashed the dinner party at Magdala. He seems to have a much deeper appreciation for women than many men, in their experience. His concern for each of them is not self-interested, but appears to be a genuine concern for their well-being. Although a few of these woman who now follow Jesus closely are blessed with husbands who love them, they all have experienced the second-class status afforded to women in that culture; they have known the lustful and impersonal attention of men. Yet Jesus is different. They can see it in his eyes. He is a man like the other men of Galilee, a handsome one at that with a charming smile, yet he treats women with more respect and dignity than they have ever experienced. Because his love seems sincere and pure, they are drawn to him; they follow along and help out by arranging places to stay, taking care of meals, and frequently doing so out of their own pockets. Yes, Jesus loves these women and all women dearly, not for what they can do for him but because they are uniquely made in the image and likeness of God, and at least one of them, Mary Magdalene, will stay at the foot of the cross in about one year from now, when all of the men have fled.

Since that eventful day of calling the first four disciples by the lakeside and curing Peter's mother-in-law and many others, we have heard little to nothing about Peter's wife or about the wives of any of the other apostles. Now that Peter constantly accompanies Jesus, where is his wife? Perhaps she too is accompanying Jesus and his apostles; more likely she is at home in Bethsaida or with her mother in Capernaum taking care of the house. From the cure of her mother to all the other miracles she has seen or heard about from her husband, she is sure Jesus is someone very special. Although domestic duties and the lack of independent means do not allow her to follow Jesus like the other women, she is happy to see her husband so clearly favored by him. Besides, she too is captivated by Jesus and the evident concern he shows her every time she sees him. He has a special affection for her as he knows the sacrifice she is making in order for Peter to travel with him. She thinks, as does her husband, that perhaps, one day soon, Peter will become famous for being so close to Jesus. The wives of his other apostles are thinking similar thoughts about Jesus and about their husbands. They all of course will be correct about becoming famous, but not in the way they envision.

There is one other very special woman about whom we have not heard much. From what will happen in a day or two, it seems clear his mother Mary has not been making these tours with him. She has remained in Capernaum and gone about her normal activities. Although we can only speculate why she has stayed there, perhaps Jesus has not wanted her subject to the crowds with which he has been dealing as he has gone throughout Galilee. In any case, we do know, from the glimpses we get of her in the scriptures, that Mary is quietly observing and listening to all that is being said about her son and is pondering them in her heart. She hears and feels the enthusiasm of the people, but there is a nagging sense in her heart about the actual depth of their commitment to Jesus. She hears the disapproving voices of the Pharisees, Scribes, and chief priests and wonders what can change their hardness of hearts. There is much to think about. How will all this work out for her son? She doesn't know, but does know he must be about his Father's business, so she puts it all in his hands.

CHAPTER TWENTY-THREE

An Eventful Day in Capernaum

After this latest tour of Galilee, Jesus arrives back in Capernaum early one morning. Everyone is up and about, and the town is excited because they have heard the news of the miracles Jesus has done since he left a few weeks ago. Travelers and merchants, as well as returning Paschal feast pilgrims, have been updating them, so they know Jesus is coming up the road from Magdala and expect his arrival today. It is mid-April and day 549 of the 909 days that changed the world. Today will be a memorable one.

When Jesus arrives, the crowd presses in on him. They ask questions about his travels through the towns, beg him to give more details of his miracles, and bring him those who are sick. Although some ask how Jesus is, most want to know about his exploits and press close to see what he might do next. For Jesus, there are no crowds, but only individuals, each whom he serves and to whom he gives complete attention. He spends a few minutes with one, longer or shorter times with others. He is so focused on them that he is unable to stop to eat (Mark 3:20). His apostles are hungry also but are taken up talking to the crowd.

Some of Jesus' relatives are in the town, and "when the relatives hear of this they set out to seize him, for they say, 'He is out of his mind'" (Mark 3:21). It is a telling use of words: "out of his mind." It shows how hard it is for these people to understand how anyone could put up with all this attention, which has little to do with Jesus as a person and much more to do with Jesus as the magician, the miracle worker. Does Jesus not see that most of these people could not care less if he is hungry, tired, in need rest? Can he not see they only want more excitement from him? Yet he treats each one with infinite patience. His relatives take control, work their way through the crowd, and tell Jesus he is to come with them to rest and get something to eat. The crowd lets out a big roar, but he and his apostles retreat to the house of one of these relatives. It is beyond the time for the normal midday meal, so they are hungry indeed. They have something to eat and drink and relax a bit, although many remain outside the door waiting for them to finish. This respite is welcome but will be brief.

In the crowd outside is a man who is both blind and mute and appears to be possessed by a demon. No one knows who he is or where he has come from, but he begins to wail and make noise, and the crowd starts to back away from him. He is dirty and unkempt. Jesus hears him and calls for them to bring him into the house (Matt 12:22). The man is invited to enter the house; no one gets near him, but he is told Jesus will see him, and so he enters on his own. Jesus has stood up and the house is quiet. The man says nothing. Jesus looks at him intently, raises his eyes to heaven, and "cures the mute person so he can hear and speak" (Matt 12:22). The man is overwhelmed as he realizes he is cured. He thanks Jesus profusely and runs out the door. The crowd, watching him leave the house and hearing him speak Jesus' praises, is astonished and asks, "Could this be the Son of David?" (Matt 12:23). Son of David—this is a reference to the Messiah, as the Jews were looking for him to come from King David's line. Can Jesus be the Messiah? Can he be the Promised One? It is an intoxicating thought as it runs through the minds of those in the crowd.

Not all of the observers are impressed. The Paschal feast has ended, and there are more Pharisees back on the scene. The Pharisees in this crowd, realizing the people are equating Jesus with the Messiah and watching their own power fade in his shadow, briefly discuss this among themselves. One of them advances a proposition meant to discredit Jesus. They shout to the crowd, "This man drives out demons only by the power of Beelzebub, the prince of demons" (Matt 12:24). It is like cold water being thrown on a hot fire. The crowd quiets down, each of them thinking about this charge. Jesus has done wonderful things, yes, but the Pharisees are men to be respected and—could it be that Jesus does all of this by the power of Satan?

Jesus from the house hears the crowd quiet down and knows what the Pharisees have just said. His eyes flash with fire, and he comes out of the door to address the crowd and the Pharisees. His apostles, in the house with him, look at one another. Where is he going? What has happened to quiet the crowd so quickly? As Jesus gets outside, everyone notices his anger; his voice is filled with indignation. Rarely, if at all, has anyone, even his apostles, seen such intensity. They all know something is about to happen, even the Pharisees are taken aback at the intensity of his angry eyes as he looks straight at them and says, "Every kingdom divided against itself will be laid waste, and no town or house divided against itself will stand. And if Satan drives out Satan, he is divided against himself; how, then, will his kingdom stand? And if I drive out demons by Beelzebub, by whom do your own people drive them out? Therefore, they will be your judges. But if it is by the Spirit of God that I drive out demons, then the kingdom of God has come upon you. How can anyone enter a strongman's house and steal his property, unless he first ties up the strongman? Then he can plunder his house. Whoever is not with me is against me, and whoever does not gather with me, scatters" (Matt 12:25-30). Jesus approaches the Pharisees and says, "Therefore, I say to you, every sin and blasphemy will be forgiven people, but blasphemy against the Spirit will not be forgiven. And whoever speaks against the Son of Man will be forgiven, but whoever speaks against the Holy Spirit will not be forgiven, either in this age or the age to come" (Matt 12:31-32).

The Pharisees are trying their best to look and remain calm, but Jesus' demeanor has them cowering, and the crowd can see it. But Jesus is not finished with these Pharisees and so continues in an equally strong voice, "Either declare the tree good and its fruit good, or declare the tree rotten and its fruit rotten, for a tree is known by its fruit. You brood of vipers, how can you say good things when you are evil? For from the fullness of the heart, the mouth speaks. A good person brings forth good out of a store of goodness, but an evil person brings out evil out of a store of evil. I tell you on the day of judgment people will render an account for every careless word they speak. By your words you will be acquitted and by your words you will be condemned" (Matt 12:33-37).

Jesus stares at the Pharisees, and his countenance seems to reveal sadness, disappointment, and disgust all at once: their hardness of heart grieves him to the quick, their failed leadership disappoints him, and their equating the Holy Spirit with Beelzebub disgusts him. What these Pharisees do not realize is they have attacked the unity of God, and Jesus will not stand for it. It will be for later generations to understand Jesus' anger here more clearly. Jesus does not cast out demons or perform any miracle "on his own." All of his power comes from the power of the love between himself and his Father. And that love, is a person, the Holy Spirit. These Pharisees, even unwittingly, may say what they want about Jesus, but he will not allow them to attack the Holy Spirit, the living personal bond of love which unites him to the Father.

The Pharisees are beaten and silenced; the crowd is also still. A few of the Pharisees, joined by some of the Scribes in the crowd, take a different tack. In a meek and almost apologetic tone, as if they are sorry for what they have said about Jesus' cure of the blind, deaf demoniac, they ask, "Teacher, we wish to see a sign from you" (Matt 12:38). A sign? It is a wonder Jesus does not explode again. The crowd half expects him to do so. Has not the cure of this demoniac man been a sign to them? Jesus knows there is nothing sincere in this question, but decides to use it as an opportunity to make his first public reference to his death and resurrection. Few, if any, will realize the significance of these words now, but many will later.

His voice becomes less angry but remains firm as he says, "An evil and unfaithful generation seeks a sign, but no sign will be given it except the sigh of Jonah the prophet. Just as Jonah was in the belly of the whale three days and three nights, so will the Son of Man be in the heart of the earth three days and three nights" (Matt 12:39-40). This prediction is lost on almost everyone there. Jesus continues, "At the judgment, the men of Nineveh will arise with this generation and condemn it, because they repented at the teaching of Jonah, and there is something greater than Jonah here. At the judgment, the Queen of the South will arise with this generation and condemn it, because she came from the ends of the earth to hear the wisdom of Solomon; and there is something greater than Solomon here. When an unclean spirit comes out of a person it roams through the regions searching for rest but finds none. Then it says, 'I will return to my home from which I came.' But upon returning, it finds it empty, swept clean, and put in order. Then it goes and brings back with itself seven other demons more evil than itself, and they move in and dwell there; and the last condition of that person is worse than the first. Thus it will be with this evil generation" (Matt 12:42-45).

Jesus' attack on these Pharisees is relentless, so the Pharisees and Scribes all slink away to lick their wounds. They are a vengeful bunch, however, and will soon be plotting other ways to undermine Jesus' hold on the people. Up until now, the Pharisees and Scribes had been nagging critics, but now, the battle lines have been drawn. Jesus is on one side, and the Pharisees and Scribes are on the other. From here on, the leaders will ratchet up their attacks and will no longer feign good will. This may be the high point of Jesus' popularity for, from now on, both Jesus and the Pharisees will invite people to choose sides.

As the Pharisees and Scribes walk away in all their finery, Jesus and the crowd remain in silence. All can see Jesus' eyes and demeanor begin to soften, and, just as he begins to say something, a woman in the back of the crowd, emboldened by what she has seen and comforted by her anonymity, shouts, "Blessed is the womb that carried you and the breasts at which you nursed" (Luke 11:27). Jesus lifts up his hands towards all the people and says, "Rather, blessed are those who hear the word of God and keep it" (Luke 11:28). Oddly, in a few hours, he will speak similar words. For now, Jesus walks back into the house and invites people in to speak to him. The rest of the afternoon passes with Jesus talking to all who wish to see him.

As the day lengthens and sunset draws closer, the crowd around the house remains large. Meanwhile, at the cottage where she is staying with some relatives, Mary, Jesus' mother, has just heard about Jesus' run-in with the Pharisees. She is upset by the reported intensity of the scene. Earlier in the morning, as Jesus first re-entered Capernaum, she had run out of her cottage to see him. He was busy with everyone, but, almost as if he sensed her approach, he had stopped, looked up, met her eyes, and smiled tenderly before turning his attention to the next person. She had decided to let him be about his Father's business and so returned to her cottage, but now this news about the Pharisees troubles her. She decides to go see Jesus, and some of her relatives accompany her.

As she approaches the house where Jesus is talking to everyone, the size of the crowd prevents her from getting inside. One of the relatives with Mary asks the people to give word to Jesus that his mother is there. The message gets passed along to the front of the crowd until someone standing close to Jesus hears it and tells him, "Your mother and brothers are standing outside, asking to speak to you" (Matt12:47). Jesus stops "and replies to the one who has just spoken to him, 'Who is my mother? Who are my brothers?' and stretching out his hands towards all his disciples he says, 'Here are my mother and my brothers. For whoever does the will of my heavenly Father is my brother, and sister, and mother'" (Matt 12:49-50).

Jesus' words hang in the air. There are some in the crowd who take Jesus' remark as a slight to Mary. They think he is snubbing his mother. Those who know him, however, realize such cannot be the case at all. They know, and have indeed seen many times, Jesus' love for his mother is profound and his concern for her far too consistent for him to be insulting to her in any way. No, those closer to Jesus realize he is not denigrating Mary at all, but raising the disciples up by saying those who would love him and thus truly be counted among his family are those who do the will of the Father. Mary is thus twice a mother—mother of Jesus' human nature, and mother because she accomplishes the will of the Father perfectly. Jesus knows the range of thoughts running through the minds of those listening and, although there is no mention of what happens next in the gospels, one can imagine his standing up and walking through the crowd to go meet his mother, whom he embraces. As the two of them walk away to the cottage where Mary is staying, Jesus turns to the crowd and his apostles and tells them he will see them in a short while. Arm in arm, Jesus and Mary disappear from the crowd's sight to spend a few moments together by themselves.

This has been a busy day; arriving in town in the early morning and ministering to the crowds, being taken away for some food and relaxation by some of his relatives at midday, curing the demoniac and being challenged by the Pharisees in a bitter confrontation, ministering more to the people in the late afternoon, and finally taking time to be with his mother. But as long as the day has been, it is far from finished. Taking leave of his mother with a smile and embrace, "on that day, Jesus goes out of the house and sits down by the sea"

(Matt 13:1). He is about to embark on a dramatic change of how he will preach to the people. As Jesus is making his way to the shore line, some notice, word spreads, and many follow him. It is a beautiful day and the sun is just beginning to set in the west, lighting up the hills and mountains on the east side of the Sea of Galilee. The crowd grows quickly and presses in on Jesus. It is hard to address them all, so, taking a page from what he did with Peter's boat a while ago, Jesus asks to use one of the boats tied up on shore. The owner gladly, proudly even, agrees to have him use his boat, so they row a short distance from the shore. It is easier now for everyone to see him, and his voice will carry well over the quiet shoreline.

As Jesus looks at the people and up at the hills behind them, he sees rows and rows of growing crops, waving in the light evening breeze, with the promise of a rich harvest soon to come. There are many footpaths that serve as a means to tend to the crops as well as for people and animals to make their way from town to town. Further down the hill, closer to town, are many crags and boulders, grey and white in the surrounding green and brown pathways. Even now, people are making their way down the hill towards the town, some with their donkeys as the evening sets in. He uses what he sees as the basis for his talk.

The crowd is hushed; all eyes are on him as he starts. "A sower went out to sow. And as he sowed, some seed fell on the path, and the birds of the air ate it up. Some fell on rocky ground, where it had little soil. It sprang up at once because the soil was not deep, and when the sun rose it was scorched and it withered for lack of roots. Some seed fell among the thorns, and the thorns grew up and choked it. But some seed fell on rich soil and produced fruit, a hundred or sixty or thirtyfold" (Matt 13:3-8). Jesus pauses for a long time. Everyone in the crowd, familiar with the imagery, wait for him to explain the story as he has done so many times before. One of the things that has made him so popular is how he uses things from everyday life to illustrate his teachings.

Jesus, however, does not explain the story. In a loud voice he merely says, "Whoever has ears ought to hear" (Matt 13:9). This is a dramatic change. All the people in the crowd, including the apostles, look at one another wondering what he means to say. For those of us who have the benefit of two thousand years of commentary on this story, the meaning seems obvious, but if we put ourselves in the shoes of these people, we can understand their confusion. To make matters worse, he continues to preach in this new way. Let us put ourselves on the shoreline, next to the apostles, and listen to Jesus, in rapid fire, deliver these parables with no explanation.

"The kingdom of heaven may be likened to a man who sowed good seed in his field. While everyone was asleep, his enemy came and sowed weeds all through his wheat, and then went off. When the crop grew and bore fruit, the weeds appeared as well. The slaves of the master came to him and said, 'Master, did you not sow good seed in your field? Where have all the weeds come from?' He answered them, 'An enemy has done this.' His slaves said to him, 'Do you want us to go and pull them up?' He replied, 'No, if you pull up the weeds you might uproot the wheat along with them. Let them grow together until the harvest; then at harvest time I will say to the harvesters, 'First collect the weeds and tie them in bundles for burning, but gather the wheat into my barn.'

"The kingdom of heaven is like a mustard seed that a person took and sowed in a field. It is the smallest of all the seeds, yet when full grown it is the largest of plants. It becomes a large bush, and the birds of the sky come and dwell in its branches.

"The kingdom of heaven is like yeast that a woman took and mixed with three measures of wheat flour until the whole batch was leavened.

"The kingdom of heaven is like a treasure buried in a field, which a person finds and hides again, and out of joy goes and sells all he has and buys that field. Again, the kingdom of heaven is like a merchant searching for fine pearls. When he finds a pearl of great price, he goes and sells all that he has and buys it. Again, the kingdom of heaven is like a net thrown into the sea, which collects fish of every kind. When it is full they haul it ashore and sit down to put what is good into buckets. What is bad they throw away. Thus it will be at the end of the age. Angels will go out and separate the wicked from the righteous and throw them into the fiery furnace, where there will be wailing and grinding of teeth" (Matt 13:24-33, 44-50).

When he finishes, he asks the boat owner to row him back to the shore. It is getting close to dusk. The crowd is perplexed about these stories, and as Jesus disembarks from the boat, most begin to make their way to their homes. Many are a touch disappointed; this was not much of an evening—no miracles, just lots of stories without any explanation. It had been a long day for most of them, so Jesus and his apostles are left to go back to their cottages by themselves without the crowd.

Getting to his cottage, Jesus knows he has confounded the apostles also. He can see it in their faces, but he can also see their faith in him and willingness to follow him no matter what. They have been whispering to one another on the walk back from the boat, so Jesus invites them all into his cottage. A candle is lit, and Jesus gets the question he knows is in their hearts: "Why do you speak to them in parables?" (Matt 13:10).

Jesus responds with a heaviness of heart. He sees the sides have been drawn clearly now after today's confrontation with the Pharisees and Scribes and knows, over the next few months, the people will have to choose on which side they stand. Knowing what is in men's hearts, he also sees that most of these people in the crowd are only following him for the thrill of his miracles, for the chance to be close to the one who will overthrow dreaded Roman rule, and for the opportunity it gives them to say they have seen or talked to someone as famous as he. Few people, save these men here, those holy woman who have followed him, and some other disciples, have an interest in hearing any message different from the one they want to hear. He knows how all this will turn out. As he addresses the question his apostles have just asked, we can hear this sorrow. "Because knowledge of the mysteries of the kingdom of heaven has been granted to you, but to them it has not been granted. To anyone who has, more will be given and he will grow rich; from anyone who has not, even what he has will be taken away. This is why I speak to them in parables, because they look but do not see and hear but do not understand. Isaiah's prophecy is fulfilled in them which says, 'You shall indeed hear but not understand, you shall indeed look but never see. Gross is the heart of this people, they will hardly hear with their ears, they have closed their eyes lest they see with their eyes and hear with their ears and understand with their heart and be converted and I heal them.' But blessed are your eyes, because they see, and your ears, because they hear. Amen I say to you, many prophets and righteous people longed to see what you see but did not see it, and to hear what you hear but did not hear it" (Matt 13:11-17).

Just as he does today, Jesus will not force anyone to seek him out; he will not force people to understand. It is up to each person to decide himself to come to know him. These apostles in the room with him have made their choice and they have decided to seek, know, and love him. He readily answers them when they next ask for clarification of the parables and patiently explains both of the sowing parables. These men may not be smarter than others, but their love for him is genuine. They will be the men to whom he will leave his ministry a year from now when he is gone. They must understand.

CHAPTER TWENTY-FOUR

Jesus Calms the Sea

The day is not yet over. It has been a long and taxing one. Jesus yearns for a little rest and time alone with the apostles, so, right after explaining some of the parables to them, he says, "Let us cross [the lake] to the other side" (Mark 4:35). His apostles are pleased to get time alone with him. The crowd has dispersed, so it is not hard for them to make their way down to the seashore relatively unaccompanied.

On their way there, however, a Scribe of good faith sees Jesus and on learning he is going to the other side of the lake says, "Teacher, I will follow you wherever you go" (Matt 8:19). Jesus smiles at him; yes, he can see this is a good man, but he answers him, saying, "Foxes have dens, and birds of the sky have nests, but the Son of Man has nowhere to lay his head" (Matt 8:20). It seems a harsh response, but Jesus is merely telling this man that he is not the Messiah for whom the Scribe is looking. Jesus is not the one who will come with power and might to set up the new political kingdom of the Jews. Since this afternoon's confrontation with the Pharisees and Scribes, he will not only speak in parables, but from now on will discourage people from thinking about him as a worldly Messiah. As they approach the shoreline, one of Jesus' disciples gets terrible news delivered to him by a messenger: his father has passed away back in his small village in Galilee. The disciple is struck with grief. He wants to follow Jesus tonight but feels compelled to return to comfort his family and bury his father. He composes himself and approaches Jesus. "Lord, let me go first and bury my father. But Jesus answers him, 'Follow me and let the dead bury their dead'" (Matt 8:21-22). Again he offers another seemingly harsh response. The disciple is visably taken aback, but Jesus is only emphasizing the need to follow him at any cost. He places his hands on the disciple's shoulders, whispers something in his ear which causes the disciple to nod in agreement, and then leaves him behind.

As Jesus gets to the shoreline, some disciples and a few others who own boats offer to take him and his apostles to the other side of the lake. They are happy to be part of this special group. They deem it an honor to spend time with him when not surrounded by masses of people. Quietly, with darkness settling in, the boats leave the shoreline. On Jesus' request, they make their way towards Gerasa, a valley and town southeast of Capernaum on the other side of the lake. Although, in general, these men do not like to be out on the lake at night, the weather is calm and the ride is smooth. Jesus himself has told them the course, so they feel all the more confident. As they move away, they look back and see many glimmering lights marking the long line of homes from Bethsaida to the north, to Capernaum and south towards Magdala. It is a charming sight. Here and there they can hear a dog bark, the distinctive noise of a band of foraging jackals, and the periodic laugh of a distant hyena. They can also intermittently hear the back and forth calls of cocks, a striking feature of these Eastern nights. Yes, all is calm and normal as they settle in for the trip across the lake. The journey should take them most of the night given the calm breeze; those not required to handle the sails or rudder, including Jesus, all prepare for sleep.

The Sea of Galilee is about fourteen miles long from north to south, and about six miles wide at its broadest point, which is opposite Genesareth and Magdala. The lake is about seven hundred feet below the level of the Mediterranean and is skirted on the east and west side by mountains, which shut it in as between two walls. On the north and south are open plains, though these too lie between mountain ridges. It is easy to see how the weather on this lake can change suddenly. Once the wind begins to pick up from the north or south, the mountains serve to funnel the wind to high speeds, causing treacherous conditions.

And so it happens tonight. Out of nowhere, with an intensity rarely seen by these rugged men, the wind begins to grow stronger from the north. The waves grow higher and higher, and the boats are difficult to control as the wind and waves are broadsiding the boats. Those asleep are rudely awakened by the sudden ferocity of the storm and the cries of the men. The boats are taking on water, and all are needed to bail the water. It is rapidly becoming a desperate situation. It is too dangerous to turn around to go back to Capernaum, so the only choice is to continue on this path or head south with the wind behind them and slowly try to maneuver the boat to the east. Neither choice is safe, though, and they realize this could be the end.

There is one person in one of the boats, however, who remains asleep. Remarkably, the weather and the cries of all the men have not stirred Jesus at all. Many of the men in the boats are kicking themselves for being out here. 'This is Jesus' fault for wanting to cross at night!' they think to themselves. How stupid of them for letting their guard down on this. Over the howls of the wind, some of the men shout out, wanting to know what Jesus thinks of this situation. Although originally not wanting to wake him up, the direness of their plight and the cries of the others compel those disciples in the boat with Jesus to wake him up. "Teacher, do you not care that we are perishing?" (Mark 4:38).

Jesus wakes up, and looks at them blankly at first, as if he has been in a very deep sleep. Standing up and holding out his arms, Jesus says in a voice that penetrates the wind and the wild sea, "Quiet, be still" (Mark 4:39). Instantly, the wind dies down, the waves subside, and "there is great calm" (Mark 4:39). The men in the boats are all stunned. Soaked from the battering waves and stressed at their apparent imminent demise, they cannot believe what has just happened. Was it really so dangerous a few seconds ago? How has this come to be? Now there is no noise but the gentle lapping of the water on the sides of the boats. Because of this quiet, Jesus does not have to raise his voice for all to hear him say, "Why are you terrified? Do you not yet have faith?" (Mark 4:40). His voice implies disappointment but also seems reassuring, as if he understands their terror and invites them to lose that terror by having more faith in him. Do not be terrified; have no fear; do not be afraid. These are words Jesus will use many times in his ministry. It is faith in Jesus that will allow his close followers to overcome their fears and accomplish great things for him, for others, and for themselves. The men in the boats, for their part, "are filled with great awe and say to one another, 'Who then is this whom even wind and sea obey?'" (Mark 4:41).

CHAPTER TWENTY-FIVE

The Healing of the Gerasene Demoniac

As dawn breaks, the boats approach their destination: the town of Gerasa. It is a little hollow between the mountains, with a few tiny villages running up the hillsides, at a distance from the shore. On those hillsides and in the valley, many crops are being grown. The mountains hold the villages in a semi-circle, with the mountain ranges coming all the way to the shoreline and ending in a steep crag both to the north and the south of this little cut-out spot. Beyond the mountains to the east of this valley lies the desert. It is a pretty yet isolated spot. The people here are mixed: some are Jews, many are not, and, although they have heard some things about Jesus by speaking to the merchants who stop for trade, the isolation of this place does not make for a well-informed community.

At the landing point where boats pull in, the land slopes upward to the villages. Jesus and his band of followers get out and secure their boats. No one asks Jesus why they have come here, but, if just to rest and to spend some time alone, this is a beautiful spot indeed. It will be nice to secure provisions from one of the villages and have a leisurely meal on the side of one of the hills surrounding the valley or even in the valley itself. There are plenty of attractive areas to choose from and not a lot of people to disturb them. After last night's scare, a restful day seems just perfect. As they slowly, almost lightheartedly, walk up the gentle slope towards the villages, they pass through an area of rough terrain filled with rock chambers and crags. Here, off to the side of the path to the villages, is a gravesite, as is clear from markings on the rock.

Suddenly on the path ahead, out of nowhere, appears a wild-looking person. This man, naked, unkempt, malodorous, and moving more like an animal than a man, frequently harasses people passing by, although he never harms them. He will also wail and scream at any time of the day or night in a voice that sounds as if there are many voices joining together. He will frequently do terrible violence to his own body, pounding and bruising himself with rocks. The townspeople have tried to constrain him with chains out of fear for themselves and pity for him, but he has always broken them. Ultimately, it was decided to leave him alone, but, as a precaution, everyone who passes this way brings a weapon just in case this demoniac man attacks.

Standing on his toes at a distance from Jesus and his disciples, this wild man sniffs at the air as if he has picked up a scent. Curling back into a ball close to the ground for a moment, he jumps up and starts running towards them, screaming something inaudible at the top of his lungs. Most of the disciples are terrified, some turn to run, but Jesus stands firm. Seeing Jesus' calmness in the face of this on-rushing madman, his followers nervously stand their ground and they hear Jesus speaking calmly, clearly, almost to himself. "Unclean spirit, come out of the man" (Mark 5:8). Speedily the man continues towards them, bounding over the rocks on the path, and then throws himself at Jesus' feet. For some long moments all is quiet except a slight whimpering from the pitiful creature. Jesus' gaze is fixed on him, and all those around inch closer to the scene, more emboldened to see what happens next.

Finally, the man raises his head and brings his arms up, shielding his face as if he is hiding from a blinding light. Then in a loud voice that hardly sounds human, he cries out, "What have you to do with me, Jesus, Son of the Most High God? I adjure you by God; do not torment me" (Mark 5:7-8). These are momentous words: "Jesus, Son of the Most High God." The devil himself is attesting to Jesus' divinity, yet, likely because of the intensity of the situation, these words just roll off the back of the apostles who hear them, even though they are the answer to the question on their minds just last night after Jesus calmed the storm, when they asked, "Who then is this that even the wind and sea obey?" (Mark 4:41).

Jesus, full of pity, asks, "What is your name?" (Mark 5:8). The answer is startling. "Legion is my name. There are many of us" (Mark 5:9). Just as Jesus raises his voice to command them to leave, this possessed man, now speaking with a voice that sounds as if it is the multitude of demons inside of him speaking together, pleads with Jesus not to send them away from that territory. The apostles shrink back from the scene again as his multiple demonic voices terrify them, their skin turning clammy.

To the right of Jesus and up the hills marking the south side of the valley, a grassy plateau ends abruptly at a cliff as it gets to the water's edge. The plateau is perfect for grazing the swine that many of the villagers owned. Legion begs Jesus to allow them to enter the swine. Those accompanying Jesus take notice of the request, because, as Jews, the law forbids them to eat swine and therefore they have nothing to do with the vile animals. Jesus waves his hand, commands them to leave the man, and allows them to take possession of the swine.

Meanwhile up on that plateau, the men who are taking care of their swine have been watching the scene below. They are too far away to hear anything, but they can see that this man and his party have confronted the crazy man, and something strange seems to be going on there. They notice the demoniac man become quiet and crawl towards Jesus, as if to cover his nakedness with the bottom part of Jesus' robe. Jesus looks down on the naked one, places his hand tenderly on his head, and others in the group start pulling off their outer garments to clothe his nakedness. They look back and forth at one another trying to make sense of what is going on when suddenly, the entire herd of swine begins to snort and act agitated. The swine begin to shake their heads and run around in circles, as if they are trying to get something out. It all happens so quickly, and then together, as if commanded by some strange force (later the herdsmen will know it is a demonic force), the animals all gallop towards the cliff overlooking the sea and run right off the edge. The men chase after them to corral them but to no avail. By the time the men get to the cliff's edge, all the animals have fallen into the sea below. As they peer over the edge, the men see many of them are dead by the fall itself, and those who are not struggle for a few seconds before succumbing. The men are devastated, for these swine were their livelihood, and terrified, for they wonder if somehow the incident of the possessed man has something to do with it. They run back to the town screaming and shouting to report the incident. Meanwhile, Jesus' companions, witnessing the sight of the swine, are flabbergasted.

A large number of townspeople come out themselves to survey the situation. They approach Jesus cautiously. Some have heard of this miracle worker, and they are wondering if this is he. As they approach him, the sight of the demoniac man, fully clothed, calmly sitting at Jesus' side, is surprising—but the sight of the dead swine floating in the sea astounds them. Most of these townspeople are seized with fear at what this man has done to the demoniac as well as to the herd. This man has cured the possessed man, yes, but at what price? What other things might he do that could be harmful to them? Better for them if he just leaves them alone, they think. The leaders of the town, fearful themselves and seeing the fear in the eyes of their fellow townspeople, thank Jesus for healing their possessed man but politely ask him to leave, and suggest he would be better served by ministering to places where the majority of people are Jewish, unlike here in Gerasa.

Jesus, as is always his way, will not force himself on these people. He listens to them, sadly shakes his head from side to side, and turns to head back to the boats. His disciples, having observed the interaction of Jesus and the townspeople, turn also and begin to follow him back towards the boats. Some of the townspeople, anxious to get rid of these men, hand the disciples some food and provisions for the next leg of their journey. No words are spoken, and all is quiet as the townspeople hope he will not change his mind and return. As the distance between Jesus and the townsfolk widens, some of the people approach the formerly possessed man. They begin to ask him many questions, but he keeps looking back and forth from the person asking the question to Jesus, disappearing in the distance. He is distracted and torn. Suddenly he turns and runs after Jesus. The town leaders call after him, commanding him not to ask Jesus to come back. The man says nothing as he closes the distance between himself and Jesus. Will he try to convince him to stay?

Calling for Jesus as he gets closer, the man catches up with him and his companions just as they are arriving at the shoreline. The man begs to go with them. He tells Jesus how grateful he is and how he wants to accompany him in his travels, to be a part of his work helping others. Jesus looks intently at the man and love emanates from his eyes. He puts both his arms on the man's shoulders, acknowledges his gratitude, but tells him, "Go home to your family and announce to them all the Lord in his pity has done for you" (Mark 5:19). Disappointed, he looks into Jesus' eyes and sees that he can help him more by going back home and doing as he asks rather than by accompanying him. Yes, he thinks, Jesus' plan will turn out better than mine. The two men embrace, and the Gerasene watches Jesus get back on the boat, hears him give the order to return to Capernaum, and stands on the shore waving as the boats leave. "Then the man goes off and begins to proclaim in the Decapolis [region] what Jesus has done for him; and all are amazed" (Mark 5:20). There are many people who will come to believe in Jesus because of this unnamed man's love and faithfulness to the vocation Jesus gives him.

CHAPTER TWENTY-SIX

Another Busy Day in Capernaum

Sailing back towards Capernaum, the boats are initially all quiet as each person reflects on the events of the previous twelve hours; last night's violent storm at sea, which Jesus calmed by a few words, and this early morning's episode with the demoniac man, the swine, and the Gerasene townspeople. There is disappointment in not being able to spend a relaxing day alone with Jesus, but, thanks to some of the Gerasenes, they do have some provisions to share on the way back to Capernaum. The water is calm, the sky blue, and as the shoreline falls out of sight, the conversations pick up, and all enjoy the ride across the lake. It may not be as charming as spending time picnicking in a beautiful valley, but it is an enjoyable and quiet time, and they all, Jesus included, revel in it. It won't last long.

Leaving Geresa as early as they had, they approach Capernaum in the mid-afternoon. By now, almost everyone in town knows that Jesus and his apostles had left last night. They wonder what might have happened to them in the violent storm that came out of nowhere. As the hours of the day tick by and Jesus does not return, there is a growing question as to whether he and his companions have met their demise. Boats landing are questioned; those leaving are asked to keep an eye out for them. As the day lengthens, there is a heaviness growing in the hearts of many in the village and a dread of what might have happened.

As Jesus and the others come into sight of the Capernaum shoreline, there are still a few townspeople from the morning watching and looking out for him. One of them recognizes the boats, and a great cheer erupts from the beach that can be heard for quite a distance over the water and into the town. On hearing the cheers, many guess Jesus must be returning and run toward the noise. As the boats approach the shoreline, Jesus stands up, smiles, and waves. The crowds follow the exact path of his boat so they will be right where he lands. On landing, the mob surrounds him. What a difference there is from one side of the lake to the other! Over there, with no enthusiasm but a lot of politeness, Jesus was asked to leave. Here with great enthusiasm and informality, he is mobbed like a celebrity.

Among those who have run down to the lake to see him is one of the officials of the synagogue, Jairus. He is a good man, likely a Pharisee, who has seen Jesus preach many times in the temple. Unlike many of the Pharisees he is not yet opposed to him but knows how leery his brethren are about him. He has heard about the very ugly confrontation between him and the Pharisees and Scribes yesterday. Although he cannot say he is his good friend, they do know each other, and he is hopeful he will not ignore him because of his bitter encounter with his fellow Pharisees. This official is distraught beyond his limit; his twelve-year-old child, an only daughter, appears to be on her death bed. She had fallen ill a few days ago; it seemed like nothing at first, but she has rapidly turned for the worse in the last twenty-four hours. The doctors say they do not know what to do. His tears have only been outdone by his wife's. Recalling what Jesus did a few weeks ago for the Roman official who helped build the temple, he decides to go to Jesus and ask his help. He is overjoyed to hear Jesus has returned to Capernaum. This is his chance to save his daughter. If Jesus saved the servant of the Roman official, surely he will cure his daughter.

Jairus' stature is such that the mob around Jesus parts as the man makes his way to the boat moored now on the shoreline. Reaching Jesus, he falls at his feet. The mob is struck by the sight of this highly respected religious leader falling at Jesus' feet. Jairus pleads earnestly: "My daughter is at the point of death. Come, please lay your hands on her so she may get well and live" (Mark 5:23). His hope that Jesus would not reject him because of the confrontation with his fellow Pharisees yesterday is rewarded as Jesus smiles at him, takes him by the hand to raise him up, and signals him to lead the way to his house. The crowd parts again as the two men walk to Jairus' house. The apostles follow behind Jesus, and the crowd, anxious to see what he will do, presses in and around all of them.

As the procession makes its way through the streets of Capernaum, it is noticed by a woman who has suffered with internal hemorrhaging for many years. She has heard about Jesus and has come to believe he can heal her. "[S]he has suffered greatly at the hands of many doctors and has spent all she has, yet she has only gotten worse" (Mark 5:26). Seeing the procession coming towards her down the narrow street, she knows she will not have to interrupt him or tell the crowd the embarrassing nature of her affliction; "If I but touch his clothes, I will be healed" (Mark 5:28). The streets are narrow; no more than four or five people can stand shoulder to shoulder walking down them. She positions herself at a corner where the street narrows even more and where Jesus will likely be turning. By staying close to the wall, she can shield herself from the people on his right and, because of the narrowness of this turn, she will likely only have to reach through one or two people to touch his garments. With all the people in the crowd constantly grasping at him along the way, no one, not even he, will notice.

And she is correct. Jesus makes the turn and there is only one person between them. She does not hesitate, reaches out, touches his garments, and immediately shrinks back to the corner from which she came. Jesus passes by a few steps. Something has happened to her. She feels it instantly; she is cured. Not only has the bleeding stopped, but she feels a strength and vigor she has not enjoyed in years. She can't believe it and is about to slip away—but Jesus stops dead in his tracks. Some behind him bump into him, and those in front continue on for a few steps before they realize he has stopped. Everyone looks at him. He looks around as if searching for someone. The crowd falls silent. Jesus asks, "Who has touched my clothes?" (Mark 5:30). He is aware that "power has gone out of him" (Mark 5:30).

Now, on hearing this, Jesus' apostles look at each other in disbelief. Who has touched his clothes? The better question is: who has not touched his clothes with this large crowd in such a small space? One of them, likely Peter, with the nodding approval of the others, says, "You see how the crowd is pressing upon you, yet you ask, 'Who has touched me?'" (Mark 5:31). But Jesus ignores the question. He continues to look around. Seeing all this, and realizing she is the one to whom Jesus is referring, the woman decides to come forward. It is a bold decision, as it requires her to "tell the whole truth" (Mark

5:33), something she has not wanted to do. Nevertheless, filled with gratitude, head bowed low with apprehension, she comes forward. As she falls at his feet, Jesus listens, impressed by her deep and humble faith. Touching her chin to raise up her eyes, he looks at her with an intensity of love she will never forget. Wanting to convey to her how her faith is more important than her physical cure, he says, "Daughter, your faith has saved you. Go in peace and be cured of your affliction" (Mark 5:34). He has cured her, but even more, her faith has not only "forced" him to cure her, her faith has saved her.

The silence of the crowd straining to listen to the conversation between this woman and Jesus is broken just as he finishes his words to her. A group of people noisily runs down the street towards them. The synagogue official, who for the brief moments Jesus was dealing with this woman has forgotten the plight of his daughter, sees the men approaching, and his heart sinks as he recalls her illness. They are messengers from his home, and he can clearly tell by their loud wailing that the news is not good. His mind is flooded with thoughts of his daughter, and his heart breaks guessing what he is about to hear. Still, he holds out hope that he is wrong. The crowd separates to let these messengers through, and, breathing heavily from their running but speaking in soft voices out of respect for him, they deliver the bad news to the official. "Your daughter has died; why trouble the teacher any longer?" (Mark 5:35). Everyone watches as Jairus stares at them for a long moment and then hangs his head, covers his eyes, and begins to sob bitterly. His love for his daughter causes even the hardest-hearted people in the crowd to bow their heads and cover their own eyes.

Jesus takes a few steps toward the man, and laying his hand on his shoulder, says, "Do not be afraid; just have faith" (Mark 5:36). Jairus looks up and sees in Jesus' eyes that his daughter is not doomed; somehow Jesus is going to make everything right. Wiping the tears from his eyes with the right arm of his elaborate clothing, he begins to walk towards his house, turning around after a few steps to see Jesus following him. The apostles follow Jesus as does the crowd, eager to see what will happen next. Jesus, Jairus, and the apostles are quiet during the walk. At first the crowd is quiet, but the noise picks up; there is discussion and anticipation about whether Jesus is going to raise this girl from the dead in much the same way he did for the widow in Naim.

As they arrive at Jairus' house, the funeral proceedings seem already to have begun. There are a number of "professional" mourners who are sitting in the outer and inner courtyard of this man's home, all wailing loudly, many beating their breasts and ripping parts of their clothes to show their sorrow. Hiring professional mourners is a custom, but the official's wife seems to have gone over the top. The crowd is hushed by the number and intensity of the wailing. Jairus' wife comes running out of the house and collapses in the arms of her husband. Jesus, seeing the official and his wife so sorrowfully in each other's arms, holds his hand up for the crowd to stop advancing, and takes a few steps into the crowd of mourners. Looking around, with a countenance that betrays discomfort at such faked emotion, asks, "Why the commotion and weeping? The child is not dead but asleep" (Mark 5:39). The reaction of the mourners is cruel and immediate. "They begin to ridicule him" (Mark 5:40).

Jesus' eyes flash a look of authority, and he tells all of them to go out of the house. The ridicule subsides, and they make a quick departure. His eyes softening, Jesus then turns to the official and his wife and summons them to follow him. He also motions for Peter, James, and John. Once again, as frequently happens when Jesus is about to do something miraculous, the crowd is totally silent and watches as Jesus, three of his apostles, and the couple enter the house. Walking into her bedroom, Jesus sees arrangements have already begun to prepare the young girl's body for funeral. She has been dressed in a beautiful dress, and attendants are working on fixing her hair. In a gentle voice, he bids them to leave the room. When it is just the six of them left with the girl, Jesus takes her by the hand and says, "Little girl, I say to you, arise" (Mark 5:41). Clutching at her husband's arm during all this, the mother screams with excitement as her daughter rises up from the bed. Can she be alive? Is this nightmare over? The girl seems disoriented, and then Jesus gently helps her to her feet. She starts to walk around, not knowing what has happened, and is searching her memory hard to remember how she has gotten where she is. As her mother and father cover her with hugs, Jesus looks on with a look of tenderness. As the couple turns to thank Jesus, knowing she has been sick for a number of days, he tells them to make sure they give her something to eat. And then, strangely, he charges them not to tell anyone about what he has just done. As Jesus, with James, John, and Peter right behind him, walks out of the house, the crowd presses him to know what happened, as they have heard the screams of joy from Jairus' wife. Jesus, however, says nothing, faintly smiles and walks through the crowd. At the same time, Jarius, his wife, and daughter come out of their house, and so the people turn their attention to them, peppering them with questions about what Jesus did.

CHAPTER TWENTY-SEVEN

Second Rejection in Nazareth; Last Tour of Galilee; Mission of the Apostles

I t has been about eight and a half months since Jesus was last in Nazareth, and they have been busy months indeed. Still stinging from his rejection there, but hoping the news of his actions in Capernaum and the surrounding Galilean towns has softened the hearts of his hometown inhabitants, he sets out for one more tour of Galilee with Nazareth as his destination (Mark 6:1). He holds Nazareth in a special place in his heart. He instructs most of the people to stay in Capernaum and to go about their ordinary work. Accompanied only by his apostles, his mother, and a few of the holy women, he begins the trip, stopping only to rest along the way. He will stay longer at these towns and villages on his way back, but for now, his sights are set on Nazareth. When he arrives at his hometown there is no fanfare at all, no crowds waiting for him. Jesus and Mary quietly make their home with one of their relatives. Accommodations are easily provided among his relatives' homes for the small group of people with him. There is excitement from his relatives and a few curious people, but unlike any of the other towns he has visited, there is not a massive wave of people moving in to see him. He rests for a day or two with his family and close friends. Then comes the Sabbath day.

Jesus gets up early and goes off to pray by himself. He prays for the people in this town that has been so much a part of his life. His heart is heavy, because he knows what today will bring. Returning to his relative's home, he readies himself, gathers up his apostles, and heads off to the synagogue. The people remember what happened last time when they drove him out of the temple to the edge of the cliff but somehow, he had avoided their grasp. Some are ashamed, and some are fearful he might seek revenge, but all are riveted to their seats to hear what he has to say. The temple has not been this crowded since the last time he was here.

When it is his turn, Jesus stands up, takes the scroll, reads it, and sits down. The temple is silent. Unlike eight months ago, the evangelists now do not tell us what passage Jesus reads or anything about his commentary, but they do say, "Many who hear him are astonished" (Mark 6:2). Jesus' words, once again, have captivated the audience. He speaks with such enthusiasm, with such power, with a tone of voice that both commands like a general but comforts like a mother.

But once again, just as before, there are some with hard hearts. They begin to ask among themselves, "Where did this man get all this? What kind of wisdom has been given to him? What mighty deeds are wrought by his hands? Is he not the carpenter, the son of Mary, and the brother of James and Joses and Judas and Simon? And are not his sisters here with us?" (Mark 6:2-3). By the time the services are over, Jesus' spell over the temple has deteriorated. Many wonder how he can speak so learnedly and yet not be a Pharisee or Scribe. Yes, there have been reports of many miracles, but there have been virtually none here, and some suspect the few he has performed are mere trickery. So as Mark sadly reports in his gospel, "They take offense at him" (Mark 6:3). As the crowd empties from the temple, Jesus waits until they are all gone. As he leaves, a very few wait to talk to him. He looks around and proclaims, not without sadness, "A prophet is not without honor except in his native place and among his own kin and in his own house" (Mark 6:4). He then turns his attention to those few who have remained to hear more. He gives himself to these people, even curing a few sick people brought to him there at the foot of the temple.

But his heart is heavy to see so many people, and his own people at that, lack faith in him, to their great loss, whether it is by judging him based on his background, or his profession, or his formal training, or some preconceived notions about how the Messiah should act. As much as he wants to give himself to them in a special way because he has known them all his life, "[H]e is not able to perform any mighty deeds there, apart from curing a few sick people by laying his hands on them. He is amazed at their lack of faith" (Mark 6:5-6).

No faith means no miracles. Jesus makes his way back to his relative's home, shares the rest of the Sabbath with them, and prepares himself and his followers to leave the town the next day. We can only imagine how quiet he is early the next morning with most people still asleep and only the occasional barking of a dog breaking the morning silence. Rejected by most of his townsmen, he walks out of his hometown knowing he is doing so for the last time in his life. A few miles outside of Nazareth, though, his spirits pick up. As they approach one of the Galilean towns, the inhabitants' enthusiasm on seeing him returning their way as he promised ignites him, and he launches into the work of preaching and healing. It is time to put Nazareth behind him.

It is sometime during this last Galilean tour on the way back from Nazareth to Capernaum that Jesus decides it is time to send his apostles out on their own. They are between villages and somewhat close to Capernaum when he stops and calls the twelve away from the others, moving off the path up the side of a little hill. He separates them into twos: Simon with his brother Andrew, James with his brother John, Philip and his friend Nathaniel, now called Bartholomew, Thomas and Levi, now called Matthew, James the son of Alpheus and Thaddeus, Simon the Cananaean and Judas Iscariot. "He then gives them power and authority over all demons and to cure diseases and he sends them to proclaim the kingdom of God and to heal the sick. He says to them 'Take nothing for the journey, neither walking stick, nor sack, nor food, nor money, and let no one take a second tunic. Whatever house you enter, stay there and leave from there. And as for those who do not welcome you, when you leave that town, shake the dust from your feet in testimony against them'" (Luke 9:1-5). With the benefit of hindsight we can see how unprepared these men are. They still have little clue as to what Jesus' mission is about; they still believe he is the promised political Messiah. Their big saving grace, however, is that they believe in the person of Jesus, not just his miracles or his powerful words. Unsure as to what his message really means, they are determined to follow him and gladly and excitedly react to his command. They are going to wield the same kind of power Jesus has exercised—and each one thinks to himself how great he is going to be in this new kingdom.

Matthew's account of this incident is much more detailed than Mark's or Luke's. Matthew records Jesus as giving a very lengthy departing talk to his apostles. As Matthew typically bunches different speeches together, it is unlikely Jesus says all of these things at this time, but much like at the Sermon on the Mount, let us not bother to try to pick these sayings apart, and let us sit behind Jesus on the ground as he faces his apostles and listen to his words. Many of these words are prophetic and concern what will ultimately happen to these apostles.

"Do not go into pagan territory or enter a Samaritan town. Go rather to the lost sheep of the house of Israel. As you go, make this proclamation: 'The kingdom of heaven is at hand.' Cure the sick, raise the dead, cleanse lepers, drive out demons. Without cost you have received; without cost you are to give. Do not take gold or silver or copper for your belts; no sack for the journey, or a second tunic, or sandals, or a walking stick. The laborer deserves his keep. Whatever town or village you enter, look for a worthy person in it, and stay there until you leave. As you enter a house, wish it peace. If the house is worthy, let your peace come upon it; if not, let your peace return to you. Whoever will not receive you or listen to your words, go outside that house and shake the dust from your feet. Amen, I say to you, it will be more tolerable for the land of Sodom and Gomorrah on the day of judgment than for that town.

"Behold, I am sending you like sheep in the midst of wolves; so be as shrewd as serpents and as simple as doves. But beware of people, for they will hand you over to courts and scourge you in their synagogues, and you will be led before governors and kings for my sake as a witness before them and the pagans. When they hand you over, do not worry about how you are to speak or what you are to say. You will be given at that moment what you are to say. For it will not be you who speak but the Spirit of your Father speaking through you. Brother will hand over brother to death, and the father his child; children will rise up against their parents and have them put to death. You will be hated by all because of my name, but whoever endures to the end will be saved. When they persecute you in one town, flee to another. Amen, I say to you, you will not finish the towns of Israel before the Son of Man comes. No disciple is above his teacher, no slave above his master. If they have called the master of the house Beelzebub, how much more those of his household?

"Therefore, do not be afraid of them. Nothing is concealed that will not be revealed, no secret that will not be known. What I say to you in the darkness, speak in the light; what you hear whispered, proclaim from the housetops. And do not be afraid of those who kill the body but cannot kill the soul; rather be afraid of the one who can destroy both soul and body in Gehenna. Are not two sparrows sold for a small coin? Yet not one of them falls to the ground without your Father's knowledge. Even all the hairs on your head are counted. So do not be afraid; you are worth more than many sparrows. Everyone who acknowledges me before others, I will acknowledge before my heavenly Father. But whoever denies me before others, I will deny before my heavenly Father.

"Do not think that I have come to bring peace upon the earth. I have come to bring not peace but the sword. For I have come to set a man against his father, a daughter against her mother, and a daughter-in-law against her mother-in-law; and one's enemies will be those of his household.

"Whoever loves father or mother more than me is not worthy of me, and whoever loves son or daughter more than me is not worthy of me, and whoever does not take up his cross after me is not worthy of me. Whoever finds his life will lose it, and whoever loses his life for my sake will find it.

"Whoever receives you receives me, and whoever receives me receives the one who sent me. Whoever receives a prophet because he is a prophet will receive a prophet's reward, and whoever receives a righteous man because he is righteous will receive a righteous man's reward. And whoever gives only a cup of cold water to one of these little ones to drink because he is a disciple, amen, I say to you, he will surely not lose his reward" (Matt 10:5-42).

These words are sobering and contain many things the apostles choose to ignore for the moment but on finishing, Jesus' countenance softens and he gently but soberly smiles at them as he sends them on their way. And so the apostles in pairs go off in different directions. On the road to the next village, the partners discuss what and how they should present themselves. On entering a town, they stop and proclaim the kingdom of God is at hand. Many people recognize them as close friends of Jesus from previous visits. Many listen and seem to want to hear more, some scoff and dismiss them, knowing the messengers' lack of credentials. Finally, the big moment comes: someone brings a sick person to the pair. Both of them together look down on the sick man; the small crowd is silenced. Encouraging each other, the apostles lay their hands on the man's head. Suddenly the sick man shouts and gets up, telling everyone he is healed as he bounds around the street. His joy knows no limit, the apostles look at each other in astonishment, and the crowd is stunned. And so, after ministering and preaching more to these people, the apostles move on to the next town on their journey. It is a time of great wonder and joy. For now, we leave not only all six pairs on their tour of Galilee but also Jesus, as he slowly makes the short trip back to Capernaum, accompanied only by his mother and some female followers.

CHAPTER TWENTY-EIGHT

The Death of John the Baptist

Something strange has been happening at Herod's castle in Machaerus. Over the months John has been imprisoned there, Herod has frequently come to visit him. John's tone has softened some and, although he does not waver from telling Herod the truth, he does so in a less threatening way. Much like a summer evening moth flies towards a light, Herod is drawn to John, and although he doesn't always like what he hears, he can't resist the pull. He, Herod Antipas, the son of the great and cruel King Herod the Great, who massacred the innocent baby boys thirty years earlier, has let John begin to stir his conscience, which has been dead many, many years. When his father died from a foul disease as a result of his scandalous lifestyle, the Romans appointed this Herod as the new Tetrarch. He was a young man at the time but quickly adopted the ways of his father and, in no time, had beaten his conscience into quiet submission. As his father before him, he is a political figurehead at best, and as long as he serves their purpose of keeping the Jews quiet, the Romans allow him to do whatever he pleases. His guards, his castle, his money are all provided by the Romans, and, knowing he is despised by his fellow Jews, he has surrounded himself with mercenaries and hangers-on. He has no friends. The Jews hate him; the Romans tolerate him.

His relatively new wife, Herodias, likely named after Herod the Great, is a beautiful woman, a number of years younger than he. She had been married to Herod's older brother Philip, and at first was pleased to be part of this "royal" family. But as the years rolled by, she became less content with the quiet, unassuming, and older Philip, and decided to make a play for her husband's younger, much more successful and exciting brother. Herod, flattered and aroused by the coy advances of this sensuous woman, responded. His brother, with his marriage to Herodias gone cold years ago, and true to his meek personality, put up no fight. Besides, his brother's position with the Romans could mean great harm could come to Philip if he got in the way. Herodias, along with her teenaged daughter, moved into the Machaerus castle amid great scandal to the Jews and no interest to the Romans.

Herod and Herodias make a grand pair. There is much revelry and partying, but over the months, as John the Baptist attacks their relationship, Herodias becomes angrier at him. She was gratified she convinced Herod to arrest John a few months ago. Now that John is in the castle, she has tried everything to get Herod to dispatch him. However, neither her words nor caresses can convince him to kill John. She has become even more anxious as she can see Herod's fascination (as she calls it) with John is dampening Herod's mood. He seems more reflective than in the past; he is more irritable and distracted, and the same pleasures that would always absorb him seem to be losing their edge. She must find a way to get rid of John. The opportunity will present itself unexpectedly very soon.

It is Herod's birthday in the spring, shortly after the feast of the Pasch, and, as usual, a big celebration is planned. Since he has taken up with Herodias, the celebrations have become even more elaborate. Invitations are sent out far and wide, and the hall is bursting at the seams with guests. None of these guests, of course, are Herod's friends; he has none. All of the guests are only there for the food, wine, and lavish entertainment, which have become a much anticipated attraction at these parties now that Herodias is involved.

The guests recline on their couches, drinking the plentiful wine and gorging on the extravagant food. Some get up and walk over to Herod and flatter him about how good he looks for his age (a lie, as he looks terrible from his life of self-indulgence), how much they are enjoying his wonderful party (more idle flattery), and how much they are looking forward to the day's entertainment. The hall is filled with noises of bawdy laughter, clinking cups as people toast one another, and waiters walking about delivering more food and drink to the guests. When everyone has had plenty to eat and the food is cleared away, one of Herod's subjects announces that the entertainment is about to begin. The guests all eagerly look to have their wine glasses refilled and settle back to see what events await them all.

The minstrels, whose background music during the dinner has been drowned out by all the noise, begin to play sultry and seductive music. The curtain separating the great hall from the rest of the castle is pulled aside, and a number of scantily dressed, beautiful, and heavily made-up women enter the hall. As the music stirs every nerve of the guests, the dancing of these women stirs every passion. The guests are mesmerized by the spell of the entire scene. A younger woman, still more beautiful than the rest, enters the room from behind the curtain. The music stops and all eyes are on her. As she makes her way to the center of the room, the other women back away towards the curtain and leave. The young girl's eyes are focused on Herod, and she knows she has not only his attention but that of everyone in the room.

The music starts again, and she begins to dance. She dances and dances, and the magnificent jewels on her body dance with her, the bracelets on her arms and ankles moving together in a way never seen before. Like a snake, she curves her little body, and her spell enters every soul there. Her dark eyes, which captivate all, boldly meet the guests' eyes as she makes her way around the room. Her laughing lips seem so inviting; her whole figure demands attention. She dances sometimes as if she is dancing for all of them, sometimes as if she is dancing for none of them, and sometimes as if she is dancing for only one of them. When she knows she has aroused the passion of everyone in the room, she turns one more time towards the person to whom she has paid the most attention during her dance: Herod. Standing in front of him, she saves her most sensuous moves for the last. The guests move their heads to get a better view as she shamelessly performs the finale. Then she stops, curtsies like a little girl, and stands before Herod with a slight smile. The applause is overwhelming. Who is this young girl? How can she be so exciting, so spellbinding?

Herod, of course, knows it is Herodias' daughter. He is not only aroused by her dancing but also proud that it is his wife's daughter who has so entertained the guests. The fact that she has done so by letting herself become an object of everyone's passion does not even enter his mind. He lost the ability years ago to see women as anything other than objects of physical gratification. Filled with bravado and not a little wine, Herod stands up, claps a little more to acknowledge his approval of her dancing, and then bids the guests to quiet down. In a loud voice meant to impress everyone he then booms, "Ask of me whatever you wish, and I will grant it to you....I will grant to you whatever you ask, even half of my kingdom" (Mark 6:22-23). Such a bold proclamation causes everyone to look at the girl and wonder what she will ask for: money, more servants, a castle of her own? Could she ask for half his kingdom, and if so, would he honor his promise? The room is filled with anticipation.

But there is one woman who knows exactly what she wants. When Herodias hears Herod's bold proclamation, she sees her chance, rises from her seat, and walks to the curtain behind where she and Herod are sitting. As she does so, she motions for her daughter to follow her. After standing there a few seconds, the young girl runs off in the direction of her mother, and both of them disappear behind the curtain. Herod follows her with his eyes and so does the crowd. What can be happening here?

Presently, the curtain separates, and the young girl comes out by herself and runs to the center of the room, facing Herod. All eyes are on her. Meanwhile, Herodias slowly parts the curtains and she makes her way, almost unnoticed, back into the great hall. Then with a voice that betrays her young age, the girl looks squarely at Herod and says, "I want you to give me at once on a platter the head of John the Baptist" (Mark 6:25).

The effect is instantaneous and has a sobering effect on the crowd. Everyone stands up. The guests, no strangers themselves to treating others cruelly, are nevertheless stunned at the request. That such a young thing would make this request causes a shudder to go down the spine of even the cruelest of guests there. Herod is crushed and turns to look at Herodias, who has a cruel smirk on her face. The excitement of the dance and the thrill of the wine are all drained from Herod now, and he is left with the consequence of his foolish promise. A bigger man would refuse the young girl's request, but Herod is anything but a bigger man. Even his growing "friendship" with John does not overcome his pride, so because of his promise and not wanting to look weak to his guests, he orders one of the guards at the curtain to bring her the head of John the Baptist on a platter.

The crowd remains standing, and very little is said for the several minutes the guard is gone. All is quiet, each guest with his own thoughts, when they can hear the footsteps of the guard. Everyone holds their breath; the curtain is swept aside and the guard, with a stoic expression, walks in with a platter. On the platter is a head with long dark hair hanging wet over the edges. A dark liquid drips down from the hair and onto the floor. The eyes are half-open but vacant and lifeless, the cheeks sunken, the lips parted as if to say something but with only some blood trickling out of either side. The guard slowly walks across the hall and hands the platter to the young girl. She is taken aback by the horror and almost drops it, but calming herself, she carries it over to her mother. As she gives the platter to her mother, Herodias smiles, gives a quick glance at Herod, and leaves the hall with her trophy. Herod's relationship with Herodias, utilitarian as it has been, will never be the same.

The music begins, more entertainment follows, but the party is over. The Baptist's death hangs in the air and cannot be forgotten. The guests leave, Herod is alone with his thoughts, and John's remaining disciples, upon hearing of his death, "come and take the body away and lay it in a tomb" (Mark 6:29). John has been silenced, but Herod's tortured conscience will not allow him to sleep. He replays John's death over and over again in his mind; he stares into space remembering thought-provoking conversations they had. How he wishes he had not made such a bold and stupid promise to Herodias' daughter!

Herod, of course, is aware of the stories of Jesus, who has been carrying on his work in Galilee. Over the last few weeks, Jesus has performed many miracles, and the stories of them are intensifying, but Herod has been busy with other things, so he has not been focused on Jesus until now. Some of Jesus' enemies, the Herodians and the Pharisees, with John now dispatched by Herod, hope to get Herod to arrest and deliver the same fate to Jesus. They tell Herod of these miracles he is performing and the following he is generating, and insinuate that he will become a threat to the status quo, much like John was, if he is allowed to continue. Surely, they think among themselves, Herod will take action. But they do not know how guilt-ridden he has become. Rather than ordering Jesus' arrest, Herod convinces himself that he is "John whom I beheaded" (Mark 6:16). In his twisted mind, Herod somehow thinks the ghost of John the Baptist has inhabited Jesus' body. The Pharisees suggest he arrest

Jesus so he can see him on his own terms as he has done with John, but, at the moment, he is too afraid to bring the ghost of John the Baptist back into his castle. We leave him there, with his wife and all of his servants trying to cheer him up and make him forget this whole incident with John. Herod wallows in the gnawing truth of his cowardice and folly as the result of his desire for a dancing teenaged girl.

CHAPTER TWENTY-NINE

Feeding of the Five Thousand

M eanwhile, Jesus has been back in Capernaum for about a week. One morning, one of his relatives runs into the house and tells Jesus the news about John. He bends over, puts his head in his hand and begins to weep bitterly. How Jesus loves this man to weep so! His mind races back to the days when they were boys and how much fun they had playing together. He thinks about that meeting at the Jordan River a year and a half ago, and how John instantly knew Jesus as the Messiah. John's death, much like Lazarus' death a year from now, touches Jesus to the core. He asks to be left alone and sits in silent prayer with his Father for some time—indeed, for the rest of the day and into the night. For the next few days Jesus' mood is clearly affected by John's death. Soon, though, the first group of his apostles comes bursting into town and running towards the house where Jesus is staying.

Their faces and voices are full of excitement, and they trip over each other's comments as they tell him all they have done in the weeks they have been away. They have not heard the news about John, and Jesus thinks this is not the time to tell them. They are intoxicated with the success of their travels. Never in their wildest dreams did they think they could cure people of their illnesses and command the attention of people the way they have. Jesus smiles, reminds them by whose power these works are being performed, and lets them enjoy the moment. Only after finishing their report does he tell them about John. Over the course of the next few days, the other six groups of apostles return, all with the same enthusiasm, their eyes wide with surprise at their successes and their voices full of confidence and conviction. These later groups, though, have heard about

John's death and, knowing Jesus' love and respect for him, express their grief and disappointment.

Whether it is because he wants to spend time mourning John's death with his apostles as Matthew (14:13) seems to imply or whether he wants to get away for some rest with his apostles as Mark (6:31) states, early one morning Jesus and his disciples walk down to the shore and board a boat to go to a deserted place near Bethsaida in the northeast corner of the Sea of Galilee. Even though John's gospel has this event happening a bit earlier, it is more likely early May and day 567 of the 909 days that changed the world. Jesus and his apostles are looking forward to being alone. As they slip away from the shore, however, some of the townspeople see them. While some run to inform the other townspeople that Jesus is leaving, others remain on the shore and follow the path of the boat. As they do so, their spirits are boosted because they see the boat is taking a northerly path. If the boat continues on that path, it will be relatively easy to keep it in sight and follow it on land by walking along the northern shore of the lake. Someone in the crowd shouts out and suggests doing this. The idea gets traction and a large crowd of people begin walking along the shore keeping their eyes on the path of his boat. There are not only a lot of townspeople, but as this group follows along the shore, they pick up other people from the hamlets and villages and the crowd swells into even larger numbers. Meanwhile, on the water, none of them hear or see the crowd following on land, and Jesus and the apostles are enjoying one another's company. Although still low over the mountains to the east, the sun has risen, the water is calm, and there is a slight and favorable breeze. The apostles know it is a glorious day to be on the water. Little do they know how glorious of a day this will turn out to be.

From the temple in Capernaum to the point where the Jordan River enters the Sea of Galilee is a walk of about one hour. Crossing the Jordan at this point is not difficult, as the water barely reaches the knees. Once across, it is about another hour of travel time, mostly made difficult by a number of streams and brooks, before reaching the plains and hills of the northeast side of the Sea of Galilee. The crowd leaders are guessing Jesus is headed somewhere there, so, while keeping an eye on the boat, the crowd makes its way to this destination. As they see the boat making a turn to head back to shore, they realize they are correct, and even better, they have actually beat him there.

As Jesus and his apostles make the turn towards the shore, they begin to hear and see the throngs of people waiting for them. The crowd gets louder and louder as the boat approaches. The apostles look at one another and are dismayed. Perhaps he will tell us to change course so we can get away from all these people for a day? But Jesus looks at the crowd and says something about their "being like sheep without a shepherd" (Mark 6:34) and instructs the apostles to land the boat. His tone of voice, acknowledging the apostle's disappointment, is filled with compassion for these people as well as a message that something important, something that needs to happen, is about to take place.

As the boat lands, the crowd pushes to get as near to Jesus as it can. He moves forward from the rocky landing area and towards the greener plain, and the crowd parts to let him through, although everyone is talking to him, some saying hello and others begging him to help them with an infirmity or other problem. Even though the crowd is crushing in on him, Jesus has a patient smile on his face. He does cure many, gives advice and consolation to others, and slowly works his way across the grassy plain until he gets to where the hill begins to slope upwards. It takes a few hours for him to cover the distance because so many people are pressing in on him, and yet he manages to treat each one as if they were the only person in the crowd. Once at the end of the plain, he tells the crowd to wait, takes his apostles who have struggled to stay next to him because of the crushing crowd, and walks a little way up the hill. The noise of the crowd begins to subside as Jesus begins walking up the hill and gradually becomes totally quiet as Jesus stops, turns back towards the crowd, and holds up his arms. The contrast is striking. A few moments ago the plain was filled with the noise of people talking and now, there is total silence. In a voice of authority, he begins to teach and instruct them. It is hard to imagine, without the aid of modern technology, how Jesus' voice carries far enough for all to hear. The crowd is mesmerized by his words and more time passes without anyone noticing.

When Jesus finishes his discourse, his apostles say to him, "Dismiss the crowd so they can go to the surrounding villages and farms and find lodging and provisions, for we are in a deserted place" (Luke 9:12). Jesus then makes a surprising request: "Give them some food yourselves" (Luke 9:13). The apostles are startled. They have no food, and the money they have in their wallets would in no way be able to satisfy such a huge crowd. "How many loaves do you have? Go and see" (Mark 6:38), he asks. So, as Jesus' teaching ends and the crowd begins to talk among themselves, the apostles make the short walk down the hill and begin to inquire what food people may have. There is little, of course, because many people didn't even think to bring some, and those who did had long ago eaten or shared what they brought. In a few minutes, the apostles walk back up the hill, and Andrew reports, "There is a boy here who has five barley loaves and two fish, but what good are these for so many?" (John 6:8-9). Jesus asks Andrew to bring the boy and his food to him. As Andrew is doing so, Jesus holds up his hands again, silence once again rules the plain, and he instructs the crowd to sit down in groups of 50 and 100. As the crowd is organizing and seating itself, he receives the young boy with a smile and seats the boy beside him. Jesus then "takes the five loaves and the two fishes and looking up to heaven, he says the blessing, breaks the loaves, and gives them to his disciples to set before the people; he also divides the fish among them" (Mark 6:41). Each of the apostles takes some of the bread and fish and puts them in their bags to distribute to the crowd, wondering how this is ever going to work.

As the apostles begin to go towards the crowd, Jesus stops one of them, Andrew, and asks him to give some bread and fish to him and the boy. Andrew puts his hand in his bag and gives some food first to Jesus and then, to his amazement, when he puts his hand back in the bag there is more there to give to the boy. Jesus encourages the boy to ask for more if he would like, and the boy does so. Again, Andrew reaches his hand in the bag and finds still more bread and fish. And what happens to Andrew is happening to all the other apostles. Everyone is amazed at the quantity (and quality) of food coming out of the apostles' bags. As the crowd is seated in groups of 50 and 100 it is relatively easy to tell there are about five thousand people, not counting women and children fed. The noise level on the plain reaches a feverish pitch as people realize what is happening. Jesus, having spent some time talking to the young boy, bids him farewell and begins to walk back down the hill to the plain and the crowd. We can only imagine how this encounter with Jesus will be played over and over again in this young boy's mind as he goes on to live the rest of his life. As Jesus walks through the crowd, the apostles gather up the leftovers and fill up twelve baskets. The plain is replete with people who are singing Jesus' praises; it is one of the few episodes recorded in all four gospels. It is the high point of Jesus' popularity—yet how quickly things change....

CHAPTER THIRTY

Jesus Walks on Water

The crowd's mood is high, recognizing this feeding is similar to the great signs of prophets in the past, like Moses with the manna in the desert and Elias multiplying the flour for the woman who fed him. Many begin to say, "This is truly the Prophet, the one who is to come into the world" (John 6:14). There is a growing movement to hail him as king. But Jesus does not want this to happen. He calls for his apostles and, with that look in his eye they cannot refuse, tells them to go back to the shore, untie the boat, and return home. He tells them he will take care of getting himself home. They all, of course, are nervous about this and filled with questions. How will he get back if we take the boat? Will he be all right alone with this crowd? It seems they want to make him king. Maybe this is the start of the new kingdom he has been speaking of. If so, why is he asking us to leave now? Despite all these questions and misgivings, the apostles obey and walk away towards the shore, frequently looking back to see what he is doing.

As they look back, they see Jesus positioning himself yet again up a bit on the mountainside. For the third time today, he raises his hands and quiets the crowd. He tells them the hour is getting late, and it is necessary for all of them to get back to their homes before it gets too dark. The crowd, like sheep in the presence of their shepherd, starts to break up, and people make their way back along the path home. The apostles stand at the shore's edge and marvel as the crowd disperses. They wait and watch as Jesus oversees the crowd scattering. Many, although not all, in the crowd who have to go all the way back to Capernaum tend to leave first; others, who live closer, leave later. There is a decent group, however, which remains and will end up spending the entire evening. The apostles wonder if Jesus will change his mind so they wait some more, but Jesus turns and walks straight up into the hills. He is going to spend the night in prayer, for just as he spent the night in prayer before he chose the twelve apostles and delivered the great Sermon on the Mount, so, too, he now feels compelled to do likewise to prepare for the radical revelation he will be making in less than twenty-four hours. Realizing he wants to be by himself, elated about the events of the day, questioning his reluctance to declare himself king, and saddened because he has stayed behind, the apostles untie the boat and leave for Capernaum as dusk is settling in. There is much to discuss among themselves as the boat leaves the shoreline.

As the apostles make their way back across the Sea of Galilee, the waters are calm—but then, much like a month ago when they tried to cross to get to Gerasa, the winds pick up, and the seas become very rough. The winds coming from the north buffet the boat and begin to blow it further south. The apostles struggle to keep the boat afloat and as closely on course as they are able. The storm, though severe, is not as bad as the one a few weeks ago; still, it is dramatically slowing down their progress. They struggle through the evening and into the early morning hours. Suddenly, as Matthew reports (14:25), "during the fourth watch," which would be somewhere between 3 a.m. and 6 a.m., the apostles see something which looks like a ghost walking on the water towards the boat. They all stop, rain pouring down on them and the wind violently rocking the boat. They look out at this mirage and are terrified, for not only does this look like a ghost, but it appears to head directly towards them. With the undulation of the heavy sea, sometimes the apparition disappears for a moment and some think, 'Maybe we are just seeing something,' but when the water crests up again, they can see it getting closer. Their terror grows. At first one and then all of them "cry out in fear" (Matt 14:26). The boat is in extreme danger now of being swamped as the apostles are frozen in fear. On hearing their cries, however, like a tender mother, "Jesus speaks to the apostles: 'Take courage, it is I; be not afraid'" (Matt 14:27). Hearing his voice so clearly, knowing he, somehow, is in this storm with them, causes them immense relief, and most are able to turn their minds back towards the task of saving their boat— most, but not all.

"Lord, if it is you, command me to come to you on the water" (Matt 14:28), says the impetuous Peter. Those who hear him are stunned. What is he asking? Does he really want to try walking on these waters? Jesus, holding out his hand, says, "Come" (Matt 14:29), and Peter, with his eyes locked on Jesus' eyes, steps out of the boat. His feet hit the water—but they do not sink. He steps forward, and his feet still do not sink. The other apostles all cry out in amazement as they see Peter actually walking on the water. Peter continues to look at Jesus even as the waves sink and rise so that sometimes Jesus is in full view and sometimes he can barely be seen. The other apostles look at one another in disbelief. Suddenly, a huge gust of wind sweeps over Peter and the apostles. Peter changes his focus from Jesus to the intensity of the wind, and he begins to fear and thinks about the insanity of his walking on the water. He starts to sink as his feet begin to slip down into the water, and in total fear cries out, "Lord, save me!" (Matt 14:30). And like a strong friend, "Immediately Jesus stretches out his hand and catches him" (Matt 14:30), and adds, "O you of little faith, why did you doubt?" (Matt 14:31). As long as Peter is focused on Jesus, anything is possible; once he focuses only on what is humanly possible, the impossible remains, indeed, impossible.

Jesus and Peter enter the boat, and the winds die down and the storm ends. The apostles, to a man, pay homage to Jesus. Once again, they marvel at the power of this man with whom they have thrown in their lot. Their hearts are quickened with yet another show of the power he possesses. But as the boat makes its way back to the western shore, Mark adds in his gospel, "They had not understood the incident of the loaves. On the contrary, their hearts were hardened" (Mark 6:52). Yes, these poor men, although more committed to him than any others (besides Mary, of course), still interpret these miracles of multiplying food, walking on water, and calming the elements as a prelude to his revealing himself as the Messiah who will raise the Jewish people and nation back to the prominence they all long for. 'And lucky me,' they all think to themselves, 'I will be among the first of his lieutenants.'

CHAPTER THIRTY-ONE

Morning of Miracles;
Afternoon of Rejection;
The "Bread of Life" Teaching

Almost immediately on the calming of the storm, the apostles see they are close to land. The bad news, though, is that, instead of being in Capernaum, they are just south of Magdala. It doesn't surprise them because they knew the wind carried them further south than their goal. They could sail up the coast to Capernaum, but Jesus indicates he wants to land here and proceed to Capernaum on foot. From the fishing villages just south of Magdala, on foot, it is about a one-and-a-half-hour trip to Capernaum. The thought strikes some of the apostles how amazing it is that a mere twenty-four hours ago they had left Capernaum in search of rest. The big crowd following them along the shore, the feeding of five thousand-plus people, and the toiling all night in the storm, hardly has made for a restful twenty-four hours. Indeed, with virtually no sleep, they marvel at how well they feel. One of them even notes that staying close to Jesus, no matter the difficulty of the circumstances, always seems to have that effect on them. They land early in the morning, and two of the apostles volunteer to take the boat back to Capernaum, while the others agree to accompany Jesus. As they disembark, some of the fishermen in the village recognize him right away and go running into the town to tell everyone he has unexpectedly arrived in their little town. This is the peak time of his popularity, and all of Galilee by now is aware of his remarkable miracles. The people immediately bring out their sick for Jesus to heal.

Meanwhile, "the crowd that remains across the Sea [of Galilee] sees that there is only one boat there, and that Jesus has not gone with his disciples in the boat" (John 6:22). They start calling out his name and walk up into the hilly area looking for him, as many remember he has a penchant for praying alone in the hills in the early morning. They search everywhere but cannot find him. They decide he must have left somehow. They guess he has returned to Capernaum and, luckily for them, see merchant vessels from Tiberias that are bound to drop off trade destined for Caesar Phillipi. As the ships will be returning home to Tiberias immediately after dropping off their cargo, the crowd is able to secure passage on them. Capernaum will not take the trade ships far off their route home.

Jesus, at the same time, is not disappointing the crowds on the western shore. He heals everyone, and news quickly spreads that he is working his way up the coastline. Much like the first night of miracles in Capernaum some five and a half months ago, which began with the cure of Peter's mother-in-law, people line up along the road to see Jesus and get his attention. As Mark reports, the people "scurry about the surrounding country and begin to bring in the sick on mats to wherever they hear he is. Whatever town or village or countryside he enters, they lay the sick in the marketplace and beg him that they may touch only the tassel of his cloak; and as many as touch him are healed" (Mark 6:53-56). It is a triumphant journey from this small fishing village south of Magdala, through the town of Gennesart, to Capernaum. The crowds are loud with anticipation as Jesus approaches them, and they give shouts of joy as he passes them having cured their sick. Even as Jesus does this, his heart is heavy, for he knows later on this very day, many of these people will be scandalized by what he will say. Much like a father who gives his children the best "things" knowing in his heart that the best things in life are not worldly goods, so too does Jesus know most of these people "love" him for the cures, the "things" he has done for them. Most do not love or believe in him.

As he makes his way up the coastline to Capernaum curing everyone, let us step away for a moment from the shouts and cries of joy and amazement and review what has happened so far. We are at a key moment in Jesus' ministry. It is after the Passover season—early May—and a little more than a year and a half since John baptized Jesus in the Jordan. At first, Jesus' ministry moved along at a slow pace. There was the miracle at the wedding feast of Cana shortly after his baptism but then nothing really to speak of, as he settled back in Nazareth before making his way over to the western shore of the Sea of Galilee fourteen months ago to travel to Jerusalem for the Passover feast. After impressing everyone there when he drove the money changers and merchants out of the temple, and then meeting Nicodemus at night, Jesus started to baptize at the spot formerly occupied by John, who had moved up the Jordan River. Ten months ago, when John was arrested by Herod, Jesus left the Jordan to return to Galilee and once again used the Samaria route on which he met the many-times-married woman at the well. On his arrival in Cana, he performed a second miracle there—a long-distance one—for the Roman official's young son. On returning to his native Nazareth, he was almost murdered after addressing the people in the temple, and so some nine months ago, Jesus and Mary moved for good to Capernaum. Starting with that Sabbath in Capernaum, when Jesus cured the demoniac in the temple, healed Peter's mother-in-law later, and spent the evening curing all the sick brought to him, the number of miracles dramatically increased as Jesus called his apostles and kicked his ministry into high gear. Now we are here, at perhaps the height of his popularity, as he makes his way north up the western shore of the Sea of Galilee with throngs of people pressing about him. In a matter of a few minutes, when he arrives in Capernaum, things will change: his popularity will begin to wane.

Spending so much time curing people on his way, the normal one-and-a-half-hour trip from Magdala to Capernaum takes Jesus four hours to make; he doesn't get into town until the early afternoon. Among the people who surround him are some of yesterday's crowd returning to Capernaum via the Tiberias merchant ships. Speaking the thoughts of most, one of them asks, "Rabbi, when did you get here?" (John 6:25). This seemingly innocent enough question provides Jesus the opportunity to unveil the real meaning of yesterday's miracle of the feeding of five thousand people. It is time for them to realize he is calling them to believe in him and not just in the things he can do for them. In a tone of voice that is a touch challenging, he says, "Amen, amen, I say to you, you are looking for me not because you saw signs but because you ate the loaves and were filled. Do not work for food that perishes but for food that endures for eternal life, which the Son of Man will give you" (John 6:26-27). Taken aback by his tone of voice and showing their lack of understanding, someone responds, "What can we do to accomplish the works of God?" (John 6:28). Jesus uses this question to cut to the quick. "This is the work of God, that you believe in the one he sent" (John 6:29). As the crowd begins to grasp more fully now that he is demanding their belief in him, someone in the crowd, almost to our disbelief given what has been happening along the coastline this morning, asks him, "What sign can you do that we may see and believe in you? Our ancestors ate manna in the desert as it is written: 'He gave them bread from heaven to eat'" (John 6:30-31). Perhaps it is a question by someone who wants to make it obvious they all should believe in Jesus, for indeed had he not symbolically brought food down from heaven yesterday to feed them? Perhaps it is a question from someone who is challenging Jesus, because Moses called down the bread from heaven whereas Jesus had more mysteriously, perhaps even by trickery, fed the people yesterday. We don't know, but Jesus uses the question to press further towards a stunning revelation.

"Amen, amen, I say to you, it was not Moses who gave the bread from heaven; my Father gives you the true bread from heaven. For the bread of God is that which comes down from heaven and gives life to the world" (John 6:32-33). Not surprisingly the crowd asks him to give them this bread always, but to their shock he replies, "I am the bread of life; whoever comes to me will never hunger, and whoever believes in me will never thirst" (John 6:35). Then raising his voice in a bit of a challenge, he says, "But I told you that although you have seen me, you do not believe" (John 6:36). The crowd is growing critical; some murmur that it is impossible that he is one who has come down from heaven; others focus on the ridiculousness of his claim to be able to satisfy their hunger for the rest of their lives; others mock the belief that Jesus will cure their thirst; and still others scoff at the level of belief Jesus seems to be demanding from them. But he will press forward. There is more to reveal.

"I am the living bread that came down from heaven; whoever eats this bread will live forever; and the bread that I will give is my flesh for the life of the world" (John 6:51). The last part of this statement, as it should, grabs the crowd's attention. What is he saying? "How can this man give us his flesh to eat?" (John 6:52). 'He can't really be saying we have to eat his flesh to be a true believer,' they think to themselves. How absurd, how repulsive, how against every tradition of Jewish law for us to eat human flesh! They press him further for an explanation. Perhaps they do not understand what he is saying. Perhaps they misheard him. Perhaps he really doesn't mean it the way it sounded. But Jesus soon shows them he is not kidding as he says in a loud voice so all can hear, "Amen, amen, I say to you, unless you eat the flesh of the Son of Man and drink his blood, you do not have life within you. Whoever eats my flesh and drinks my blood has eternal life, and I will raise him up on the last day. For my flesh is true food and my blood is true drink. Whoever eats my flesh and drinks my blood remains in me and I in him. Just as the living Father sent me and I have life because of the Father, so also the one who feeds on me will have life because of me. This is the bread that came down from heaven. Unlike your ancestors who ate and still died, whoever eats this bread will live forever" (John 6:53-58).

Unbelievable! There we have it. It is clear to the crowd Jesus is not kidding. He is talking about their actually eating his flesh and drinking his blood as a necessity. It is too much to believe, too much to do. Many in the crowd cry out in disgust at these last words; many shake their heads at the apparent nonsense of what he is saying; still some quietly reflect on his words. One of the more thoughtful ones in the crowd, looking for more help in grasping this, asks, "This is a hard saying; who can accept it?" (John 6:60). But Jesus does not back off. He does not tell them this is a joke. He does not tell them not to be bothered with this revelation. Instead, he challenges them yet again. "Does this shock you?" (John 6:61). No, Jesus is serious about the words he has just spoken. It all started with a simple question from an adoring crowd—"Rabbi, when did you get here?"—but now they are divided. Many in the crowd wave their hands as if to say "you are crazy," and turn and walk away. As they do so they tell others farther back what a madman this Jesus is. "He is telling us we need to eat his flesh and drink his blood!" Many of those also turn and walk away, although some press closer to Jesus to hear for themselves. Still, Jesus does not back down, and as he does not, more and more of the crowd leaves. It is such a turning point that John points out that "as a result of this many of his disciples returned to their former way of life and no longer accompanied him" (John 6:66).

Not surprised, but deeply grieved, Jesus watches as the crowd dramatically thins out. He can hear the ridiculing comments of many of them as they walk away. He has known all along, of course, how divisive his comments would be, yet still he feels sorrow to see how little faith, despite the plethora of miracles performed even just this morning, the people have. They don't understand, so they will not believe. With heaviness in his heart and vulnerability in his voice, Jesus turns to his apostles and asks, "Do you also want to leave?" (John 6:67). The apostles, of course, are equally stunned by the words they have just heard. Each of them, in his own mind, wrestles with his faith in Jesus in the face of the difficulty understanding his recent words. Each is lost in his own thoughts, asking 'How can this be?' None can find a quick answer, but Jesus' turning to them and asking if they want to leave draws them out of their inner thoughts and requires an answer. Who will be the first to speak?

It is Peter. He has no unique insight into what these words really mean. Despite the seeming absurdity of Jesus' words, Peter knows Jesus and has full faith in him. His love for Jesus is such that he decides the difficulty is not in Jesus' words but in Peter's understanding of them. He then voices the consensus of most (save one) of the apostles and declares in a strong but calm voice, "Master, to whom shall we go? You have the words of eternal life. We have come to believe and are convinced that you are the Holy One of God" (John 6:68-69). The change on Jesus' face is immediate. He smiles at Peter and the other apostles, knowing that they have freely chosen him. Their motives may not be totally pure, but they choose him, even though they don't understand everything . Their choice pleases Jesus very much indeed. But his smile is tempered as he looks at the one apostle who wavers more than the others. This apostle thinks these words cannot be true and, although too committed to the cause at the moment, suffers an irreversible crisis in his faith. We can only wonder if Judas knew to whom Jesus was referring when he responds to Peter's declaration of faith by saying, "Did I not choose you twelve? Yet is not one of you a devil?" (John 6:70). His comment hangs in the air for a second but then is almost forgotten as Jesus suggests they return to his house and spend the rest of the afternoon resting. It has been a busy thirty-six hours.

Chapter Thirty-Two

Jesus Confronts the Pharisees

Meanwhile, in Jerusalem, the chief Pharisees have been intensely and jealously listening to all that everyone is saying about Jesus. It has been over a year since he caused such chaos in the temple area, and the Pharisees have continued to hear mostly marvelous reports about him. He did not show up for the Paschal feast this year, and they are unsure if they are grateful or not about his absence. They have been regarding him as a growing threat. But now, they hear some encouraging news: people are speaking about this absurd claim he has made about eating his flesh and drinking his blood, and about his coming down from heaven. The Pharisees immediately dispatch an envoy to Capernaum to see if they can capitalize on this rumored decline in Jesus' popularity.

The moment they arrive in Capernaum, these Pharisees can sense there has been a noticable change in the town's attitude towards Jesus. Although most are busy during the day, as it is now harvest season, there are not the throngs of people following Jesus around as they did in the past. There are still plenty of people who want to be near him, but there is a definite coolness in the air about him. For his part, Jesus seems to be taking a lower profile, and likely because so many have lost what little faith in him they had, he does not perform many miracles. It is as if the miracle spigot has been turned off since the day of the "Bread of Life" sermon a month ago.

After a few days of general observation, the Pharisees decide to go on the offensive. In these rural areas, most Jews do not perform, in all their rigorous details, the customary Jewish cleansing laws. Where there is so much work going on, especially now during harvest season, it is impractical to observe every minutiae of these rituals, but the Pharisees see this as a good point on which to attack Jesus.

One day, as they watch from across the street, they see some of his apostles not washing their hands before they eat their mid-day meal. With a new boldness in their voice, they call across the street to him. "Why do your disciples break the tradition of the elders? They do not wash their hands when they eat a meal" (Matt 15:2). Jesus stops eating and conversing with his apostles and looks up at the Pharisees with a perturbed look on his face. It is June and day 603 of the 909 days that changed our world, and since that day a few months ago when another group of Pharisees accused him of working through the power of Beelzebub, Jesus' tolerance for them has thinned. He sees into their hearts and knows they are only, once again, trying to trick him and lead even more people away from believing in him. He counterattacks: "And why do you break the commandment of God for the sake of your tradition? For God said, 'Honor your mother and your father,' and 'Whoever curses his mother or father shall die.' But you say, 'Whoever says to father or mother, "Any support you might have had from me is dedicated to God," need not honor his father.' You have nullified the word of God for the sake of your tradition. Hypocrites, well did Isaiah prophesy about you when he said: 'This people honor me with their lips, but their hearts are far from me; in vain do they worship me, teaching as doctrines human precepts.'" (Matt 15:3-9).

The Pharisees, seeing the look in Jesus' eyes and hearing the tone of his voice, decide not to press the point. Instead, they huff and roll their eyes in disapproval as they walk away. Some turn around and look back, smirking at Jesus. They know they may have been bested here, but they sense the tide is turning in their favor. As they leave, Jesus gets up and goes outside and addresses the few people who have witnessed this exchange. The apostles, too, get up from their meals and walk outside. Jesus, in a voice loud enough for the Pharisees who are walking away to hear, says, "Hear and understand. It is not what enters one's mouth that defiles that person, but what comes out of the mouth is what defiles one" (Matt 15:10-11). Those in the small crowd nod their heads, not really understanding what Jesus is talking about; they walk away and return to their normal activities. Jesus does not elaborate on his words but turns to return to his meal.

The apostles too, of course, have noticed Jesus' waning popularity, and it causes them noticeable consternation. If his popularity is decreasing, maybe he should be a little more tolerant of the Pharisees? Maybe, they think, he shouldn't be so aggressive in his dealings with them. Besides, they know these specific Pharisees are on a mission from the chief priests of Jerusalem. Maybe it would be wise to be a little friendlier. Once back inside, therefore, the disciples, ask, "Do you know that the Pharisees took offense when they heard what you said?" (Matt 15:12). Jesus' response is quick. "Let them alone; they are blind guides of the blind. If a blind person leads a blind person, both will fall in the pit" (Matt 15:14). Jesus' tone indicates he is not in a compromising mood. The Pharisees are choosing not to see the truth, and they will take with them those who are equally unwilling to see the truth. So be it. The battle lines have been drawn, and people will have to choose sides. Will it be the Pharisees, their empty traditions and hard hearts—or will it be Jesus, his new teachings and compassionate heart? Most of the apostles quietly choose Jesus, but Judas, considered to be the most prudent of the bunch, worries about the formidable opposition of the leaders. His commitment to Jesus weakens a little more.

Peter, looking to change the mood of the room and referring to Jesus' recent comments to them and the crowd, asks Jesus, "Explain this parable to us" (Matt 15:15). The Jewish law is filled with prohibitions about what a good Jew can and cannot eat. What was Jesus saying about these laws in his statement? Jesus looks lovingly at Peter and says, "Are you even still without understanding? Do you not realize that everything that enters the mouth passes into the stomach and is expelled into the latrine? But the things that come out of the mouth come from the heart and they defile. For from the heart come evil thoughts, murder, adultery, unchastity, theft, false witness, blasphemy. These are what defile a person, but to eat with unwashed hands does not defile" (Matt 15:16-20). Years later, Peter will remember these words when, as the first leader of the church, he will ease the dietary laws to be followed by the growing number of Gentiles who become Christians. For now, it is clear the mood in Capernaum has changed, yet Jesus shows no sign of reversing any of his teachings. The Pharisees are spreading their poison, so, a few days later, Jesus first tells his mother and then his apostles about his desire to take a trip into some places less heavily dominated by Jews. He announces his desire to travel to the Mediterranean to the region of Tyre and Sidon and asks if any of them would like to come with him. To a man, the twelve decide to join him. His mother wants also to join him, but he asks her to stay in Capernaum. With her eyes and lips she pronounces, yet again, her "fiat" to the will of God. When the morning of departure arrives, Jesus embraces his mother and tries with his smile to wipe away the worry on her face. As he and his apostles leave the city, a certain sadness lingers. There are some townspeople who bid him good-bye and ask where he is going, but for the most part, he and his companions leave town with little fanfare. They will not return for three months.

Chapter Thirty-Three

Jesus Travels to the Tyre and Sidon Region

The trip from Capernaum to Tyre starts out in loud silence. The apostles think about what has recently happened in Capernaum and try to figure out, each in his own way, how this trip will have anything to do with Jesus revealing himself as the Messiah. He is lost in prayer as he unites his will with his Father's, knowing the time is growing short for him to accomplish his mission. He prays intensely for his apostles, knowing how disappointed they will be at how things will end less than a year from now. He prays for strength for them to carry on his mission after he is put to death, rises, and ascends back to heaven. After a long period of silence and at a good distance from Capernaum, Jesus engages them in conversation, smiling, and once again, they know that somehow, all will turn out for the best.

Tyre is a busy city and a center of shipping commerce. Mostly populated by Gentiles, jobs are plentiful and so a number of Jews have migrated here over the years. As Jesus arrives, some Jews recognize him, because they have seen him in Galilee, returning to visit relatives or making the trip to Jerusalem for a feast. Jesus does take someone up on an offer to house him and his apostles. He is intent on being alone with the apostles, as Mark reports: Jesus "enters the house but wants no one to notice" (Mark 8:24). Nevertheless, the news quickly spreads about his presence, and many, Gentile and Jew alike, come to see him, enticed by the stories of his miraculous cures and special powers. Jesus "cannot escape notice" (Mark 8:25). Here, there is much curiosity and little faith, but at least he does not have to deal with the Pharisees. He does, however, greet everyone warmly and makes them feel special. From Mark and Matthew's gospel texts, it doesn't appear as if Jesus performs many miracles here, but there is one woman, though, who will move Jesus to action.

Having heard about Jesus from some of her Jewish neighbors, a middle-aged woman from the outskirts of town goes to see him. Her daughter has been afflicted with a demon for some time. Her husband has long been dead from an accident at the shipping docks. She makes an honest living by doing domestic jobs for the wealthier people in the city who have taken pity on her. Hers is a hard life. Mark takes pains to tell us that this woman is not a Jew, but "a Greek, a Syro-Phoenician by birth" (Mark 8:26).

It is only the second day since Jesus has arrived in Tyre when the woman comes to the home where he is staying. As she works her way to the front of the crowd, she shouts to him to have pity on her daughter. She is so loud and so persistent that the apostles ask him to just dismiss her but on reaching Jesus, she throws herself at Jesus' feet, "and begs him to drive the demon out of her daughter" (Mark 8:26). Jesus looks down at this woman. Her face worn beyond her years from work and worry over her daughter elicits compassion from him. Her eyes, green and shining brightly from her tired face, look at him piercingly. He can see it—she believes he can heal her daughter. He can see she wants it done because her love for her suffering daughter far outweighs the pain and difficulty it has caused her. In his love, he tests her faith even more, in order to generate abundant grace for her and teach a lesson to the others in the crowd. Looking directly into her eyes but in a voice loud enough for all to hear, he replies, "Let the children be fed first. For it is not right to take the food of the children and throw it to the dogs" (Mark 8:27). It appears to be a rejection and alludes to the primacy of the Jewish people over the Gentiles. Jesus' response takes those within earshot aback. They think this is the reason he is not performing any miracles here. He must be prejudiced against us Gentiles, but, on further thought, why is he not doing any of his miracles for the Jews in the crowd? While the others are mulling over Jesus' comment, the middle-aged woman responds in a very strong voice, much stronger than her original request. "Lord, even the dogs under the table eat the children's scraps" (Mark 8:28). Ah yes, this woman does believe Jesus can cure her daughter and is willing to acknowledge it by humiliating herself before him. He looks back down at her. This is the kind of faith he seeks. His countenance softens as he leans over and says, "For saying this you may go. The demon has gone out of your daughter" (Mark 8:29). The woman shouts and cries for joy, stands up, and knowing her daughter is cured, thanks him through tears and runs back to her house. The apostles and the others in the crowd are silent. Why has he treated her so specially? And she has such confidence in his promise that her daughter is healed. Many are more than curious to see the end result of this, and some even follow her home to see for themselves. "When the woman gets home, she finds the child lying in bed and the demon gone" (Mark 8:30). She hugs her daughter and quickly brings her outside for all to see. The neighbors all attest to the fact that the daughter seems to be cured—her eyes are as clear as they have been in years—, and, as the days go by and the girl remains calm, sane, and happy, everyone becomes certain of it. By then, though, Jesus and his apostles have moved on.

Chapter Thirty-Four

Miracles in Decapolis; The Feeding of the Four Thousand

When Jesus leaves Tyre, "he goes by way of Sidon to the Sea of Galilee into the district of Decapolis" (Mark 7:31). On leaving Tyre, Jesus passes through the city of Sarepta, famous for the visit of Elias. Continuing on north he reaches Sidon, a city that was prosperous in the past but has lost much of its luster. From there, he turns back southeast until he gets to Caesarea-Philippi, and from there, he goes south until he reaches the land of Decapolis. There is no mention of any miracles taking place as he is making this journey with his apostles. Although there are pockets of Jewish people along the way, these territories are mostly Gentile. He does not engage the inhabitants too much as he travels through these towns. The pace seems almost to be leisurely and the intent just to spend time together. There is a good reason for this. Without the presence of the crowds and the Pharisees, Jesus is able to spend a long while forming his apostles. In nine months, he will be gone and they will be the ones to carry on his mission. So he teaches them much along the way. True, most of what he teaches them goes over their heads, but he builds closer intimacy with each of them. Later they will remember what he is saying now and realize the full meaning of his words. It is enough now to instruct them and to love them. It is an enjoyable time for all of them as over two months come and go.

On arriving in Decapolis, however, things change. It has been four months since Jesus was here on that day when he dismissed the devils from the wild man into the swine on the hill. The apostles are somewhat worried as they enter this territory, remembering how the people had calmly but firmly asked Jesus to leave. Would they still be the same way? No one is sure what to expect. Unbeknown to the apostles though, Jesus' reputation here is strong. From the time he left Geresa, the man from whom he had driven out the devils had taken seriously his charge to "go home to your family and announce to them all the Lord in his pity has done for you" (Mark 5:19); he has done his job well. Although this is a primarily Gentile area, many people have been moved to want to learn more about this Jesus on seeing and listening to this converted wild man. There also have been stories and first hand testimonies about the many miracles taking place all over Galilee, although there have been no reports of recent miracles as no one seems to be sure about Jesus' location.

All of sudden, though, here he is. Some recognize him immediately, and when he confirms his identity, the word spreads like wildfire. The apostles see that their worries are for naught. Many of these Gentiles over the last months have come to believe he can cure them and their loved ones from their ills, so all the excitement and attention are focused on that. And because of this location and the Gentile population, there is no contingent of Pharisees attempting to throw cold water on the proceedings or to turn the people against him.

Jesus and his apostles make their way up into the hills which rise above the sea, and the people begin to gather. Some "bring him a deaf man who has a speech impediment and beg him to lay his hand on him" (Mark 7:32). The deaf man looks like a deer in headlights; he is frozen to the spot and looks at Jesus with a blank stare. Although the people who have brought him think Jesus can cure him, the deaf man's eyes are empty. Likely it is because he doesn't have anywhere near the same faith as the woman in Tyre, but something strange happens here, and the apostles note it. Rather than just saying the words or laying his hands on him, this time Jesus takes the man and walks a little distance away from the crowd, signaling that he does not want them to follow him. "He puts his fingers in the man's ears and, spitting, touches his tongue; then he looks up to heaven and groans and says 'be opened,' and immediately the man's ears are opened, his speech impediment is removed, and he speaks plainly" (Mark 7:33-35). Somehow this miracle takes more effort from Jesus than others. Perhaps it is because less faith somehow requires Jesus to do more work. The once-deaf man thanks Jesus quickly, almost as if he views him as some kind of miracle machine, and turns to run back to tell all about what has happened to him. As the man is turning to leave,

Jesus orders him and the others "not to tell anyone," (Mark 7:36) but to no avail. Jesus knows they are all excited about what he can do for them physically. Most care little about who Jesus is or what he can do for them spiritually. Jesus understands this and, much like in the early days of his Capernaum mission, heals the great crowd of people who come to him over the course of the afternoon. They bring the sick, the lame, the infirm, the crippled, the possessed—and he cures them all. It is a wonderful afternoon of miracles, and the apostles seem drunk with the enthusiasm generated by the crowd. This is just like the old days, with Jesus performing miracles in Galilee and everyone lauding him as the foretold Messiah. True, most of these people are Gentiles, but they are all united, for the moment, in their admiration of his talents. Surely, they all think, he is destined for great things. And just like he did for the Jewish people of Capernaum who had followed him around the northern shore of the sea months ago, so, too, will he do, soon, for these Gentiles.

Jesus stays here on the hillside for a few days. Every day is filled with healings and miracles. Some people leave after being cured, others stay to see more miracles, and a few stay even longer, over-night, or for a few days to be close to him. On the third day of his stay here in Decapolis, something remarkable happens. Just like his walk from south of Magdala to Capernaum before the "Bread of Life" sermon was the high point of his popularity with the Jews, so today will we witness the high point of his popularity with the Gentiles. He and his apostles, most of the people who have stayed with him, and many newcomers are without sufficient food. Looking north to the place where a little over three months ago he had fed the five thou-sand, Jesus calls together all his apostles, emphasizing the importance of what he is about to do, and says, "My heart is moved with pity for the crowd, because they have been with me now for three days and have nothing to eat. If I send them away hungry to their homes they will collapse on the way and some of them have come a great distance" (Mark 8:2-3). This is not the Promised People on whom he has pity, but the Gentiles. His disciples, focusing again as they did before on the absurdity of the feeding of the five thousand but remembering the miracle that followed, tell him there is not enough to feed all these people. Yet, just as he had done before, now, too, he asks them to see how much food is available. As before, they enter the crowd and come back with their report: "Seven [loaves of bread], and a few fish" (Matt 15:34). The apostles see this coming and most of them marvel at the fact that he is going to do this miracle for a Gentile crowd.

"Then Jesus takes the seven loaves and the fish, gives thanks, breaks the loaves, and gives them to his disciples, who in turn give them to the crowds. They all eat and are satisfied. They pick up the fragments left over—seven baskets full" (Matt 15:36-37). He has performed the very same miracle for these Gentiles as he had for the mostly Jewish crowd a short time ago. What can he mean by doing this? Are the Gentiles as important as the Jews? How can that be, as they are not the Chosen People? The apostles' minds are filled with these questions as they collect the excess food. The people, some of whom have heard about Jesus' doing a miracle like this before, shout with pleasure. Although their enthusiasm is high, unlike the Jews before, they do not move to make him a king. They are content to give him their gratitude and affection and wait to see what he will ask of them. At the moment, though, he asks nothing but for them all to go back to their homes. He sees them off, looking directly into the eyes of those who come to say "good-bye" to him personally, and watches as the field slowly empties out. He smiles to himself. Someday his apostles will realize that this last tour with them through these Gentile regions, including this "repeat" miracle, is a sign of his and their call to preach the good news to all people of good will, and not just the Jews. For now, though, as the crowd leaves, Jesus and his apostles "get into the boat and go to the region of Dalmanutha" (Mark 8:10). It is mid-August, day 675 of the 909 days that changed the world.

CHAPTER THIRTY-FIVE

Jesus Confronts the Pharisees in Dalmanutha

Dalmanutha is in the southern part of the Sea of Galilee. It encompasses the area where people traveling from Galilee to Jerusalem cross the Jordan River to continue south on the Decapolis and Perea side of the river. It was here, just over one year ago, where John was arrested by Herod's guards. Today, after a smooth and relaxing sail down the Sea of Galilee, Jesus and his apostles disembark. It has been a little less than three months since they left Capernaum on this tour which began in Tyre. As noted before, they have been dealing more with Gentiles than with Jews, and they have not been hounded by any of the Jewish leaders. On landing, however, they see a group of Pharisees and Sadducees approaching them. The apostles, remembering Jesus' last confrontation with the Pharisees back in Capernaum, once again have their fears and concerns intensified as it looks like these leaders have been on the lookout for Jesus. This has the makings of another uncomfortable confrontation; that much is obvious by the gait and countenance of the approaching men....

These Pharisees and Sadducees, however, are making a trip from Jerusalem and just happen to be there as Jesus and his apostles arrive. They have been talking about Jesus from time to time, as many have, and have been wondering where he has been these last few months. There have been some stories of his being in the land north of Galilee but not much talk of miracles. Some of the Pharisees recognize him as he gets out of the boat and point him out to the others. Knowing his popularity with the Galileans has decreased and thinking perhaps his "miracle" powers are fading also, they decide to question him. Dressed impeccably, heads held pompously high, these leaders provide a striking contrast to Jesus and his apostles who, for their part, look common, dressed in working clothes. The leaders go on the attack. With the number of people decreasing who say Jesus is the Promised One, the Pharisees and Sadducees push him on the point and "begin to argue with him, seeking from him a sign from heaven" (Mark 8:11).

Jesus' heart is heavy, and "he sighs from the depths of his spirit" (Mark 8:12). These men are so intent on trying to take Jesus down. They are so full of their own authority that they are blind to the possibility of their being wrong. Their lack of good will exhausts him, even though he has not had to deal with these kinds of men for a while. He turns away from them and looks around at his apostles. Their faces are deeply marked with concern. He will address these Pharisees and Sadducees and then be gone again with his apostles. Turning back to the leaders, he replies, much as he had to the Pharisees back in Capernaum when they accused him of using the power of Beelzebub, "An evil and unfaithful generation seeks a sign, but no sign will be given it except the sign of Jonah" (Matt 16:4). His voice conveys utter indifference for their opinion, yet he has given them a clue. Let them ponder the sign of Jonah. Perhaps some of them, after his death and resurrection, will remember and then come to believe. For now, he turns his back on them and walks to the boat.

As quickly as Jesus and his apostles have landed, they now leave, and he instructs them to set sail north to Bethsaida. Although many of them wonder why they had sailed south in the first place, no one asks. They suspect the sudden arrival of the Pharisees and Sadducees has changed Jesus' plans. Jesus, although he knows what is on their minds, decides not to answer their nonverbalized questions as the apostles begin to discuss another issue which will provide a more important teaching experience.

As they have left Dalmanutha so suddenly, they have not secured more provisions, and "they only have one loaf with them in the boat" (Mark 8:14). As they are making their way north on the calm sea, it dawns on them that they have almost nothing to eat. Searching around the boat and finding only this one loaf, the apostles are wondering if they should pull in along the eastern shore to secure provisions or just wait until they finish the four-hour trip to Bethsaida. As if reading their minds, Jesus says, "Look out and beware of the leaven of the Pharisees and Sadducees" (Matt 16:6). Thinking Jesus is perhaps asking for some of their bread, the apostles look at Judas, who is usually in charge of getting provisions. They tell Jesus there is only one loaf of bread on board. Jesus, of course, is not referring to real bread at all. Jesus says to them, "You of little faith, why do you conclude among yourselves that it is because you have no bread?" (Matt 16:8). Then, as if to remind them he can change one loaf into more than enough bread, he continues, "Do you not yet understand, and do you not remember the five loaves for the five thousand, and how many wicker baskets you took up? Or the seven loaves for the four thousand, and how many baskets you took up? How do you not comprehend that I was not speaking to you about bread?" (Matt 16: 9-11). The light bulbs do go on in some of the disciples' heads as Jesus concludes by repeating, "Beware of the leaven of the Pharisees and Sadducees" (Matt 16:11). Then they understand that "he is not telling them about bread but of the teaching of the Pharisees and Sadducees" (Matt 16:12).

They continue the smooth sail up the eastern side of the Sea of Galilee. They pass the place where Jesus fed the four thousand mostly Gentile people only yesterday, and slightly further north, they pass the Gerasene area where he, almost four months ago, had cured the demoniac, allowing the legion of demons to take over the swine and hurl them into the sea. Finally, they arrive at Bethsaida and see the plain where he fed the mostly Jewish five thousand over three months ago. It was right after that miracle, when he gave his "Bread of Life" sermon in Capernaum the following day, that things began taking a turn for the worse. Yes, this east coast of the Sea of Galilee holds many memories. They are all lost in their own thoughts, but quietly and efficiently they guide their boat to shore.

Chapter Thirty-Six

The Blind Man at Bethsaida

Mark is the only one who records what happens next as they enter Bethsaida. When Jesus fed the five thousand, most of the people were from Capernaum and the surrounding areas and had hiked along the northern shore of the Sea to get to this area. Now, it is just the regular natives there, a number of whom are non-Jewish. Jesus' reputation, though, is very strong here as these Gentiles see Jesus as someone who can cure their sick, not concerning themselves with any of the religious disagreements of the Jews. In addition, of course, a number of apostles live here and their families have been constantly talking about Jesus. As Jesus and his apostles get out of the boat and proceed into town, some townspeople run to find an ill-fated neighbor, hoping to have Jesus cure his blindness. The man has mysteriously lost his sight recently; no one can figure out why or how it happened. The man has become depressed; his wife and family are distraught. A fisherman by trade, he has been unable to work, and the family has been relying on the generosity of friends and family to help them live.

Jesus and his apostles stop for some supplies in the village. It appears they are merely passing through Bethsaida. Some ask if they will stay, and he tells them they can remain only a brief while, as they are heading north towards Caesarea-Philippi. Most people, including the apostles, are surprised and even shocked that Jesus is going to a city known for its moral depravity.

It is at this time that the blind man is led into Jesus' presence. The blind man's friends, with genuine concern in their eyes, beg Jesus to touch him. They are not bold enough to ask for a cure; they only hope that Jesus will touch him and somehow, out of pity for the man, make him see. Jesus can see this selfless concern for the blind man in their eyes. He can also see the man's wife in the background, hands together almost as if praying in hope of some miracle. Finally, he can see a ray of hope in the darkness of despair in the blind man's soul. Taking him by the hand, Jesus leads him away from the people to the outskirts of the city, with only his apostles in tow. The villagers watch as Jesus spits in his hands and lays them on the blind man's eyes. Much like the miracle he did for the deaf mute in Decapolis, this miracle appears to require more effort on Jesus' part. He asks, "Do you see anything?" (Mark 8:23). The man replies, "I see people looking like trees and walking" (Mark 8:24). Jesus places his hands on the man's head and then once again on his eyes and looks up to heaven, and the man "sees clearly; his sight is restored and he can see everything distinctly" (Mark 8:25).

The man is ecstatic. The villagers in the distance hear his shouts of joy and see him excitedly thanking Jesus. He is cured. He can see. The hearts of the blind man's friends burst with gratitude. The man's wife comes running and throws her arms around her husband's shoulders. He can see! He can see! With tears streaming down her face, she turns her attention to Jesus and can hardly find the words to thank him. Jesus tells the man to go home and be about his normal life. Amidst all the requests of the townspeople to stay with them in Bethsaida, Jesus insists they cannot stay now. It is as if he is pushing forward in anticipation of an important encounter. Indeed, there will be an important encounter shortly, as Peter will utter something that will signal another turning point in Jesus' ministry.

CHAPTER THIRTY-SEVEN

The Confession of Peter

Jesus and his apostles depart from Bethsaida later the same afternoon to make the twenty-mile journey to Caesarea-Philippi. The city of Caesarea-Philippi is ruled by Philip, a son of Herod the Great. This Philip is not the same Philip whose ex-wife Herodias engineered the death of John the Baptist. The city had been called Paneas, but Philip had rebuilt much of it and changed the name to Caesarea-Philippi, "Caesarea" to honor Caesar and "Philippi" to honor himself. It is a city heavily influenced by Greek culture. The apostles can think of no reason why they would visit this place of iniquity, but say nothing. Although not able to make it all the way to the city before nightfall, they do find a safe place to camp some miles outside the city.

In the morning, Jesus, as frequently is his custom, gets up earlier than the others and goes away by himself to pray. The air is heavy, and it is a particularly hot summer morning. As the apostles awaken, they notice Jesus is not in camp but are not alarmed, figuring he is alone, praying. As they are preparing breakfast, he comes back into camp and his face bears a very determined look. After breakfast, they break camp and make the final leg of the journey to Caesaria-Philippi and arrive mid-morning at the outskirts of the city. There they can see on a bluff two temples; one built in honor of Caesar and the other built in honor of the Greek god, Pan, for whom the city had originally been named (Paneas). The latter temple is the worldwide center for worshipping Pan and is the site of many lewd acts performed as devotions to the god. Next to the temple of Pan is a crevice, called the "Gates of Hell," believed to be the entrance way where all the dead spirits come and go from hell. This whole area is an abomination to the Jews.

Jesus motions for everyone to stop and then points up at these temples and the crevice. The apostles still cannot make any sense of why they are here and why he is pointing out this place of degradation. He turns around to face the apostles and with the temples and crevice behind him solemnly asks, "Who do people say that the Son of Man is?" (Matt 16:13). His words are sharp and his eyes piercing. They respond, "Some say John the Baptist, others Elijah, and still others Jeremiah or one of the prophets" (Matt 16:14). He looks even more intensely at them and asks, "But who do you say I am?" (Matt 16:15). Struck by the seriousness of Jesus' countenance and uncomfortable with the pagan background, the apostles are not quite sure how to respond. This feels like a test. They have called him many great things since the two years or so when Peter, Andrew, John, Philip, and Nathaniel had met him on the Jordan riverside. They know he is not John the Baptist, nor Elijah, nor Jeremiah, nor one of the prophets. They all do believe that he is much more than those men, but they are not quite sure what to say or how to respond. Does this city and this backdrop have something to do with the answer? They are all lost for words, except one.

Much like a student who has been studying a writer for a long time without really understanding the depth of the author's message finally "sees it," finally "gets it," so now the light goes on in Peter's head. Jesus is the antithesis of the lies behind his shoulders! He has called Jesus the Son of God before, but now, for a moment, he sees what that means with clarity. His heart expands with love and full confidence in Jesus and who he is, as he states, "You are the Christ [Messiah], the Son of the Living God" (Matt 16:16). It is not so much the words themselves as it is the conviction in his voice that signals the conviction of his heart and mind. It is a like a wife whose husband says, "I love you." There are some times when he says those words by force of habit, but there are other times when he says those words with such intensity in his voice and eyes, she feels the words are coming from his soul. Jesus immediately hears and sees the words coming from Peter's soul, and he is very pleased. This is what he has been waiting for. Yes, Peter is weak and will make many more mistakes along the way, but his heart and mind belong entirely to Jesus. He fully believes in Jesus as the Son of God, the Christ, the Savior of the world, and Jesus knows Peter has been showered with this grace by his Father in heaven. Jesus smiling looks at Peter and says, "Blessed are you, Simon son of Jonah; flesh and blood have not revealed this to you, but my heavenly Father. And so I say to you, you are Peter and upon this rock I will build my church, and the gates of the netherworld shall not prevail against it. I will give you the keys to the kingdom of heaven. Whatever you bind on earth shall be bound in heaven, and whatever you loose on earth shall be loosed in heaven" (Matt 16:17-19).

These words are made all the more powerful in front of the two temples: one temple of pride and vanity to Caesar; the other, of depravity and false godhood to pan, and then there is the crevice of exit and entrance to hell. Jesus anoints Peter the first vicar, the first pope of his ministry, although the full importance of these words will only become evident after Jesus' death. For now, he slowly moves his gaze to each of the apostles as if to emphasize what he has just said to Peter. Peter, impetuous, hot-tempered, but full of love, is the man Jesus has chosen to lead his Church. With the exception of one of them, the apostles are fine with his choice. Peter is a good man, clearly loves Jesus, and speaks and acts with courage. Yes, they think, if not me then Peter is a good choice. Only one—Judas—thinks he would have been the better choice and scoffs at Jesus' choice of Peter. Doesn't Jesus see how imprudent and childish Peter can be? How can he ever choose such a person to be his second in command? 'Utterly ridiculous!' he thinks to himself, and his commitment to Jesus weakens more.

Jesus' spirits are high and the apostles know it, but they don't know that Peter's confession has signaled a change in Jesus' ministry. With the certainty that his Father has given Peter the graces he will need to lead his church after his death, resurrection, and ascension, he is now ready to embark on the final leg of his mission. Much to the relief of the apostles as they stand at the footsteps of this city, he tells them they will not continue on, but will turn around and head back south. Unbeknownst to his apostles, they will return to Galilee for a month or so of more intense instruction, and then he will make his way to Jerusalem, ready to begin the final showdown with the Jewish leaders. He will be dead in less than seven months.

CHAPTER THIRTY-EIGHT

The First Prophecy of the Passion

As the group retraces its steps along the smooth and easy road back to the Sea of Galilee, Jesus falls into silence again. The breeze has picked up and cooled things off some. It is a beautiful day, and the apostles enjoy the walk. As they continue to travel in silence, Jesus begins to speak to them about the future. He tells them, "He must suffer greatly and be rejected by the elders, the chief priests, and the scribes, and be killed and rise after three days" (Mark 8:31). The contrast of his words and his mood from a mere few hours ago startles the apostles. What can he be saying? Most of them reason that he is telling them a parable of sorts, and he will soon explain the real meaning of all these foreboding predictions. But he doesn't explain the "parable"; he goes back over again the fact that he will be scorned by the leaders, put to death, and rise again in three days. With no further explanation of this account, the apostles become despondent, for they all have been assuming that Jesus will unite all of the Jews in the task of eliminating the hated Roman rulers to once again restore Israel to all its former glory. This talk of rejection, suffering, and death, even though followed by a resurrection, depresses them. It depresses them all the more, of course, because they have noticed Jesus' popularity waning among the Jewish people and the growing toxic relationship with the Pharisees, Sadducees, and other Jewish leaders. Besides, if Jesus is going to be killed, it is safe to assume their lives will be at risk also.

Peter, the "rock," views himself now as the leader of the apostles, so he decides he needs to tell Jesus to cut out this kind of talk or explain himself more clearly. Peter thinks that Jesus doesn't know how much his words are depressing the apostles. Moreover, he is being encouraged by Judas and a few others to tell him to stop such silly talk. Peter therefore asks to rest for a while, and the others all agree. Walking over to Jesus, Peter comes alongside him and walks him a short distance from the apostles. "Peter then begins to rebuke him, saying, 'God forbid, Lord. No such thing shall ever happen to you'" (Matt 16:22). Peter's voice is more pleading than demanding but speaks with the confidence of his knowing what is best in this situation. The effect of Peter's words is instantly registered on Jesus' face. His brow wrinkles up and his eyes widen as if he is seeing the personification of evil itself. Peter takes a step back. He is overwhelmed by what he sees in Jesus' face. Jesus turns his back on Peter, looking back at the other apostles who can see his severe countenance. He then turns back to Peter and cries out in a loud voice, "Get behind me, Satan. You are an obstacle to me. You are thinking not as God does, but as human beings do" (Matt 16:23).

Peter, the one whom a few hours ago Jesus had clearly anointed as leader of the apostles, is now being compared to Beelzebub. This is no small charge from the man who so violently reacted to the Pharisees when they accused him of acting with the power of Beelzebub. Peter is embarrassed and unsure of what to do, and all the apostles are confused about what this means about Peter's leadership. Those apostles knowing Peter had taken Jesus aside to ask him to tone down the depressing rhetoric wonder now if Jesus' predictions are to be taken literally. One of them, Judas, wants no part of the fate Jesus is outlining for himself and for them. His commitment to Jesus weakens more again.

In a matter of a few moments, though, the look on Jesus' face softens. He motions with his head for Peter to follow him and makes his way back the short distance to the other apostles. His anger seems to have evaporated. He asks them all to sit in front of him and as they do, he sits down facing them. Jesus' face takes on that look of power and authority. While the sun is brightly shining in the late morning sky, Jesus teaches, "Whoever wishes to come after me must deny himself, take up his cross and follow me. For whoever wishes to save his life will lose it, but whoever loses his life for my sake will find it. What profit would there be for one to gain the whole world and forfeit his life? For the Son of Man will come with his angels in his Father's glory, and then he will repay everyone according to their conduct" (Matt 16:24-27). It is Jesus' promise to them that they will be rewarded for their faithfulness if they choose to suffer for his sake. Most of them focus on the "repay everyone" part of his instruction and so their spirits are lifted up again. Yes, they think, we will do battle with him, we will be by his side and reap the rewards. Jesus, after giving his apostles a minute or so to digest these words, smiles and suggests they have something to eat before they continue their journey back to the northern shore of the Sea of Galilee.

CHAPTER THIRTY-NINE

The Transfiguration

Finishing their meal, Jesus and the apostles continue south along the Jordan River until they get close to the Sea of Galilee. On reaching the Sea of Galilee, they make a right turn and cross the river at the same spot the five thousand crossed when following Jesus from Capernaum. They take the same path along the northern shore back towards Capernaum. The apostles are all very excited to be returning, as they have not been home for the better part of three months. Jesus tells them they will be spending the next four or five days with their families. Because it is late and they have been away for a while, they make the trip down the coastline mostly unnoticed. John and James are the first to leave the others as the group travels along the outskirts of Bethsaida, and the two young men depart for their parent's home. They call out to their parents as they get close to the house. Looking at each other with excited smiles, their parents both drop what they are doing and run out to meet the boys. As the four of them embrace, they are overwhelmed with joy, and as they walk arm in arm back towards the house, their mother wants to know everything they have been doing. Down the path in Bethsaida, Philip leaves the others to return to his house. No one is inside when he gets there as they are all tending to chores. He waits within, and shortly his mother comes back to prepare the evening meal. Dropping the bowl she is carrying, she lets out such a cry when she sees him that the others come running as fast as they can. Here, too, the family reunion is one of great joy. How they love each other!

It is early evening by the time the others get to Capernaum. When Peter arrives at his mother-in-law's house where his wife is still staying, he quietly slips inside and puts his arms around his unsuspecting wife. Turning around in confusion at first, her eyes open wide on seeing him and she literally jumps into his arms. As it is for these, it is the same for all the apostles. It is good to be home. The apostles' families are overjoyed to see them. They ask many questions about Jesus, about what they have been doing these last few months, and about what the future will bring. Most are thrilled because they are hopeful he is the Messiah, but some family members express concern because they have seen how the tide has turned against him since the "Bread of Life" discourse. They also note how much bolder the Pharisees have become in their criticism.

Jesus goes to his house where his mother is staying with relatives. He stands outside the door and calls. She instantly recognizes his voice, stands up, and starts running towards the door just as he walks in the house. She almost bowls him over, pulls back for a second, looks at him with all the love she has in her heart, and starts crying. Jesus, thrilled to be home, enfolds her lovingly in his arms. They walk arm in arm for a few moments until Mary hears his stomach growling and realizes he has not eaten the evening meal yet. She promptly prepares one for him as he cleans up from his travels. It is over this meal they begin a conversation that lasts long into the night.

The next morning, word of Jesus' return spreads quickly, but the response is muted. Some come to see him, but the poison spread by the Pharisees over the last few months has seeped into the minds of the townspeople. A number now believe he is somehow working with Beelzebub. Over the next few days, of those who come to see him, there are requests for miracles, but Jesus, gracious and friendly, performs none. This causes even more people to doubt; they become skeptical. More family members of the apostles begin to question them, asking if they are sure this Jesus is going to be the new leader of the Jewish nation's revival. A few even press further by asking if following him is a wise move as they think there may be more risk than reward in being one of this man's apostles?

Despite family concerns, after the several days' visit, all the apostles return to where Mary is staying, ready for the next move. To a man, they all agree to follow Jesus forward, although one, Judas Iscariot, agrees, but with hidden reservations. He has heard all the criticism of Jesus from others and from his own family and, having already begun to doubt he is the Messiah, finds his enthusiasm waning a little more. Jesus smiles warmly at each as they return. He has, as he always does, respected their freedom and even now allows them the choice to stay here at Capernaum or to follow him. They still are in, so with all twelve with him for now, he leaves Capernaum early in the morning and heads south.

At the end of a relatively long and uneventful day, they arrive at the foot of Mount Thabor. It is early September—day 693 of the 909 days that changed the world. Thabor stands alone, attached to no other mountain or hills, and has a singularly conical shape, almost as if someone just dropped the mountain there. Climbing to the top provides breathtaking views in all directions. To the west Mount Carmel and the great sea are visible; to the north are the stretch of mountains behind which lie Nazareth and Cana; to the northeast, there is a break between the hills that allows a view of the northern corner of the Sea of Galilee. A strategist would likely think whoever controls this mountain could control the surrounding area. Indeed, many years later, this mountain will become one the Crusaders fortify with walls when they are fighting the Saracens. The Saracens will agree that Thabor is a strategic stronghold and will attack it with vigor, finally breaking through the walls and massacring the Crusaders to a man. The foundations of these walls are still visible to this day.

Jesus tells the apostles to make camp in the village at the foot of the mountain, and then selects Peter, James, and John to go up the mountain with him for the evening. The other apostles have seen him take these three aside a number of times before, so with the exception of Judas, none of them is surprised or disconcerted. As they get close to the summit, Jesus tells the other three to pray while he goes ahead alone. At first the apostles are fine but, as it has been a long day and it is getting dark, they all begin to doze.

They are awakened by a bright light, and "he is transfigured before them, and his clothes become dazzling white, such as no fuller on earth could bleach them" (Mark 9:3). They have to shield their eyes at first but then gradually get used to the light and, as they do, realize Jesus is not alone. "Elijah appears to them along with Moses, and they are conversing with Jesus" (Mark 9:4). The apostles are overwhelmed, dumbfounded, terrified, and lost for words. Finally, Peter, as is usually the case, speaks up. "Rabbi, it is good we are here. Let us build three tents: one for you, one for Moses, and one for

Elijah" (Mark 9:5), but instead of a response from Jesus, the apostles get this sense of a cloud overshadowing the three apostles "and out of the cloud comes a voice: 'This is my beloved Son. Listen to him'" (Mark 9:7). As quickly as it has all happened, the cloud lifts, the light disappears, Moses and Elijah are gone, and Jesus, the man they know, is standing in front of them. It is now close to daybreak, and Jesus tells them it is time to go back to the others. As they walk down the mountain, however, Jesus "charges them to not relate to anyone what they have seen, except when the Son of Man has risen from the dead" (Mark 9:9). As St. Mark relates, the apostles still do not comprehend the prediction of his death, as the three "keep the matter to themselves but question what rising from the dead means" (Mark 9:10). This vision is something these three apostles will always remember and will be a great source of strength to each of them when they are preaching the good news after Jesus' death and resurrection.

CHAPTER FORTY

The Demoniac Boy

Coming down the mountain, they draw closer to the little town where the other apostles have spent the night, and they can see and hear a commotion going on. As they get a clearer view, they see most of the other nine apostles in active and heated dialogue with Scribes and others. Off to the side, a smaller gathering of people looks down on something in the midst of them. Both groups are so focused that neither of them notices Jesus finish the descent from the mountain and walk into the town.

One of the nine sees Jesus and lets out a cry of joy. He is back! It has not been a pleasant morning for the nine. When the townspeople awoke and realized Jesus' apostles were there, one man had brought them his son who was possessed by a demon. He had begged the apostles to cure him, but try as they might, they were unable to do so. The news of their failure spread quickly in the town, and the local Scribes came out to see the events. Instantly, the Scribes went on the attack and have been arguing for quite some time about the power of their leader, Jesus. As the Scribes are more learned in the Jewish scriptures and traditions than the nine, this battle is not going well for the apostles. The Scribes are making them look unintelligent and taunting them for their inability to help the boy. Meanwhile, the other group close by consists of the boy, his father, and a few neighbors. The boy is on the ground, exhausted from his rantings and surrounded by these people, who all look down on him in pity.

When the father of the boy hears the cry of one of the apostles acknowledging Jesus' return, he runs towards Jesus. His disciples failed to cure his son, but maybe Jesus can to it. Falling at Jesus' feet, the man says, "My son is possessed by a mute spirit. Whenever it seizes him, it throws him down; he foams at the mouth, grinds his teeth, and becomes rigid. I asked your disciples to drive it out, but they were unable to do so" (Mark 9:17-18). Jesus looks at the man in pity and then, raising his eyes and looking around at the crowd staring at him now, groans, "O faithless generation, how long will I be with you? How long can I endure you?" (Mark 9:19). He knows there will be a great lesson of faith taking place here momentarily, and again he wants to emphasize how important it is to have faith in Jesus, the person, the man, the God. So looking back down on the boy's father, he says, "Bring him to me" (Mark 9:19). The man gets up, excited because he is becoming hopeful, and runs over to where his son is lying on the ground. He takes him by the hand and raises the boy up. The boy can't see Jesus at first, but as soon as he gets around those blocking his view, his reaction is violent. "The spirit immediately throws the boy into convulsions. As he falls to the ground, he begins to roll around and foam at the mouth" (Mark 9:20). The father tells Jesus, "This has been happening since childhood. It has often thrown him into fire and water to kill him, but if you can do anything, have compassion on us and help us" (Mark 9:21).

"If you can do anything"; these words stick in Jesus' mind. Clearly this man does not have the kind of faith Jesus desires. The man is looking for magic. He doesn't understand that Jesus is looking for unconditional faith no matter what the circumstances. Jesus looks down on the boy who has spent himself again and lies whimpering on the ground with his hands around his head as if to protect himself from Jesus, then Jesus turns his gaze back to the father. Firmly but gently he says, "If you can! Everything is possible to one who has faith" (Mark 9:23). The boy's father, looking directly into Jesus' eyes with his own tear-filled ones, utters, "I do believe; help my unbelief" (Mark 9:24). He gets it. He knows how imperfect his faith is; he knows how his faith is largely driven by what he wants from Jesus; he knows he is more interested in the miracle than the man, but he is honest enough to know more is demanded of him, and he desires to give it. "I do believe; help my unbelief." And it is enough. It is not perfect—but it is honest, repentant, and a big move in the right direction.

Jesus smiles at the father while putting both hands on his shoulders and then turns his gaze to the boy, rebuking the spirit to leave. Once again the boy begins shouting and going into convulsions, but then all of a sudden, he falls limp to the ground and "becomes like a corpse, which causes many to say, 'He is dead'" (Mark 9:26). All eyes in the crowd go back and forth from the boy to Jesus. Only the boy's father has not taken his eyes off Jesus. He has seen his son convulse like this many times; never has he seen such a look of concern and authority as he does now in the face of Jesus. After what seems like an eternity but is only a few seconds, Jesus walks over to the boy and "takes him by the hand, raises him, and the boy stands up" (Mark 9:27). Gently Jesus leads the boy over to his father and puts the boy's hand in his father's. The father is so happy, the son acts as if he has no idea of what has been taking place, and the crowd observes all in stunned silence. Jesus tells the father and son to go home, the Scribes shrink away, and the crowd dissipates. The father will never tire of telling everyone about Jesus.

As the crowd disappears and Jesus and his disciples prepare to move on, some of his apostles ask, "Why could we not drive the spirit out?" (Mark 9:28). His reply is mysterious and reminiscent of some of his other miracles, which seemed to require more work or more effort. He says to them, "This kind can only come out through prayer" (Mark 9:29). As there is an order of good, he is indicating there is also an order of evil. Some evils are harder to eradicate than others.

CHAPTER FORTY-ONE

Jesus Makes a Mini-Tour of Galilee

It is getting into mid-September. In a month, it will be the Feast of Tabernacles, which is kind of a double celebration, as it commemorates the journey of the Jews through the desert on the way to the Promised Land as well as the completion of the fall harvest. While waiting for the feast, Jesus begins a mini-tour of the Galilean territory. This time, though, he wants to do so quietly. As he goes from town to town, we mostly hear about his instructions to the apostles and others. The time of great miracles has come and gone. It is a clear sign Jesus wants people to believe in who he is, not in what he can do for them.

It is on this tour that, for the second time, he tells the apostles about his upcoming death. "The Son of Man is to be handed over to men and they will kill him, and three days after his death, he will rise" (Mark 9:31). How more clearly can he state it? Nevertheless, the apostles still don't quite get, or refuse to believe, what he is saying to them, "as they do not understand the saying and are afraid to question him" (Mark 9:32). We can only imagine how disconcerting these words, if taken literally, would be to the apostles. After all, they have committed their lives to him and his cause. Talk of death is incomprehensible. Quickly they begin to set their minds on the glory of the new kingdom. As they are making their way to Capernaum after touring Galilee for about a week, the apostles begin to talk about which of them "is going to be the greatest" (Mark 9:34). Oh yes, they know Jesus has clearly chosen Simon Peter, but they begin to argue among themselves as to what heights of power they will each achieve. Jesus is a bit ahead of them, surrounded by some town people who have seen them coming, so the apostles think he is out of earshot. Arriving in town, he immediately goes to the home where his mother is staying. The apostles follow him as does a small crowd of people. Gone are the days of throngs of followers. The poison of the Pharisees is spreading. Still, enough support remains to create a minor stir.

As Jesus stands outside his mother's house, he looks at his apostles and asks them, "What were you arguing about on the way?" (Mark 9:33). They are startled and feel like little boys who have been found out. Had he heard their discussion about who was the greatest among them? They all look at the ground. Even Peter cannot bring himself to say anything. Jesus turns his gaze from the apostles and, looking around the small crowd, walks over to a young child whose mother had pushed him to the front so he could see better. Jesus gets down on one knee so he is at eye level with the child, and in a loud yet tender voice says, "If anyone wishes to be first, he shall be the last of all and the servant of all" (Mark 9:35). Standing back up, walking behind the child, and putting his hands on his shoulders, he continues, "Whoever receives one child such as this in my name, receives me; and whoever receives me, receives not me, but the One who sent me" (Mark 9:37). It is a profound lesson, but one mostly lost for the moment on the crowd as well as the apostles who are each feeling embarrassment. Being first means putting yourself last, but they will only fully learn it after Jesus is gone. Indeed, it is a lesson hard to learn even today.

John, the beloved John, feels the sting of Jesus' knowledge of the apostle's vain conversation, attempts to change the topic, and, referring to a recent incident that happened on this latest tour of Galilee, blurts out, "Master, we saw someone casting out demons in your name and we tried to prevent him because he does not follow in our company" (Luke 9:49). Jesus' reply is quick. "Do not prevent him, for whoever is not against you is for you" (Luke 9:50). Yes, the Holy Spirit will move where he will, but that is a different lesson for a different day. For now, Jesus does not want to be distracted and has more to say and teach. With his hands still on the boy's shoulders, and in a voice that gets progressively louder as he delivers these words, he says, "Whoever causes one of these little ones who believe in me to sin, it would be better for him if a great millstone were put around his neck and he were thrown into the sea. If your hand causes you to sin, cut it off. It is better for you to enter into life maimed than with two hands to go into Gehenna, into unquench- able fire. And if your foot causes you to sin, cut it off. It is better for you to enter into life crippled than with two feet to be thrown into Gehenna. And if your eye causes you to sin, pluck it out. Better for you to enter into the kingdom of God with one eye than with two eyes to be thrown into Gehenna, where the worm does not die, and the fire is not quenched" (Mark 9:42-48). The crowd is silenced by the tone of his voice and the severity of his words. As Jesus turns the boy around and smiles at him, the crowd begins to dissipate, as no one dares ask him if he really means these hard teachings. But many in the crowd observe how "severe" Jesus is becoming in his words lately and, sadly, even more people begin to wonder if the Pharisees are correct about him.

While Jesus and his apostles are staying in Capernaum, as Peter is leaving his mother-in-law's house, one of the tax collectors approaches him and asks, "Doesn't your teacher pay the temple tax?" (Matt 17:24). Peter is taken aback. Never have the authorities in the past been so bold as to require Jesus to pay the temple tax. Peter correctly interprets this as another sign of Jesus' waning popularity and the increasing boldness of his detractors. Not wanting to create anymore animosity, Peter simply replies, "Yes" (Matt 17:25), but as he walks back to see Jesus, he wonders how he is going to bring this up. He begins to think perhaps he should not have said "yes." Maybe Peter spoke too soon.

"As Peter approaches the house, before he has time to speak, Jesus asks him, 'Simon, what is your opinion? From whom do the kings of the earth take tolls or census taxes? From their subjects or from foreigners?'" (Matt 17:25). Peter realizes right away Jesus is aware of his encounter with the tax collector. He answers, "From foreigners." Jesus then replies, "Then subjects are exempt. But that we may not offend them, go to the sea, drop in a hook, and take the first fish that comes up. Open its mouth and you will find a coin worth twice the temple tax. Give that to them for me and for you" (Matt 17:26-27). Peter is in awe and immediately leaves, makes the short walk to the sea, puts in a line, immediately catches a fish, opens its mouth, and finds the coin as Jesus foretold. The miracle amazes Peter, and he wonders why Jesus chose to pay the tax. A negative thought creeps into his head. Could Jesus be worried about the authorities and his decreasing popularity also?

Jesus and his apostles stay only a few days in Capernaum, and then they leave again to seemingly roam around Galilee. It is clear this is a time of instruction for his apostles. We hear from Matthew as he relates some of the parables and teachings Jesus gives the apostles as they travel around Galilee for well over three weeks. It is on this trip that he tells them the parable of the lost sheep (Matt 18:10-14), indicating how much Jesus loves each sinner and how they should treat brothers who are sinning (Matt 18:15-20). He also tells them the parable of the wicked servant who had his huge debt forgiven by his master but himself had one of his fellow servants thrown in jail for a much smaller amount due him (Matt 18:21-35). The themes of loving everyone and forgiving everything are predominant in this special time of instruction. In five months, Jesus will offer the prime example of loving and forgiving everyone when he is hanging from the cross.

Chapter Forty-Two

Journey to the Feast of Tabernacles

Jesus and his apostles return to Capernaum just as the caravans are forming to depart to Jerusalem for the Feast of Tabernacles. It is early October, day 729 of the 909 days that changed the world. Some wonder if this is the time Jesus will travel to Jerusalem to proclaim himself the leader of the new kingdom he has been preaching about. It is troubling that Jesus has not been around as much in the last four months, that the number of miracles performed is down, and that the minds of many have become more skeptical of him. There are those who still hold on to the belief that he may be a great prophet or even the Messiah, but there is growing impatience to see just what he has in mind. "So some of his brothers say to him, 'Leave here and go to Judea so that your disciples also may see the works you are doing. No one works in secret if he wants to be known publicly. If you do these things, manifest yourself to the world'" (John 7:3-4). The goal is clear here. These people, likely cousins or others that have known and more or less followed him for quite a while, want to push to see if he is the Messiah and challenge him to go to Jerusalem and fully reveal himself. As John succinctly puts it, they say these things "because they do not believe in him" (John 7:5). Jesus sees into their hearts and says, "My time is not yet here, but the time is always right for you. The world cannot hate you, but it hates me, because I testify to it that its works are evil. You go up to the feast. I am not going because my time has not yet been fulfilled" (John 7:6-8). There is some grousing, some more cajoling, but ultimately, they realize he does not plan on going to the feast, and they leave him and his apostles behind.

In the caravans traveling down the Perean side of the Jordan River, there is much talk about Jesus. Although some of his apostles, with his blessing, join the caravan with their families and go to the feast, most stay behind with him. For those apostles who stay behind, their family members who are travelling to the feast discuss among themselves if, indeed, their loved ones are making the best choice by remaining with Jesus. Are they working for a crazy man and a losing cause?

We now come upon a major turning point in Jesus' ministry. After spending a night in prayer, with most people having left for the feast, Jesus makes a surprising announcement to his apostles. As Luke points out (9:51) and John implies (7:1), he decides it is now time to turn his face to Jerusalem and to confront the Jewish leaders. He tells the apostles he has changed his mind and is going to the feast. He doesn't tell them now, but later they will realize that this trip to the Feast of Tabernacles is the beginning of his death march. Just as surprising, he tells them he is going to Jerusalem by way of Samaria. With the Samaritans celebrating the same feast at their major temple, Temple Gerizim, and therefore present in large numbers and perhaps more than a little influenced by the wine of the celebrations, the apostles realize it is a particularly risky time to take that path. They may be subject to immense ridicule, even physical danger, as the Samaritans see them passing on the road to Jerusalem. Jesus, however, cannot be convinced to change his mind, so the apostles go along with him and reluctantly, nervously agree to take the Samaria route.

The trip from Capernaum to Samaria is about a full day. As evening approaches, while most of them are taking a break, Jesus sends two apostles a short distance ahead to secure a place to stay in one of the Samaritan villages. It is not a welcome task, as they suspect they will not be well received. Indeed, in a short time, the two return and report they have been unsuccessful, as the Samaritans would not welcome them "because the destination of their journey is Jerusalem" (Luke 9:53). When they hear the news, John and James, both indignant, ask Jesus, "Lord do you want us to call down fire from heaven to consume them?" (Luke 9:54). It is interesting these words come from a man, John, who in his old age will insightfully and constantly insist to "love one another." At this moment though, he has revenge on his mind. But Jesus has no need of revenge and rebukes John and James. This is the second time in a few short days he has had to straighten things out in John's mind about how to deal with people who are not part of his "group." Jesus and his apostles get up from their resting spot and walk through this unnamed town, listening to the snickers and insults hurled at them by the town people. Down the road, they find a place to stay. As it happens, they run into a family who met Jesus in the town of Sychar some fifteen months ago. They have moved a bit north to this area of Samaria, are thrilled to see Jesus, and strongly insist that he and his apostles spend the night with them. Jesus and his apostles are treated to a wonderful meal, and they all share a delightful evening.

The next morning, they are up early to continue the journey to Jerusalem, but they are not the first ones up and out. One of the sons of their host, with his father's blessing, has already left to inform all the people of Sychar that Jesus will be passing by soon. Jesus asks Judas to offer money to their hosts. When Judas quietly seeks out the head of the household, the host insists he will not take any money—so happy he and his family have been to be able to spend time with Jesus. Bidding good-bye and thanks to their hosts, Jesus and his apostles resume their journey. As they make their way south on the road, by mid-morning they arrive at the Well of Jacob with the village of Sychar nearby. As the news of Jesus' coming has already reached them, many from the town are waiting for him as he rounds the bend in the road. Even though it has been well over a year since they have last seen him, great enthusiasm for him remains. There is a cheer from the crowd when he comes into view. Jesus smiles at their affection and concern. No miracles here, no long speeches, just a few days' visit a long time ago, and see how they flock to him. How can Jesus not contrast in his mind these faithful Samaritans, with whom he has spent so little time, with his skeptical countrymen, with whom he has spent so much more time? They press him to stay but know his need and desire to move on to Jerusalem. They are able to convince him to stay for a short rest. Sitting down on a spot a bit off the road, Jesus and his apostles enjoy the food and drinks offered by these good people.

While Jesus is carrying on a conversation with the townspeople, he is approached by one who had met him last year and whose heart has been haunted by Jesus ever since. The man tells him he wants to join him and says, "I will follow you wherever you go" (Luke 9:57). Jesus smiles but shakes his head. "Foxes have dens and birds of the sky have nests, but the Son of Man has nowhere to rest his head" (Luke 9:58). Following Jesus is not easy, and quickly will become difficult. Indeed, Jesus says these words for the apostles to hear as much as he does to respond to the man. After leisurely enjoying their company and refreshments and thanking them for their hospitality, Jesus stands up to leave. As he leaves, he has two noteworthy encounters.

He begins to walk back to the road from his resting place, and turns to one man in the crowd whom he recognizes from his previous visit but who has a deeply burdened look on his face. Jesus says, "Follow me. But the man replies, 'Lord, let me go first and bury my father'" (Luke 9:59). The man's request is sincere, as his father has just died, and he is deeply mourning the loss. He has just come out to see Jesus before getting back to the sorrowful task of burying his father. Jesus puts his hand on the man's right shoulder and answers, "Let the dead bury the dead but you, go, and proclaim the kingdom of God" (Luke 9:60). The man and those who hear these words are a little stunned at the first part of Jesus' response. Surely Jesus understands this man must take care of his dead father's body? He then turns his gaze on another man and repeats the command to follow him. This man, young and strong and with a big smile on his face, really wants to follow Jesus but "first let me say farewell to my family at home" (Luke 9:61). Jesus takes his gaze off the man and turns to his apostles and, raising his voice, says, "No one who sets a hand to the plow and looks back to what is left behind is fit for the kingdom of God" (Luke 9:62). Some more strong words from Jesus for men who are making seemingly reasonable requests—but the words are mostly directed to his apostles. It will be only a short time before he will be gone, and everything will be demanded of them. They will be consumed by zeal for the kingdom, and they will have no time to look back. Everything in their lives will be subordinated to spreading the message of his being the Son of God. For now though, Jesus walks back to the man who has to bury his father and whispers something, causing him to smile faintly while nodding in agreement with Jesus' words. Jesus then goes over to the young man who wants to say good-bye to his family, and says something to him which causes the young man to nod in sober agreement. Turning to the entire crowd, Jesus bids them all a warm farewell as he and his apostles continue on the road to Jerusalem.

CHAPTER FORTY-THREE

Jesus Arrives at the Feast of Tabernacles

The rest of the trip through Samaria takes place without any major issues or problems. Meanwhile, back in Jerusalem where the feast has begun, there is much discussion and varying opinions about Jesus. "Some are saying, 'He is a good man,' while others are saying, 'No, on the contrary, he misleads the crowd.' Still, no one speaks openly about him because they are afraid of the Jews" (John 7:12-13).

As Jesus and the apostles approach the city of Jerusalem from the west, some people along the way recognize him and scurry off to the city to announce his arrival. Instead of entering the city right away, Jesus and his apostles skirt off to the north and go around it to first make camp near Mt. Olivet, as it is the customary camping spot of many Galileans who do not have relatives in the city. It is mid-October—day 738 of the 909 days that changed the world. They find the camp largely empty, as most of the people are already inside the Jerusalem city gates. There are, however, some stragglers still in the camp who immediately recognize Jesus. In no time, between the people who had seen him approaching the city from the west and the people in the camp who run into the city, there is a buzz in Jerusalem that Jesus has arrived. Most eyes in the city frequently steal a glance at the Golden Gate to see if he is entering through yet.

It is very important to understand the mood of the city towards Jesus. There are generally four groups of people in the city. As we have already noted, on the one hand, there are "some who say he is a good man" (John 7:12). These are mostly Galileans who have not succumbed to the poison the Pharisees have been spreading, but this group also includes a few Judeans who, for diverse reasons, are favorably disposed towards him. On the other hand, the second group consists of "others who say, 'No, he misleads the crowd'" (John 7:12). These are the people—Galilean and Judean alike—who have come to believe what the Pharisees have been saying about Jesus. The third group, mostly Judeans, is the largest and consists of those who have not made up their mind and are anxious to hear and see more of him. They are open to being moved one way or the other. They have heard the miracle stories as well as the biting criticism of the Pharisees and other leaders, and want to learn more about this man who is generating such controversy. Many remember him from his driving the merchants out of the temple area over a year and a half ago, but as Jesus has spent so little time in this part of Israel, they want to see more for themselves. The fourth group, the Jewish leaders, almost to a man is bitterly opposed to him, and the few, like Nicodemus, who do admire Jesus generally keep quiet because of the intensity of the hatred of their fellow leaders.

And then it happens. Jesus walks through the Golden Gate into the same temple courtyard where he had caused such havoc a year and seven months ago. Immediately people surround him as he pushes more towards the center. The crowd around him grows bigger and bigger as the news of Jesus' arrival spreads like wildfire. After nearly ten minutes, the growth of the crowd slows down and Jesus gets himself in a position where most can hear him. He raises his voice and begins to teach, interpreting scripture passages. The crowd quiets down, the people all marvel at his preaching, and, for a short period of time, Jesus seems to be winning them over. It is an amazing scene. The beautiful deep blue October sky, the coolness in the air tempered by the warmth of the autumnal sun, and a huge group of people surrounding Jesus in the temple area quiet and listening intently to his words. The Pharisees, however, in an attempt to break the magic of the moment, begin to move around and whisper into the ears of the people standing in the back of the crowd. Some of those people nod their heads in approval and repeat the Pharisees' words to others: "How does he know scripture without study?" (John 7:15). Slowly, like a spreading infection, the skepticism of the crowd begins to grow, and the magnetic hold Jesus has over the crowd begins to wane. Jesus notices this, of course, and in his response we now see a change in how he will deal with crowds from now until his death. Yes, he has affection for them all, but no longer will he lead them ever so gently along, but he will challenge them more, speak the truth more directly, and force people to take sides, knowing full well it will shortly lead to his demise. Responding to this criticism, Jesus says, "My teaching is not my own but is from the one who sent me. Whoever chooses to do his will shall know whether my teaching is from God or whether I speak on my own. Whoever speaks on his own seeks his own glory, but whoever seeks the glory of the one who sent him is truthful, and there is no wrong in him" (John 7:16-18). There is a direct challenge in both the words and his tone of voice. Many in the crowd, and certainly the Jewish leaders, realize this is a claim that his teaching comes from God. The leaders are indignant, and many in the crowd ask themselves how someone can make such a bold and crazy claim; yet as they mull this over in their minds, Jesus raises his voice even more loudly and challenges them further, saying, "Did not Moses give you the law? Yet none of you keep the law. Why are you trying to kill me?" (John 7:19). Although the leaders know the killing part is true, and there are many in the crowd who suspect or have heard that the Jewish leaders want to do away with Jesus, they are stunned at his direct accusation. Someone in the crowd cries out, "You are possessed! Who is trying to kill you?" (John 7:20). Jesus does not directly answer the question but addresses the accusation leveled against him by the leaders. Referring to his cure of the crippled man by the pool at the Feast of Pentecost a year ago last May, he responds, "You are angry with me because I made a whole person well on a Sabbath? Stop judging by appearances but judge justly" (John 7:23-24). It is an appeal to the common sense of the Pharisees; it is a challenge to the crowd to take sides.

His words cause the crowd to discuss among themselves what has been said. A few of the Judeans look at one another and ask, "Is he not the one they are trying to kill? And look, he is speaking openly and they say nothing to him. Could the authorities realize he is the Messiah?" (John 7:25-26). For these Judeans, who have not had much personal experience with Jesus, it is a start, the beginning of siding with him over the authorities. Alas, most of them take a quick step backwards as they reflect on (and take pride in) their personal interpretation of the scriptures and say, "But we know where he is from. When the Messiah comes, no one will know where he is from" (John 7:27).

Jesus takes the challenge higher still. Knowing what is being murmured in the crowd and to quiet them all yet again, he cries out in a loud voice. The effect is immediate. With all eyes and ears trained on him, he boldly and clearly states, "You know me and know also where I am from? Yet I did not come on my own, but the one who sent me, whom you do not know, is true. I know him because I am from him, and he sent me" (John 7:28-29). These words are so powerful that the crowd buzzes again as they discuss them among themselves. There are those in the crowd who take these words to mean that Jesus is equating himself with God, and consider it an egregious blasphemy. Some rush to take hold of him to have him arrested, but he somehow slips out of sight, so "no one lays a hand on him because his hour has not yet come" (John 7:30). He seems to disappear into thin air. Everyone turns their heads around looking for him. He was just here—where has he gone? Jesus has accomplished his mission, though. He has gotten people to think, and "many of the crowd believe in him and say, 'When the Messiah comes, will he perform more signs than this man has done?'" (John 7:31). Meanwhile, in the background, the Jewish leaders have been observing all that is going on. They have heard all of Jesus' words and see the confusion in the crowd. They think this will be a good time to try to have him arrested, so they send some guards fanning out into the crowd to find him. Mysteriously, after vanishing out of sight a short time ago, he reappears and proceeds directly towards a group of the guards. People come running over to the spot where he and the guards are standing to see what will take place. As these guards are being egged on by some who tried to arrest Jesus themselves, Jesus holds up his hands and, looking over the crowd, says, "I will be with you only a little while longer, and then I will go to the one who sent me. You will look for me but not find me, and where I am you cannot come" (John 7:33-34). As the guards move forward to arrest him, he turns his back and somehow again disappears in the crowd, leaving the guards and the crowd wondering where he has gone. After a few minutes of looking around, the guards return to report their failure to the Jewish leaders, and the crowd disperses with many saying, "Where is he going that we will not find him? Surely he is not going to the dispersion among the Greeks to teach the Greeks, is he? What is the meaning of this saying, 'You will look for me and not find me and where I am you cannot come?'" (John 7:35-36).

Today has been a momentous day. Jesus has polarized the city. No miracles occurred—just challenging words compelling people to choose either to believe in him or in the Pharisees. Jesus is at the center of every conversation in every home or camp in and around Jerusalem…and their opinion of him divides many families and leads to discussions that last deep into the night.

CHAPTER FORTY-FOUR

Jesus at the Feast of Tabernacles

The next few days of the feast pass a bit more quietly. Jesus is in the temple area preaching and spending time speaking to people in smaller groups as opposed to addressing the entire court-yard. The evenings are spent at his camp where many people sur-round his campfire late into the night. Jesus even gets another night time visit from Nicodemus. He is smiling a lot more now and, as he looks into peoples' eyes while he answers their questions and interprets the scriptures, many more become all the more favorably disposed towards him. His popularity grows, especially among the Judeans, and becomes more problematic for the Jewish leaders, so they decide to try one more time, on the last day of the feast, to have him arrested. Little do they know, Jesus plans to make one more public appeal.

On that last day of the feast, Jesus' face takes on a more serious look as he approaches the temple courtyard. His gait is quick and his eyes are fixed on the temple gates. Those walking with him can sense something is about to happen. It is a beautiful, sunny, autumn day as he enters the courtyard. As people engage him, he insists on walking into the center where he taught the first day he arrived at the feast. The crowd begins to quiet as it anticipates his teaching to all assembled in the courtyard. In no time, the crowd hushes. At the same time, the guards positioned in the courtyard by the Jewish leaders move in on him. The leaders themselves stay on the temple steps awaiting Jesus' arrest. 'Finally,' they think, 'we will be able to arrest him, then bring him before the Roman curate and have him killed or at least banished from the territory.'

As Jesus looks around with a gaze of authority and power and the crowd remains silent, the soldiers stop in their tracks, frozen by the look on his face. He raises his voice, and in a clear reference to Moses, to whom he has been referring in his teachings at this feast, says, "Let anyone who thirsts come to me and drink. Whoever believes in me, as scripture says, 'Rivers of living water will flow from within him'" (John 7:37-38). With those words only, he lowers his eyes to the ground and waits for the crowd to soak them in. The power of these words are lost on most modern readers but, to the studied Jew of the day, his words are reminiscent of many Old Testament passages linking the Messiah with overflowing water: Isaiah 12:2-3, Ezekiel 36:25, Joel 3:18, and others. The effect on the crowd, especially this learned Judean crowd, is as Jesus suspects. Slowly the murmuring picks up once again. His words spur many in the crowd to think he "must truly be the prophet" (John 7:40). Yes, his words, his miracles about which they have heard (or maybe even seen), the power of his personality, all point to his being the one to announce the upcoming new kingdom. There are others in the crowd, however, who draw an even bigger (and correct) conclusion. "This is the Messiah" (John 7:41); this is the one who is going to lead us in the formation of the new kingdom. The noise grows in admiration for Jesus until, much like the first day, there are some voices, informants of the Pharisees, who loudly proclaim, "The Messiah will not come from Galilee, will he? Does not scripture say that the Messiah will be of David's family and come from Bethlehem, the village where David lived?" (John 7:41-42). Unlike the other day, this time Jesus does not respond at all. It is an old objection, and he has already addressed it. Then something very striking happens.

A few in the crowd come forward to arrest him, but others in the crowd stand in their way as if to guard him from those who want to detain him. The guards sent to arrest Jesus, strangely, are all glued to the ground and do not move. He has confused the minds and touched the hearts of most of these Jewish guards and they cannot proceed against him. The noise of the crowd intensifies as the two groups, those who want to see Jesus arrested and the much larger group of those who are protecting him, shout back and forth at each other. The soldiers don't quite know what to do. In a mighty voice, Jesus tells everyone to quiet down, and they all do, turning to look back at him. At first his look is severe but soon brightens. As the crowd is silenced, the guards relax, and Jesus turns to leave the courtyard, slowly making his exit as he stops to talk to people along the way. His smile returns, his mood is lighter, and his affection for the people is obvious. Although many in the crowd still do not believe in him, he has turned the tide in his favor over the last few days—it is obvious by the noise and enthusiasm of the crowd—and the Jewish leaders are furious as they watch from the temple steps.

When the guards approach them, the incensed Jewish leaders shout, "Why did you not bring him here?" (John 7:45). The response given by one of the guards riles the leaders even more: "Never has anyone spoken like this one" (John 7:46). The leaders are apoplectic. With dripping sarcasm, one of the Pharisees says to the guard, "Have you also been deceived? Do any of the authorities or Pharisees believe in him? But this crowd, which does not know the law, is accursed" (John 7:47-49). Nicodemus, emboldened by his recent visit with Jesus, speaks up in his defense. "Does our law condemn a person before it first hears him and finds out what he is doing?" (John 7:51). The wrath of the majority of the leaders is now directed at Nicodemus. "You are not from Galilee also, are you? Look and see, no prophet arises from Galilee" (John 7:52). Nicodemus knows the scriptures also and knows they have a valid point. He is silenced for the moment, but somehow knows his fellow leaders are wrong. Despite Jesus' being from Galilee, Nicodemus knows there is something very special about Jesus. He will bide his time. The rest of the leaders, though, are up in arms. Can this day go more wrong? Rather than having Jesus safely in jail, they can see how the majority of the crowd is moving towards him. He is increasing and they are decreasing, and they can have none of that. What to do? The opportunity to trap Jesus arises immediately.

CHAPTER FORTY-FIVE

The Woman Caught in Adultery

The Pharisees are approached by some men with a woman who has been caught in the act of adultery. What has happened to the man with her, we do not know, but this woman is dragged in front of the Pharisees for their permission to stone her, which is the customary punishment for adultery. The woman, her head down and sobbing, is fearful of the fate that awaits her. She is pretty, with dark hair disheveled by her rough handling by these men, hastily redressed in a colorful outfit, with bracelets and rings on her arms and fingers. She turns her eyes up to the leaders and looks at them with pleading. Even in these hard-hearted men, she elicits pity from a number of them. These men accusing her seem to make a habit of catching women in the very act of this sin. Although nothing has ever been proven, it makes the leaders a little suspicious.

One of the Pharisees looks at the crowd around Jesus and comes up with an idea. He informs the others of a conversation he and a few other Pharisees had with him earlier in the week. He tells them they had approached Jesus to test him and asked, "'Is it lawful for a husband to divorce his wife?' Jesus responded, 'What did Moses command you?' They replied, 'Moses permitted him to write a bill of divorce and dismiss her.' But Jesus told them, 'Because of the hardness of your hearts he wrote you this commandment. But from the beginning of creation, 'God made them male and female. For this reason a man shall leave his father and mother and be joined to his wife, and the two shall become one flesh. So they are no longer two but one flesh. Therefore what God has joined together, no human being must separate.'" (Mark 10:2-10). Since Jesus is so opinionated about marriage, they say, "Let's bring this woman's case to him. If he condemns her as our laws require, perhaps the crowds' enthusiasm for him will dampen. If he says she should not be condemned, he will put himself at odds with the law. Yes, they all agree at once. It is well worth the try."

Quickly, they all leave the temple steps and work their way through the crowd to get to Jesus, who is leaving the courtyard. The crowds make way for the leaders, and the noise level drops as they all try to figure out what is about to take place. The leaders get close to Jesus, whose back is still towards them as he is talking to a group of people. The leaders position the woman between them and Jesus and call him, saying, "Teacher, this woman was caught in the very act of committing adultery. Now in the law, Moses commanded us to stone such a woman. So what do you say?" (John 8:4-5). The Pharisees gloat to themselves. He has been referring to Moses for the last few days, and here they will use the Law of Moses against him. Jesus slowly turns around as they are speaking and looks at the Pharisee speaking. Slowly he moves his eyes over each of these Jewish leaders. Nicodemus is there, but he is way in the back and his eyes are lowered. Jesus then turns his attention to the woman. He can see sorrow, pain, hurt, fear, and some hope all at once in her eyes. He sees into her heart and knows all the reasons that have brought her to this place—and he has pity on her. He looks into her eyes and, although there is no smile and no one else senses a thing, she knows he sees her to her core—and yet is concerned for her.

He then bends down and begins to draw in the sand with his finger. All are silent until finally some of the Pharisees press him for an answer. Slowly getting up, he looks at the leaders and says, "Let the one among you who is without sin be the first to throw a stone at her" (John 8:7). With that, Jesus bends down once more and continues to write in the dirt. Some of the Pharisees press him for a more definitive answer, but he says nothing. After a minute or so, slowly, beginning with the elders, the leaders walk back towards the temple. They have been defeated, for they all know they, too, are not without sin themselves. The younger ones almost decide to stone her on their own, but as they look around at the crowd and reflect on what their elders have done, they also walk away. The crowd falls silent, and all attention is on Jesus and this woman.

When all the leaders are gone, Jesus straightens up again and looking at the woman says, "Woman, where are they? Has no one condemned you?" (John 8:10). With a smile that speaks of gratitude as well as astonishment, she responds, "No one, sir" (John 8:11). Jesus, his countenance warm but serious, tells her, "Neither do I condemn you. Go and from now, do not sin anymore" (John 8:12). The woman thanks him and disappears into the crowd, thankful for her life and determined to do better going forward. We will not hear from her again, but like so many people Jesus gets to know in a brief meeting, this moment will change her life. The people in the crowd begin to talk among themselves. What did Jesus just do, and what does it say about the Law of Moses? Yes, some think, she is a pitiable woman, but she broke the law and the law demands her death, but some others grasp the meaning of what they've just witnessed. We are all sinners, and those who are genuinely sorry for their sins will be forgiven.

Jesus continues making his way out of the temple area and leaves the city gates to return to camp. As he leaves the city, he does not go directly back to camp but instead takes the road to a place called the "Garden of Gethsemane." It is a pleasant garden spot, and Jesus dismisses those who follow him with the exception of his apostles. This is the exact place where he will be betrayed with a kiss. For now, though, among other things, he explains to them his conversation with the Pharisees about the sacredness of marriage. He then takes the apostles deeper into the garden and asks them to pray while he goes off by himself to engage his Father in prayer. Meanwhile, the Pharisees and other Jewish leaders return to the temple and collectively lick their wounds yet again. It has been a bad day. They have to figure out some way to get rid of Jesus—to turn the tide of popular opinion against him. All the work they have done against him since he began baptizing in the Jordan two years ago seems to have been for naught. Little do they know, it will only be a short six months before they will have their way—but only because Jesus will then allow it.

Chapter Forty-Six

Last Hours of the Feast of Tabernacles

T he next opportunity for the Jewish leaders to try to get at Jesus happens more quickly than they imagine. After spending a good part of the afternoon in the Gethsemane garden, Jesus tells his apostles he wants to go back to the city for the last hours of the feast. As they walk back into the city, the people once again begin to crowd around him. Seeing him back in the temple courtyard, the Jewish leaders are ready for yet another attack. Once again a group of them, those deemed the best debaters, prepare to make their way down the temple steps to approach Jesus, but, as luck would have it, he seems intent on making his way directly to them. So they wait. He walks up the temple steps and, pointing to the candles in the temple area, says, "I am the light of the world. Whoever follows me will not walk in darkness, but will have the light of life" (John 8:12). By the look in his eyes and the tone of his voice, the Jewish leaders sense he is here for a confrontation, and they launch into it. Let us follow the words of John as we see how the Jewish leaders attempt to outdo Jesus in a debate in front of this crowd of people. Imagine the crowd listening to their leaders, all dressed in their rabbinical best, attempting to feign an air of superiority over this commonly dressed, uneducated man from Galilee. Listen how Jesus, consistent as he has been in dealing with the Judeans in this city, will not mince words, and will not back down.

"So the Pharisees say to him, 'You testify on your own behalf, so your testimony cannot be verified.' Jesus answers and says to them, 'Even if I do testify on my own behalf, my testimony can be verified because I know where I came from and where I am going. But you do not know where I come from and where I am going. You judge by appearances, but I do not judge anyone'" (John 8:14-15). Jesus' last sentence is likely referring to the woman caught in adultery whom the leaders presented to him earlier in the day. He continues, "And even if I should judge, my judgment is valid, because I am not alone, but it is I and the Father who sent me. Even in your law it is written that the testimony of two men can be verified. I testify on my behalf and so does the Father who sent me.' So they say to him, 'Where is your father?' Jesus answers, 'You know neither me nor my Father. If you knew me, you would know my Father also.'…He says to them again, 'I am going away and you will look for me but you will die in your sin. Where I am going you cannot come'" (John 8:16-22). Now some of the Jewish leaders, whispering to each other in a tone of wishful thinking, say, "He is not going to kill himself is he?" (John 8:22). Jesus, however, picks up on those whispers and uses them to stun the audience. He proclaims, "You belong to what is below; I belong to what is above. You belong to this world, but I do not belong to this world. That is why I told you that you will die in your sins" (John 8:23-24). Then making a reference to Moses as he has been doing at this festival, he makes the statement that none of the leaders or people in the crowd can mistake: "For if you do not believe that I AM, you will die in your sins" (John 8:24).

These are startling words because Jesus is clearly equating himself with Yahweh, the great I AM who revealed himself to Moses in the burning bush. The Jewish leaders ask for clarification, scarcely believing the audacity of this man equaling himself to God. Jesus responds, "What I told you from the beginning. I have much to say about you in condemnation. But the one who sent me is true and what I have heard from him I tell the world. When you lift up the Son of Man, then you will realize that I AM, and that I do nothing on my own, but I say only what the Father taught me. The one who sent me is with me. He has not left me alone, because I always do what is pleasing to him" (John 8:25-29). As John indicates, in the midst of this battle with the Jewish leaders, many in the crowd come to believe in him more firmly (John 8:30).

But the battle continues. Jesus turns away from the Jewish leaders, faces the crowd, opens his arms and, looking over the crowd—some would say looking directly at each one of them—he loudly proclaims, "If you remain in my word, you will truly be my disciples, and you will know the truth and the truth will make you free" (John 8:31-32). Some of the Jewish leaders roll their eyes and almost mockingly say, "We are descendents of Abraham and have never been enslaved to anyone. How can you say 'You will become free?'" (John 8:33). Jesus is tiring of these stubborn, proud, selfish leaders. Still facing the people in the courtyard below, he says, "Amen, Amen, I say to you, everyone who commits sin is a slave to sin. A slave does not remain in the household forever, but a son always remains. So if a Son frees you, you will truly be free" (John 8:34-36). Quickly turning around now and facing the Jewish leaders, he sternly lowers his voice to them alone and says, "I know you are descendents of Abraham, but you are trying to kill me because my word has no room among you. I tell you what I have seen in my Father's presence; then do what you have heard from the Father…. If you were Abraham's children, you would be doing the works of Abraham. But now you are trying to kill me, a man who has told you the truth that I heard from God. Abraham did not do this. If God were your Father, you would love me for I came from God and am here; I did not come on my own, but he sent me. Why do you not understand what I am saying?" (John 8:37-43). Jesus is about to accuse them of what they falsely accused him many months back. He continues, strong and firm in his voice, "Because you cannot bear to hear my word. You belong to your father the devil, and you willingly carry out your father's desires. He was a murderer from the beginning and does not stand in truth, because there is no truth in him. When he tells a lie, he speaks in character, because he is a liar and the father of lies. But because I speak the truth you do not believe in me. Can any of you charge me with sin? If I am telling the truth, why do you not believe me?" (John 8:43-46). Turning away from the leaders and facing the crowd again, Jesus shouts, "Whoever belongs to God hears the words of God" (John 8: 47), but then quickly turning back to the leaders he continues sternly with them, "For this reason you do not listen, because you do not belong to God" (John 8:47).

The leaders are incensed. Jesus is giving them a verbal thrashing, and they worry what the crowd is thinking. They try to turn Jesus' criticism back on him. Capitalizing on a general myth that some Samaritans have mystical demonic power, one of the leaders shouts out to Jesus, "Are we not right in saying you are a Samaritan and are possessed?" (John 8:48). Jesus responds, "I am not possessed. I honor my Father, but you dishonor me" (John 8:49). Knowing many in the crowd have heard this accusation, Jesus turns towards the crowd and continues, "I do not seek my own glory; there is one who seeks it, and he is the one who judges. Amen, Amen, I say to you, whoever keeps my word will never see death" (John 8:50-51). The crowd and leaders are all incredulous. What are these words? What can he possibly mean by someone never tasting death? Everyone dies. What kind of promise is this? Is this man crazy?

The Jewish leaders feeling the weight of those words hanging over the crowd, and sensing an opportunity to discredit Jesus, scoff all the more and taunt him by saying, "Now we are sure you are possessed. Abraham died as did all the prophets, yet you say, 'Whoever keeps my word will never taste death.' Are you greater than our father Abraham who died? Or the prophets who died? Who do you make yourself out to be?" (John 8:52-53). Most of them know perfectly well Jesus is equating himself with God and are hoping by pushing the point that they can turn the crowd against him. After all, does this Jesus look like the great I AM? He responds, looking out over the crowd again, saying, "If I glorify myself, my glory is worth nothing, but it is my Father who glorifies me of whom you say, 'He is our God.' You do not know him but I know him" (John 8:54-55). Then turning back to the leaders, he continues in a voice loud enough for all to hear, "And if I would say that I do not know him, I would be like you, a liar" (John 8:55). Then turning again towards the crowd, he goes on, "But I do know him and I keep his word. Abraham your father rejoiced to see my day. He saw it and was glad" (John 8: 55-56). This last sentence again jolts the crowd. How is it possible that Abraham has seen Jesus' day? How can this be? Once again, picking up on the noise of the crowd about these last words of Jesus, one of the leaders shouts out, "You are not yet fifty years old and you have seen Abraham?" (John 8:57).

Many in the crowd nod in agreement with this question. This Jesus is claiming quite a few unbelievable things here, is he not? Equating himself with the great I AM, promising that whoever keeps his words will not die, and now claiming to have seen Abraham. It is too much. Some in the crowd begin to waver and think he really is a bit crazy. Maybe he is possessed? As the crowd murmurs the question of the Jewish leader, Jesus waits a few moments. It looks like the leaders finally have him stumped—but then he raises his hands, and the crowd falls silent. All ears and eyes are upon him. In his strongest and most solemn voice, seemingly as if his voice is amplified by some mysterious power, Jesus says, "Amen, amen, I say to you, before Abraham came to be, I AM" (John 8:58). There it is again—a clear, direct declaration that he predates Abraham and is God. There are those in the crowd who see this as total blasphemy, and some pick up rocks to stone him. The leaders smile as they watch the commotion. Maybe this will all end right now.

Such, however, is not to be the case. All of a sudden, Jesus walks down the temple steps into the crowd and seems to disappear, as he has done a few times during this feast. No one can find him. A cry goes up from the crowd. "Where has he gone? How did he disappear from our midst so quickly?" A bewildered astonishment reigns at first, but slowly the crowd quiets down and, more slowly still, disperses. This afternoon has had the affect of steeling the Jewish leaders all the more against Jesus and causing many in the crowd to rethink, once again, their opinion. Who is he? Can he really be who he says he is? Once again this evening, Jesus will be the center of conversations that last long into the night.

CHAPTER FORTY-SEVEN

The Man Born Blind

T he next day most of the people organize their caravans to begin the trip back to their homes. Jesus has spent a busy night with people coming to see him to press him further on his "I AM" remarks, but he only calmly reiterated his words from that afternoon and offered little more explanation. Rising this morning while it is still dark, he sits at his campsite in silence and prays until the first of his apostles wake up. As they prepare breakfast, he tells them he is going to stay in Judea for now. The twelve apostles all agree to stay with him, as do a good number of his other disciples and even some non-local Judeans, but most must go back home with their families. There are others who stay there, but for them it is a matter of spending more time with relatives or pursuing business or other interests. For the next few days, Jesus remains camped outside of the city, generally coming into the city for some time every day.

As it so happens, on the first Sabbath day after the feast, when Jesus is walking through the city with his apostles, he passes by a man blind from birth. It is yet another beautiful sunny and glorious October day—day 747 of the 909 days that changed the world. Some of his disciples ask him, "Rabbi, who sinned, this man or his parents, that he was born blind?" (John 9:2). They are expressing the common belief that physical calamities are punishment for sins— either sins committed by the person or by one of his ancestors. It is still an attitude that many cling to today—that of a vengeful God waiting to punish as soon as he sees sin. But Jesus sets them straight. "Neither he nor his parents sinned; it is so that the works of God might be made visible through him. We have to do the works of the one who sent me while it is day. Night is coming when no one can work" (John 9:3-4). Then once again referring to himself as the light of the world, the light out of the darkness, he continues, "While I am in the world, I am the light of the world" (John 9:5). Then, to emphasize how he is the light that can make all people see things with more clarity, he leans down, spits on the ground, makes some mud with his spittle, stands up, and applies it to the blind man's eyes. Those observing wonder what he is doing. He tells the blind man, "'Go wash in the Pool of Siloam' (which means Sent)" (John 9:7). In addition to the literal meaning of his words, he is figuratively saying go wash in the pool of the one who is sent, that is Jesus himself. The blind man is led to the pool, washes, and sees. He is overcome with joy. He rushes back to find Jesus, but he is gone. Seeing the blind man with full eyesight, his neighbors and all who recognize him inquire as to how he was healed. He tells them the story. Some of these people sympathetic to Jesus take the man to the Pharisees to show them what Jesus has done. The man gladly obliges, as he feels indebted to Jesus.

It is mid-afternoon when the neighbors and the man arrive at the temple steps. They explain the situation to the Pharisees, but they receive the reaction that some predicted. The Pharisees' pompous response is "This man is not from God because he does not keep the Sabbath" (John 9:16). But some in the crowd, bending down so as to not be seen by the leaders for fear of chastisement, call out, "But how can a sinful man do such signs?" (John 9:17). Many in the crowd raise their voices in agreement. This is a good question indeed. Presently the Pharisees quiet everyone down and question the man himself. He tells them the entire story in a straightforward manner. The Pharisees, at a loss, tell the crowd they cannot be sure the man was really blind from birth, so they decide to call for the man's parents. Many wait, although some wander off; in a short time, the man's parents are brought before them. They confirm their son was born blind, but for fear of retaliation from the leaders, they tell them to ask him themselves how he has come to see. Their fear of the ramifications causes them to flee from the truth, as it does for many still today. Once again, the Pharisees turn to speak to the blind man, this time starting out with the warning, "Give God the praise. We know this man [Jesus] is a sinner" (John 9:24). The once-blind man, however, is not afraid of the truth. He sees the light (literally now, of course, as he will come to see it figuratively later this day) and speaks it as he sees it. "If he is a sinner, I do not know. One thing I do know is that I was blind and now I see" (John 9:25). The Pharisees then ask him to repeat the whole story, but, tired of their obstinate attitude, the former blind mans stings them by saying, "Why do you want to hear it again? Do you want to become his disciples, too?" (John 9:27). The Pharisees can hardly contain their anger in the face of this man's audacity. They attempt to ridicule and intimidate him. "You are that man's disciple; we are disciples of Moses. We know that God spoke to Moses, but we do not know where this one is from" (John 9:28-29). This former blind man, however, does not cower easily and almost mockingly responds, "This is what is so amazing; that you do not know where he is from, yet he opened my eyes. We know that God does not listen to sinners, but if one is devout and does his will, he listens to him. It is unheard of that anyone ever opened the eyes of a man born blind. If this man were not of God, he would not be able to do anything" (John 9:30-33). Feeling again beaten yet attempting to save face, the Pharisees, their voices dripping with disdain, respond, "You were born totally in sin and are you trying to teach us?" (John 9:34). But the man just stands there and looks at them, so the Pharisees call the guards and have the man removed from the temple area. The man walks away shaking his head at these leaders' stubbornness. Most of his neighbors and friends who have witnessed this exchange question why the leaders are so much against Jesus, and the leaders know they have been bested by a lowly blind man.

It is later on this same day when Jesus seeks out the formerly blind man. As Jesus approaches him, the man smiles from ear to ear. Followed by a crowd of people including his apostles and even some of the Pharisees, still looking for more evidence against him, Jesus walks up to the man, returning his smile. Jesus asks him, "Do you believe in the Son of Man?" (John 9:35). The man answers, "Who is he, sir, that I may believe in him?" (John 9:36). We see how strong this man's faith is. He has so much faith in Jesus that he will believe and do whatever he tells him—a good lesson. So, Jesus, looking deeply into his eyes, responds, "You have seen him and the one who is speaking with you is he" (John 9:37). Having had his visual sight restored yesterday, the man now gets a supernatural light from Jesus and responds, "'I do believe,' and he worships [Jesus]" (John 9:38). It is a poignant moment as all around watch this man worship Jesus.

Jesus puts his hand on the man's head and then looking around at the crowd says, "I came into this world for judgment, so that those who do not see might see, and those who do see, might become blind" (John 9:39); turning his head towards the Pharisees for the last part of these words. Feeling challenged, the Pharisees respond, "Surely we are not also blind, are we?" (John 9:40). Jesus, with sadness in his voice and lowering his head, tells them, "If you were blind, you would have no sin, but now you are saying, 'We see,' so your sin remains" (John 9:41), acknowledging the hypocrisy of these Pharisees, who feign interest in him.

CHAPTER FORTY-EIGHT

The Parable of the Good Shepherd; The Mission of the Seventy-Two

I t is late in the day, and Jesus, his apostles, and others make their way outside the city again to spend the night at their campsite. As they do, Jesus looks up into the hills and sees some shepherds beginning to herd their sheep for the approaching darkness. As is his custom, he uses what he is looking at to teach an important lesson, emphasized, as he frequently does, by his double "Amen." Stopping and pointing to the shepherds in the hills, he says, "Amen, Amen, I say to you: whoever does not enter a sheepfold through the gate is a thief and a robber. But whoever enters through the gate is the shepherd of the sheep. The gatekeeper opens it for him and the sheep hear his voice as he calls his own sheep by voice and leads them out" (John 10:1-3). Jesus is referring to the practice of the shepherds each morning going to the area where sheep from multiple owners have been spending the night inside a pen for safety with a guard posted at the gate. In the morning, the owners of the sheep each approach the gatekeeper, enter the pen through the gate, and call for their own sheep, who amazingly recognize the voice of their masters. Jesus continues, "When he has driven out all his own, he walks ahead of them, and the sheep follow him because they recognize his voice. But they will not follow a stranger; they will run away from him because they do not recognize the voice of strangers" (John 10:4-5). This is evident enough to all those listening to him. No one, though, gets that he is trying to make a point here, so after a few seconds, he gives them an explanation known so well by all Christians.

"Amen, Amen, I say to you, I am the gate for the sheep. All who come before me are thieves and robbers, but the sheep do not listen to them. I am the gate. Whoever enters through me will be saved and will come in and go out and find pasture. A thief comes only to steal and slaughter and destroy; I come that they may have life and have it more abundantly" (John 10:7-10). But not only is Jesus the gatekeeper, he goes on to say he is something even more valuable and powerful than that. "I am the good shepherd. A good shepherd lays down his life for his sheep. A hired man, who is no shepherd and whose sheep are not his own, sees a wolf coming and leaves the sheep and runs away, and the wolf catches and scatters them. This is because he works for pay and has no concern for the sheep. I am the good shepherd, and I know mine and mine know me, just as the Father knows me and I know the Father, and I will lay down my life for the sheep" (John 10:7-15). Then in what in time will be understood as an obvious reference to the Gentiles and all other non-Jews, he continues, "I have other sheep that do not belong to this fold. These also I must lead, and they will hear my voice, and there will be one flock and one shepherd. This is why the Father loves me, because I lay down my life to take it up again. No one takes it from me, but I lay it down on my own. I have power to lay it down, and power to take it up again. This command I have received from my Father" (John 10:16-18). These words have a big impact on those listening to him. What can he possibly mean by having the power to lay his life down and take it up again? Do his words make sense or is he just babbling nonsense? Indeed, some in the crowd say, "'He is possessed and out of his mind; why listen to him?' Others say, 'These are not words of one possessed; surely a demon cannot open the eyes of the blind, can he?'" (John 10:20-21). The crowd continues to be divided. Many in the crowd turn around and go back into the city to their homes for the evening, discussing and arguing among themselves who this Jesus really is. Others, both Galileans and Judeans who have remained behind with him at the end of the festival, make their way back to their campsites for the night. They, too, discuss among themselves what these words mean. Night falls before what will be a very busy day tomorrow.

When the morning sun rises, Jesus is already up and in prayer. He will be making some important appointments today and therefore has spent a good portion of the early morning in union with his Father. As the disciples and others wake up and are making breakfast, Jesus returns to the campsite. He seems to be in a light mood. Over breakfast, he tells the apostles of his plan. He is going to appoint six new disciples to accompany each of the apostles and have all twelve groups scatter into the Judean towns and villages and announce the kingdom of God. Meanwhile, Jesus will stay camped here with a few Galileans, waiting their return and strengthening himself through prayer.

By mid-morning, a number of people have gathered in and around Jesus' camp. Along with the apostles, there are some of his disciples, as well as Galilean and Judean pilgrims who decided to stay a few extra days when they heard Jesus was going to do so. There are also a few Judeans from Jerusalem, very interested in Jesus and not content to wait until he enters the city again, who come out of the city early in the morning to see him. He has been conversing with various groups of these people, answering their questions, and encouraging them in their faith. It is a happy group as it is a bit too early for any of the Jewish leaders to be there hounding him.

Jesus then raises his voice and asks for everyone's attention. He separates his twelve apostles from the others and announces that he is going to appoint six men to accompany each of the twelve apostles, a total of seventy-two. Each of the twelve groups will go to the various towns in Judea and announce the kingdom of God. He tells them they will have special powers. His words stir up excitement. There are more than seventy-two people there, so many shout out hoping to be chosen. Others, not so sure, say nothing and hang back. Jesus, eyes ablaze and looking determined, walks into the crowd and points to one, puts his hand on the shoulder of another, motions to follow him to a third. In a matter of a few minutes, he has chosen the seventy-two and has them each standing next to his lead apostle. There are those who have not been chosen who are upset, while others not chosen are secretly happy. Most who have been chosen are pleased, although a few protest because of this, that, or another obligation or excuse. These are replaced. Jesus does not force people to follow him, he will not do so now, and he does not do so today.

As the crowd disperses, Jesus is left with his apostles and the seventy-two, and he gives them these instructions: "The harvest is abundant, but the laborers are few; so ask the master of the harvest to send out laborers for his harvest. Go on your way; behold, I am sending you like lambs among wolves. Carry no money bag, no sack, no sandals; and greet no one along the way. Into whatever house you enter, first say, 'Peace to this household.' If a peaceful person lives there, your peace will rest on him; but if not, it will return to you. Stay in the same house and eat and drink what is offered to you, for the laborer deserves his payment. Do not move about from one house to another. Whatever town you enter and they welcome you, eat what is set before you, cure the sick in it, and say to them, 'The kingdom of God is at hand for you.' Whatever town you enter and they do not receive you, go out into the streets and say, 'The dust of your town that clings to our feet, even that we shake off against you. Yet know this: the kingdom of God is at hand.' I tell you it will be more tolerable for Sodom on that day than for that town" (Luke 10:2-12).

Even with the promise of working miracles, these words nevertheless are hard ones. We can see that Jesus is intent on making people take sides. He wants people either for him or against him. Unlike earlier in his ministry, when he was gentler, now there is no middle ground. Almost to make the point even more strongly, Jesus continues, "Woe to you, Chorazin [a town not otherwise mentioned in the gospels but believed to be up the mountain a bit to the north and west of Capernaum]! Woe to you Bethsaida! For if the mighty deeds done in your midst had been done in Tyre and Sidon, they would long ago have repented, sitting in sackcloth and ashes. But it will be more tolerable for Tyre and Sidon at the judgment than for you" (Luke 10:13-14). These are harsh words, indeed, but he saves his hardest words for the city where he has spent most of his public ministry. "And as for you, Capernaum, will you be exalted to heaven? You will go down to the netherworld" (Luke 10:15). Raising his hands now over all of them, Jesus finishes by saying, "Whoever listens to you, listens to me. Whoever rejects you rejects me. And whoever rejects me, rejects the one who sent me" (Luke 10:16). With those words, his voice calms, his demeanor softens, and he bids good-bye individually to each of the groups, sending them off in varying directions. When they are all gone, Jesus walks further up the side of the mountain and prays.

CHAPTER FORTY-NINE

The Return of the Seventy-Two

The seventy-two are gone for only a short while. Seven days after they have left, the first group returns to the campsite on Mt. Olivet. They are filled with enthusiasm and rejoicing. "Lord, even the demons are subject to us because of your name" (Luke 10:17). As the other groups return over the next few days, the campsite is overrun with excitement as the groups share their stories with one another. Jesus lets them revel in the success, much as he did when he sent the twelve out two-by-two in Galilee just about a year ago. When all the groups have arrived back in the camp and someone notes, again, their ability to drive out demons, Jesus decides to use this as a teaching moment. "I have observed Satan fall like lightening from the sky. Behold, I have given you power to tread upon serpents and scorpions and upon the full force of the enemy, and nothing will harm you. Nevertheless, do not rejoice because the spirits are subject to you, but rejoice because your names are written in heaven" (Luke 10:18-20). Jesus is pleased to see the enthusiasm of this new group of his disciples. After spending so much time forming his twelve apostles, he has given his power to these seventy-two others and, like the apostles, wants them to realize it is about more than just the power. The real reason for their rejoicing should be because they are now his friends. He has called them to a special relationship with him and his Father such that, now, their names are written in heaven. It is likely few, if any, realize the depth of his words, but it is no matter. Much like the apostles, over time each of them will realize the honor of his invitation.

Although some of these disciples (a few Galileans) have spent significant time following Jesus, most have not. True, each group had one of the apostles with them on tour, but, in general, these new disciples are like babes in the woods. There is still so much for them to learn. Doesn't it seem an incredible leap of faith Jesus is taking in giving his power to these people? Doesn't it seem risky to trust these people, many of whom have not known him for long at all? Yet after telling them the real reason to rejoice, he holds up his arms high to the sky, raises his eyes to heaven, and loudly proclaims, "I give you praise, Father, Lord of heaven and earth, for although you have hidden these things from the wise and the learned you have revealed then to the childlike. Yes, Father, such has been your gracious will" (Matt 11:25-26). Jesus is happy with and grateful for this group. Lowering his arms and his eyes and now looking over them all, his smile widens as he continues, "All things have been handed over to me by my Father, and no one knows the Father except the Son and anyone to whom the Son wishes to reveal him" (Matt 11:27). It is to these men standing in front of him that he is choosing to make the Father known. Yes, he is happy to make the choice and is happy for the enthusiasm he sees in the hearts of these chosen disciples. These are childlike people with little guile in their hearts. Over time, they will be tested, and sometimes they will fail, but most of them will come back to him in their hearts and bodies and try again. Almost as if anticipating their failures and frustrations in the future, and as words of comfort today, Jesus affectionately speaks some of the most consoling words recorded in the gospels: "Come to me, all you who labor and are burdened, and I will give you rest. Take my yoke upon you and learn from me, as I am meek and humble of heart, and you will find rest for yourselves. For my yoke is easy, and my burden light" (Matt 11:28-30). Little do these followers know how severe the trials will be going forward, but they will learn. They will also come to know how trusting in Jesus eases the burden of all the inevitable pains of life.

Finally, as if to remind them how fortunate they each are to be standing here with him, he concludes, "Blessed are the eyes that see what you see. For I say to you, many prophets and kings desired to see what you see, but did not see it, to hear what you hear, but did not hear it" (Luke 10:23-24). They believe they are blessed because Jesus has given them these powers and they feel invincible at the moment. How far from the truth they are! These men are blessed because Jesus is offering himself to them; he is standing right there in front of them. Jesus still offers himself today, but we cannot be blamed for feeling a twinge of envy towards those who had the fortune of seeing him face to face as these did.

Chapter Fifty

The Parable of the Good Samaritan

Jesus knows the news of what the seventy-two have accomplished will steel the resolve of the Jewish leaders even more against him. After a few days, Jesus decides to leave the campsite of Mt. Olivet. Staying this close to Jerusalem will only invite harassment. Many of the newly appointed seventy-two have to return to their homes. Jesus lets them go with a fond farewell and a reminder of their special calling, but tells them they should not attempt to use any of his special powers for now. Although most go, there are some who are able to stay with him. It is now mid-November, day 765 of the 909 days that changed the world, and the rainy season has begun. Jesus has less than five months to live. He will spend these last months moving from town to town in Judea and the lower part of Perea. His time in Galilee is over; the final days of his ministry will take place in Judea.

One day as he is visiting one of the towns along the road from the Jordan River to Jerusalem, a Scribe approaches him. It is important to note as Jesus travels in and around Judea, there are some leaders—Pharisees, Sadducees, Scribes, and others—still trying to make up their own minds about him. However, it is well known that the leaders in Jerusalem are out to get Jesus, and so it is politically risky for anyone in authority to voice a favorable opinion of him. Being in Judea, he is now almost daily shadowed by the opposition. This Scribe has a good heart and wants to know more about Jesus but, out of fear of the leaders standing around, asks a question in a tone of voice that appears testing. "Teacher, what must I do to inherit eternal life?" (Luke 10:25). Jesus looks into this man and sees the pressure he is under. He responds with a question of his own: "What is written in the law? How do you read it?" (Luke 10:26). The Scribe, drawing on his close reading of the scriptures and the kind of life he has tried to live, pauses for only a second before he answers, "You shall love the Lord, your God, with all your heart, with all your being, with all your strength, and with all your mind, and your neighbor as yourself" (Luke 10:27). Amazing! In this small village somewhere in Judea, an unnamed Scribe summarizes the totality of the law. Jesus smiles, marvels at his answer, and says, "You have answered correctly; do this and you will live" (Luke 10:28). But as attracted as he is to Jesus, with the anti-Jesus leaders in the crowd, the Scribe is a bit uncomfortable with Jesus' smile and apparent favor towards him, so he asks a follow-up question. "And who is my neighbor?" (Luke 10:29). His question elicits one of the great parables of Jesus' ministry. Nodding toward the road visible from the village, he begins his story.

"A man fell victim to robbers as he went down from Jerusalem to Jericho. They stripped him and beat him and went off leaving him half-dead. A priest happened to be going down the street, but when he saw him, he passed by on the opposite side. Likewise, a Levite came to the place, and when he saw him, he passed by on the opposite side. But a Samaritan traveler who came upon him was moved with compassion at the sight. He approached the victim, poured oil and wine over his wounds, and bandaged them. Then he lifted him up on his own animal, took him to an inn, and cared for him. The next day he took out two silver coins and gave them to the innkeeper with the instruction, 'Take care of him. If you spend more than what I have given you, I shall repay you on my way back.' Which of these three, in your opinion, was the neighbor to the robbers' victim?" (Luke 10:30-36). The crowd is silent; the answer is obvious, but it implies complimenting one of the hated Samaritans, even if this is only a story. The Scribe thinks for a brief moment, feeling trapped. "The one who treated him with mercy" (Luke 10:37) is the Scribe's somewhat shy reply. "Go and do likewise" (Luke 10:37) are Jesus' bold and final words to the Scribe. Jesus' challenging parable angers the leaders all the more. The Jews dislike all Samaritans, but the one in this story would be even more loathed because he is a businessman on his way to Jerusalem for some mercantile transactions. Of course, to make matters worse, Jesus is also clearly indicating the Samaritan's actions are far superior to the actions of the Jewish leaders (priest and

Levite). The leaders listening to the story realize he is directing this story at them, challenging them to be more compassionate. Most reject the message as they reject him. They say nothing, though, and the Scribe is lost in his own thoughts as the crowd dissipates. We can only guess how this encounter with Jesus will change the life of this Scribe. We will hear no more of him, so can only wonder if he overcomes his fear of human respect and ends up following Jesus. Will he acquire the same boldness as that of the man born blind, who challenged the religious leaders just a few weeks ago, or will he let his fear of the Pharisees cause him to act much the way the parents of the man born blind acted?

CHAPTER FIFTY-ONE

Jesus Dines with Martha and Mary

One day late in November—day 774 of the 909 days that changed the world—Jesus visits the home of Martha and Mary, who live in Bethany, a little residential town on the east side of Mt. Olivet. We cannot be exactly sure how Jesus became such good friends with Martha, Mary, and their brother Lazarus. Many scholars believe this Mary is the same Mary of Magdala who washed Jesus' feet with her tears, anointed them with precious oil, and wiped his feet with her hair in the house of Simon the Pharisee last December, as indeed the gospel of John (11:2) indicates. Others think this Mary is a different person. Maybe Martha, Mary, and Lazarus are one of the Judean families who have heard him in Jerusalem and become close to him. Perhaps they have followed him as he has made his way through Judea the last month or so. In any event, it is clear by the story as related by St. Luke that Jesus has a special friendship with this family. He visits them more than once in these last few months of his life; he clearly is very comfortable and "at home" with them.

This day Jesus accepts an invitation to dine with Martha and her sister Mary at their house. Martha is the elder and the leader of the household. Neither is married. Both women are excited about his visit and work hard to prepare a special meal. When Jesus arrives, there is still work to do, so they leave Jesus and the few apostles he brings along with him sitting by themselves while the women finish preparing the meal. Bethany, being on the east side of the mountain, provides an excellent view of the Jordan River. We can imagine Jesus waiting for the meal and silently contemplating all that has transpired in the last two years as he looks towards the river valley. He can remember how it all started, when he was baptized by John, and can even catch a glimpse of the castle on the other side of the river where John was imprisoned and beheaded. Behind him is Jerusalem, where in a few months he will lay down his own life. Jesus is lost in his thoughts until Mary comes in, offers Jesus an appetizer, and sits down at his feet. Jesus smiles warmly at her and engages her in conversation. Mary has her eyes pinned to his as if there is no one else in the world and as if nothing else in the world is more important than being with him. After a few minutes, though, Martha notices Mary is not helping and sees her sitting at the feet of Jesus. There are still things to do to finish preparing the meal and with a certain frustration says, "Lord, do you not care that my sister has left me by myself to do the serving? Tell her to help me" (Luke 10:40). The look on Martha's face clearly indicates she is fully expecting Jesus to tell her sister to get up and help. But he will surprise her.

He turns his gaze from Mary and looks at Martha. He loves Martha deeply, and appreciates her active service in preparing the meal and the other things she has done for him. She is a woman of action, and he knows he needs such women, then as now. On the other hand, these actions matter only as much as the purpose they serve. Without denigrating the importance of Martha's work, Jesus says to her in a gentle voice, "Martha, Martha—you are anxious and worried about many things. There is need of only one thing. Mary has chosen the better part and it will not be taken from her" (Luke 10:41-42). Martha does not feel chastised; she basks in the love he communicates through his eyes, and she understands instantly. She sees her work as being important, but realizes she must not lose sight of the person for whom she is doing the work. As is true for most, it is easy for her to let her work become an end in itself, instead of a means to an end: loving Jesus and others. It is a profound lesson.

Mary, however, gets up and helps her sister make the final preparations for the meal. Dinner is served, and they all enjoy the food, wine, and most importantly, the time spent together. As the dinner progresses, the rain moves in but the sound of the rain gently hitting the roof only seems to make the gathering inside feel all the more cozy and intimate.

CHAPTER FIFTY-TWO

Another Turning Point: Jesus Dines with a Judean Pharisee

It is now early December, and Jesus is continuing to make his way around Judea visiting many towns. He is accompanied by his apostles, a number of disciples, and some of the holy women. As we have noticed before, Jesus is intent on having people choose sides. It is either belief in him or belief in the Jewish leaders. One day, while in one of the towns, a Pharisee invites Jesus to dine with him and a number of his fellow Pharisees and local leaders. Like so many other men of Judea, this unnamed Pharisee is trying to figure out if Jesus is something special. Jesus accepts his invitation.

The Pharisee's house is full when Jesus arrives, and people are excited to see him and hear what he will have to say. This scene is reminiscent of the one about nine months ago when Jesus dined with Simon the Pharisee in Magdala and had his feet washed and anointed by the woman. Like then, the guests are all excited about seeing him, but unlike then when Simon offered Jesus none of the ritualistic greetings, this Pharisee has them all available. When he enters the room, however, Jesus does not stop to do the prescribed washings before the meal. The host is taken aback by his action, which is also noted by a number of the guests. He knows what they are thinking and is choosing to make a point, attacking the Pharisees for being more concerned about external appearances than internal attitudes. Notice how much harsher Jesus' words are here than they were in Simon the Pharisee's house. Gone are the days of instruction; now are the days of making a choice. Let us listen to Jesus' stinging words. "Oh, you Pharisees! Although you cleanse the outside of the cup and the dish, inside you are filled with plunder and evil. You fools! Did not the maker of the outside also make the inside?" (Luke 11:39-40). Challenging words, indeed, although he does offer an antidote: "But as to what is within, give alms, and behold, everything will be clean for you" (Luke11:41). But he is not finished with his condemnation. "Woe to you Pharisees! You pay tithes of mint and of rue and of every garden herb, but you pay no attention to judgment and to love for God. Those you should have done without overlooking the others. Woe to you Pharisees! You love the seat of honor in synagogues and greetings in the marketplaces" (Luke 11:42-43). As the Pharisees' anger rises, Jesus finishes addressing them with bitter words, referring to how they debase their unsuspecting followers. "Woe to you! You are like unseen graves over which people unknowingly walk" (Luke 11:45).

The place is in an uproar. How rude of him to attack the host and his other guests! One of the scholars of the law in the room, almost incredulous about what he has heard, speaks up. "Teacher, by saying this, you are insulting us, too" (Luke 11:45). Jesus, however, does not back down, and vehemently responds, "Woe also to you, scholars of the law! You impose on people burdens hard to carry, but you yourselves do not lift one finger to touch them. Woe to you! You build the memorials of the prophets whom your ancestors killed. Consequently, you bear witness and give consent to the deeds of your ancestors, for they killed them and you do the building. Therefore the wisdom of God said, 'I will send to them prophets and apostles;' some of them they will kill and persecute in order that this generation might be charged with the blood of all the prophets shed since the foundation of the world, from the blood of Zechariah who died between the altar and the temple building. Yes, I tell you, this generation will be charged with their blood. Woe to you, scholars of the law! You have taken away the key of knowledge. You yourselves did not enter and you stopped those trying to enter" (Luke 11:46-52). The room is on its feet in anger. How arrogant of him! They are all yelling back at him, hurling insults at him and his apostles. Jesus' demeanor does not change; his eyes are on fire as he turns his back on the room and walks out of the house.

This is another turning point. Whereas Jesus had been relentless with the leaders in Jerusalem at the Feast of Tabernacles a month and a half ago, he has never challenged the leaders of the other towns of Judea as he has just done now. Why does he attack these men so harshly? Some of them likely are good men in their own right and are trying to make up their own minds about him. Why is he so aggressive? It is four months until his death, and he wants these men to confront the truth about themselves much like he wants us to confront the truth about ourselves. Sometimes it takes harsh words to make that happen. We can only wonder how many Pharisees and Scribes in the room, upon reflection and soul searching, will realize the truth in his words, much as our own reflection on hard words or difficult situations may help us realize the truth. But there is another reason Jesus is so challenging to the Pharisees.

Although he has not worked many miracles at all, the common people of Judea are favorably disposed towards him. They are impressed with how he has fearlessly taught, even with his opposition watching him so closely. Jesus knows it is important that the crowd learns the same lesson he is trying to impress on the Pharisees. As he leaves the house, there are a number of people there. They see the fire in his eyes and most of them have heard the confrontation. Jesus stops and at first addresses his words to his apostles, but quickly widens his gaze to all the people gathered around him. With many of the Pharisees and Scribes he has just challenged looking out at the crowd, Jesus warns everyone, "Beware of the leaven—that is the hypocrisy—of the Pharisees" (Luke 12:1). He does not mince words. He has everyone's attention, and so he presses onward. "There is nothing concealed that will not be revealed, nor secret that will not be known. Therefore, whatever you have said in the darkness will be heard in the light, and whatever you have whispered behind closed doors will be proclaimed from the housetops" (Luke 12:2-3). What a clear message he delivers on the importance of the rightness of heart. The thought of having everything said or thought in secret proclaimed from the housetops causes most of them (and us) to think deeply. But there is more to say. Jesus knows following him will be difficult. He realizes they will face many persecutions if they do, and so as both a warning and a comfort to them (and to us), he continues, "I tell you, my friends, do not be afraid of those who kill the body but after that can do no more. I shall show you whom to fear. Be afraid of the one who after killing has the power to cast into Gehenna; yes, I tell you, be afraid of that one. Are not five sparrows sold for two small coins? Yet not one of them has escaped the notice of God. Even the hairs on your head have all been counted. Do not be afraid. You are worth more than many sparrows. I tell you everyone who acknowledges me before others the Son of Man will acknowledge before the angels of God. But whoever denies me because of others will be denied before the angels of God" (Luke 12:4-9). Finally to emphasize the importance of the Holy Spirit in the upcoming days of challenge, Jesus closes his teaching with these words: "Everyone who speaks a word against the Son of Man will be forgiven, but the one who blasphemes against the Holy Spirit will not be forgiven. When they take you before the rulers and authorities, do not worry about what your defense will be or about what you will say. For the Holy Spirit will teach you at that moment what you should say" (Luke 12:10-12). Yes, it is so clear Jesus is pushing people to choose sides. As news of this confrontation makes its way through Judea, most of the leadership of all Judea, and not just Jerusalem, turns on Jesus.

CHAPTER FIFTY-THREE

Jesus Continues His Tour of Judea

The storm clouds are getting thicker as Jesus continues his tour of the Judean countryside. Many parables and passages in St. Luke's gospel are included here, which almost exactly mirror parables and passages related earlier in St. Matthew's account of Jesus' life. Although there are some scholars who believe St. Matthew's timing is correct, most believe Luke's placing of these passages is more accurate. For one reason, Matthew has a tendency to lump passages and parables together, whereas Luke seems a bit more interested in the chronology of the events. Moreover, the nature of these passages fit much more neatly here in the Judean ministry, where Jesus is more demanding and exacting than he was in his Galilean ministry. In any event, it is December, and, as Jesus tours through another town, he is approached by someone who wants him to make a judgment for him against his brother in splitting an inheritance. With the growing chasm between Jesus and the leaders, some of the common folks are looking to see if he is willing to assume some of the responsibilities of the Jewish leaders. Jesus will have no part in usurping the authority of the Jewish leaders, so he responds to this man, "Friend, who appointed me as your judge and arbitrator?" (Luke 12:14). It is an interesting response, because, although he wants the Jewish leaders to judge with purer hearts and sounder minds, he will not do it for them. He is not looking to take away their authority but rather to help them better exercise it.

The man's question, though, provides Jesus a good opportunity to teach about the importance of material things. He looks at the group around him and says, "Take care to guard against all greed, for though one may be rich, one's life does not consist of possessions"

(Luke 12:15). Some heads nod in agreement, but many look blankly back at him, as most believe material possessions are a sign of God's favor. Jesus presses on with a parable to explain. "There was a rich man whose land produced a bountiful harvest. He asked himself, 'What shall I do, for I do not have enough space to store my harvest?' And he said, 'This is what I shall do: I shall tear down my barns and build larger ones. There I shall store all my grain and other goods, and I shall say to myself, "Now as for you, you have many good things stored up for many years; rest, eat, drink, and be merry."' But God said to him, 'You fool, this night your life will be demanded of you; and the things you have prepared—to whom will they belong?' Thus will it be for the one who stores up treasure for himself but is not rich in what matters to God" (Luke 12:16-21). The lesson is clear: God is more important than things. But Jesus wants to build on this point, so he continues, his tone of voice becoming almost solicitous, as if he is beseeching them to follow his advice. "Therefore I tell you, do not worry about your life and what you will eat, or about your body and what you will wear. For life is more than food and body more than clothing" (Luke 12:22-23). Pointing to some birds flying by them in the sky, Jesus goes on, "Notice the ravens: they do not sow or reap; they have neither storehouse nor barn; yet God feeds them. How much more important are you than birds! Can any of you by worrying add a moment to your life span? If even the smallest things are beyond your control, why are you anxious about the rest? Notice how the flowers grow. They do not toil or spin. But I tell you, not even Solomon in all his splendor was dressed like one of them. If God so clothes the grass in the field that grows today and is thrown into the oven tomorrow, will he not much more provide for you, O you of little faith? As for you, do not seek what you are to eat and what you are to drink, and do not worry anymore. All the nations of the world seek these things and your Father knows that you need them. Instead, seek his kingdom, and these other things will be given you besides. Do not be afraid any longer, little flock, because your Father is pleased to give you the kingdom. Sell your belongings and give alms" (Luke 12:24-32). He pauses for a long moment now, for he wants them to get this next point. "Provide money bags for yourselves that do not wear out, an inexhaustible treasure in heaven that no thief can reach or moth destroy. For where your treasure is, there also will your heart be" (Luke 12:33-34). His tone of voice is so inviting, because he knows this is a hard message to comprehend and accept, yet is crucial for the happiness of every human being. Things will not make humans really happy—entertained, yes, distracted, maybe, but really happy, no.

In another town during this tour, as Jesus is walking down a street, he responds to someone's question about the coming of the kingdom. Jesus stops, and, as he addresses the small crowd following him, his tone of voice becomes stern, knowing he is issuing a warning. "Gird your loins and light your lamps and be like servants who await their master's return from a wedding, ready to open immediately when he comes and knocks. Blessed are those servants whom the master finds vigilant on his arrival. Amen, I say to you, he will gird himself, have them recline at table, and proceed to wait on them. And should he come in the second or third watch and find them prepared in this way, blessed are those servants. Be sure of this: if the master of the house had known the hour when the thief was coming, he would not have let his house be broken into. You must be prepared, for at an hour you do not expect, the Son of Man will come" (Luke 12:35-40). With that, Jesus continues to walk down the street.

This parable produces utter confusion in the minds of those who hear it. Although this is familiar imagery, it is not the kind they expect to hear about the new kingdom they are anticipating. They are looking for imagery of war, conflict, and battles won, not wedding imagery. And what of this talk of the master girding himself and serving the servants? What can he mean by that? And what does the thief breaking into the master's house have anything to do with this new kingdom? No one, however, asks for clarification; most just shake their heads and watch him walk away.

As they are walking along, Peter is also trying to figure out the parable, so he asks if it is intended for everyone or just for the apostles and other close followers of Jesus. Jesus stops again and uses strong language to impress on Peter and the others how much will be riding on their faithfulness and how much will be demanded of them. They do not fully appreciate these words now, but they will after he has died, risen, and ascended into heaven. We can hear in Jesus' tone the urgency with which he is trying to teach them. He knows his time is short and getting shorter, so he responds to Peter's question:

"Who then is the faithful and prudent steward whom the master will put in charge of his servants to distribute the food allowance at the proper time? Blessed is that servant whom his master on arrival finds doing so. Truly, I say to you, he will put him in charge of all his property. But if that servant says to himself, 'My master is delayed in coming,' and begins to beat the menservants and the maidservants, to eat and drink and get drunk, then that servant's master will come on an unexpected day and at an unknown hour and will punish him severely and assign him a place with the unfaithful. That servant who knew his master's will but did not make preparations nor act in accord with his will shall be beaten severely; and the servant who was ignorant of his master's will but acted in a way deserving of a beating shall be beaten only lightly. Much will be required of the person entrusted with much, and still more will be demanded of the person entrusted with more" (Luke 12:42-48).

Rarely have we seen Jesus demand so much from the apostles as he does here. The apostles see the seriousness of these words in his eyes, and they dare not ask him anymore questions. There is one of them, however—Judas Iscariot—who recoils at these words and asks himself yet again if it is smart to have his future tied up with this man.

CHAPTER FIFTY-FOUR

More Strong Warnings from Jesus in Judea

It is now late December—day 810 of the 909 days that changed the world. Jesus' messages during this tour of Judea seem severe, and the crowds following him have been dwindling. There have been no miracles since the blind man was cured in Jerusalem about two months ago, and his words have been hard to take—more challenging than comforting—so the enthusiasm for Jesus abates. It so happens during these days, in yet a different town, that he fires off another disturbing speech. "I have come to set the earth on fire, and how I wish it were already blazing! There is a baptism with which I must be baptized, and how great is my anguish until it is accomplished! Do you think that I have come to establish peace on earth? No, I tell you, but rather division. From now on a household of five will be divided, three against two and two against three; a father will be divided against his son and a son against his father, a mother against her daughter and a daughter against her mother, a mother-in-law against her daughter-in-law and a daughter-in-law against her mother-in-law" (Luke 12:49-53). As with his other warnings, no one, not even his apostles, really understands what he is talking about, but the tone of his voice and the look in his eyes are a clear indication that he is dead serious. These speeches are having the desired effect, as they force people to choose whether or not to follow him. Unfortunately, more and more people are choosing not to do so. Later on, the apostles will see many of these speeches as a warning of the struggles, both internally and externally, people who choose to follow Jesus will face.

All along, the Jewish leaders have been shadowing him and are happy to see his hard words are having the affect of dampening the people's enthusiasm. They consider if he is in the process of self-destruction, so they bide their time, say nothing, and just observe. On another occasion during this tour, Jesus challenges the crowd, "When you see a cloud rising in the west you say immediately that it is going to rain, and so it does; and when you notice that the wind is blowing from the south you say that it is going to be hot, and so it is. You hypocrites! You know how to interpret the appearance of the earth and the sky; why do you not know how to interpret the present time? Why do you not judge for yourselves what is right? If you are to go with your opponent before a magistrate, make an offer on the way; otherwise your opponent will turn you over to the judge, and the judge hand you over to the constable, and the constable throw you into prison. I say to you, you will not be released until you have paid the last penny" (Luke 12:54-59). The Jewish leaders know, as usual, Jesus' words are directed more at them than at the crowd, but they take great delight in seeing the confusion these words cause in the people. He is challenging the leaders, yes, but he is also challenging the crowds, and since the crowd doesn't quite get what he is saying, it makes it seem as if it is Jesus against all. 'Perfect,' they think. If the price of alienating the crowd is some insults hurled at them, the Jewish leaders are happy to make that trade.

As we have mentioned, the greatest cause of confusion among the people is trying to figure out if Jesus is the leader who will restore the glory of Israel and overthrow the dreaded Roman rule. Looking to get more clarity, the next day some people ask him his opinion about the recent killing of some Galileans in the temple by Pilate's soldiers. They are looking to see if this injustice will serve to rile him up against the Roman rulers. Yet again, however, he vexes the crowd. "Do you think that because these Galileans suffered in this way, they were greater sinners than all other Galileans? By no means! But I tell you, if you do not repent, you will all perish as they did!" (Luke 13:2-3). Then, referring to a recent accident in Judea, he continues, "Or those eighteen people who were killed when the tower at Siloam fell on them—do you think they were more guilty than everyone else who lived in Jerusalem? By no means! But I tell you, if you do not repent, you will all perish as they did" (Luke 13:4-5). The idea is merely to ascertain if Jesus sees the injustice of the Romans, and instead, he fires back a warning about the need for them to repent with nary a remark about the Romans. Not only is it a call to repentance, it comes across almost as a threat. In an attempt to soften the blow a touch, he tells them a parable meant to show God's justice as well as his patience with sinners. Looking around he notices a fig tree which, as is customary this time of year, has no fruit on it and points to it.

With a softer voice, he begins, "There once was a person who had a fig tree planted in his orchard and when he came in search of fruit on it but found none he said to the gardener, 'For three years now I have come in search of fruit on this fig tree but have found none, so cut it down. Why should it exhaust the soil?' He said to him in reply, 'Sir, leave it for this year also, and I shall cultivate the ground around it and fertilize it; it may bear fruit in the future. If not, you can cut it down'" (Luke 13:6-9). Not a soul in the small crowd gets the point that Jesus is saying he is the gardener who wants to help every person bear good fruit. Yes, Jesus is challenging them to repent and wants them to know the importance of repentance, but he also wants them to know God doesn't give up easily on anyone—no one then and no one now.

Chapter Fifty-Five

Jesus Cures a Crippled Woman on the Sabbath

Since the end of the Feast of Tabernacles and his curing of the blind man, Jesus' popularity has been waning; there have been no miracles and lots of challenging speeches. The crowds have decreased, and the leaders are happy with the current direction of events. It all changes on the next Sabbath day.

Jesus is attending Sabbath services, and, as frequently happens, he is asked to read and interpret a scripture passage. He does so with the usual effect. The people all marvel at how he proclaims the scriptures and his thoughtful commentary on them. Despite his decreasing popularity, he still is able to hold a Sabbath crowd spellbound. As he finishes his commentary and makes his way back to his seat, he notices a woman bent over, completely unable to stand up. She has long been widowed and lives with one of her daughters. Her condition has worsened over the years, yet she has mostly been a cheerful woman and is very well liked by all in her village. When the services end, Jesus is standing outside talking when the woman exits the synagogue along with her daughter and her family. Jesus excuses himself from the people to whom he is speaking, walks over to the woman, calling out as he approaches, "Woman, you are set free of your infirmity" (Luke 13:12). Arriving at her side, "He places his hands on her and she at once stands up straight and glorifies God" (Luke 13:13). The crowd is stunned; they know this woman has been ill for many, many years. This is clearly a miracle and the first one seen by most of these people. They all begin to glorify God for having sent them this…prophet, king, maybe even savior. Enthusiasm for Jesus begins to mount.

The leader of the synagogue, though, not a believer in Jesus himself, tries to throw some cold water on the proceedings by "blaming" the people (he is too cowardly to blame Jesus) for the miracle. With some of his fellow Scribes and Pharisees standing next to him, he calls out to the crowd, "There are six days when work should be done. Come on those six days to be cured, not on the Sabbath day" (Luke 13:14). In the hardness of their heart, they insist on the letter of the law, while a miraculous cure of a poor woman who has suffered for years stares them right in the face. The crowd is taken aback by the leaders' attack, but Jesus wastes no time defending them, as well as himself—the real target of the leaders' criticism. In a voice that commands silence, Jesus replies, "Hypocrites! Does not each one of you on the Sabbath untie his ox or his ass from the manger and lead it out for watering? This daughter of Abraham, whom Satan has bound eighteen years now, ought she not to have been set free on the Sabbath day from this bondage?" (Luke 13:15-16). It is a commonsense point that most in the crowd see instantly, and it makes the leaders' position look foolish. The leader acts as if he is about to say something—but does not. Humiliated and beaten, the synagogue leaders turn and walk back into the temple while the crowd rejoices in the miracle. News of this miracle spreads like wildfire, and the Jewish leaders' recent optimism is reversed as they see the people respond to news of this miracle.

CHAPTER FIFTY-SIX

The Feast of the Dedication

Jesus' popularity is back on the upswing with the healing of the crippled woman. In addition, his challenging remarks become more aimed, once again, at the Jewish leaders and not as much at the people themselves. It is the end of December and time for the Feast of the Dedication (otherwise known as the Feast of Lights or Hanukkah), which commemorates the Maccabees' rededication of the altar and temple in Jerusalem around 164 BC. Because it is in the middle of the rainy season, this feast does not draw as many pilgrims, especially from Galilee, as the traveling conditions can be difficult. As Jesus has been touring through Judea, he makes his way towards Jerusalem for the feast. Along the way, Luke records two important parables and one important speech that he gives to his followers as he sets his sights on Jerusalem. He has been speaking about the kingdom of God, its arrival, its not being all about an earthly kingdom, and what it takes to be part of the kingdom. These continue to be hard concepts for the people (and the apostles) to grasp.

In one of the towns where he stops, he is enjoying a drink and eating some bread under a huge mustard tree that provides him and his listeners some shelter from the light rain. It gives him an idea. There are no Jewish leaders in the crowd today to harass him or try to trip him up in his words, so the crowd can hear the affection for them in his voice as he calls out, "What is the kingdom of God like? It is like a mustard seed that a person took and planted in the garden. When it was fully grown, it became a large bush and the birds of the sky dwelt in its branches" (Luke 13:18-19). Then holding up the piece of bread he is eating he looks at it and continues, "To what shall I compare the kingdom of God? It is like yeast that a woman took and mixed in with three measures of wheat flour until the whole batch of dough was leavened" (Luke 13:20-21). Yes, the kingdom of God will start small like a mustard seed, almost hidden like leaven, but will grow much bigger. By contrast, of course, he is telling them to not look for fireworks or quick overthrow of Roman rule. The kingdom of God will start in the quiet of each man and woman's heart and grow from there. These two parables are hard to understand but will provide much opportunity for the followers of Jesus to ponder today—and down through the centuries.

In another town, right before he gets to Jerusalem, someone asks him a telling question: "Lord, will only a few people be saved?" (Luke 13:22). From the question it is apparent that some are beginning to understand that he is not just talking about an earthly kingdom. Here, however, by the intensity of his response we can tell Jesus is being observed yet again by the Jewish leaders. He looks at the man who asks the question and replies, "Strive to enter through the narrow gate, for many, I tell you, will attempt to enter but will not be strong enough" (Luke 13:24). Then moving his eyes towards the leaders lurking in the background, he continues in a stronger tone of voice, "After the master of the house has arisen and locked the door, then will you stand outside knocking and saying, 'Lord, open the door for us.' He will say to you in reply, 'I do not know where you are from.' And you will say, 'We ate and drank in your company and you taught in our streets.' Then he will say, 'I do not know where you are from. Depart form me, all you evildoers!' And there will be wailing and grinding of teeth when you see Abraham, Isaac, and Jacob and all the prophets in the kingdom of God and you yourselves cast out" (Luke 13:25-28). The leaders' eyes fire back at Jesus, but their lips speak no words. Pausing a second, Jesus then turns his gaze back to the crowd, softens his voice, and slowly, as if hoping the speed with which he says these words will allow them to sink in better, finishes by saying, "And people will come from the east and the west and from the north and the south and will recline at the table in the kingdom of God. For behold, some are last who will be first, and some are first who will be last" (Luke 13:29-30). His words are so hard for the people listening to grasp, as they are almost counter to everything they have ever believed. Some of the first being last and some of the last being first? Some even wonder the unthinkable. Could he be saying this new kingdom may include other people than the Jews? How can that possibly be?

Jesus tells them he is on his way to Jerusalem, and he and his followers leave the town. It is late in the day, but they can easily get to the outskirts of Jerusalem in less than an hour and set up camp. The heavy rain on the road makes the trip bothersome, but luckily the rain lets up when they arrive at Mt. Olivet, so they are more easily able to make camp, have dinner, and retire for the evening.

The next day, Jesus and his followers enter the city for the feast. The rain has picked up once again and, in spite of the feast, there is a sense of foreboding in the air. What will happen now between Jesus and the authorities? He has been traveling all over Judea the last two months with his message of a new kingdom, with strong words for the Jewish leaders, and with challenging words for the crowds. The opinions about him are almost as numerous as the number of people in the city. With the exception of the hatred of the majority of the leaders, there is no consensus about him among the townspeople and pilgrims in Jerusalem.

Jesus makes his way to the Portico of Solomon in the city and like many others seeks shelter from the rain under the porch. The leaders decide to press him on the issue of his being the Messiah, the one to save Israel. "How long are you going to keep us in suspense? If you are the Messiah, tell us plainly" (John 10:24). Everyone in the crowd stops. They all come at attention to hear what he will say to the leaders. It is a poignant moment. He easily sees the evil intent in these men's hearts. They only mean to make trouble for Jesus. Everyone who is close enough can see the fire in Jesus' eyes, and all in the crowd can hear the frustration in his voice as he focuses on the leaders all gathered together. "I told you and you do not believe. The works that I do in my Father's name testify to me. But you do not believe because you are not among my sheep" (John 10:25-26). Then looking away from the leaders, he much more gently says to the people gathered there, "My sheep hear my voice. I know them and they follow me. I give them eternal life and they shall never perish. No one can take them out of my hand. My Father who has given them to me is greater than all, and no one can take them out of the Father's hand" (John 10:27-29). Then turning his gaze once again towards the leaders, he calmly and sternly says, "The Father and I are one" (John 10:30).

With those words some of the younger Pharisees among the leaders gasp in disbelief, step out from underneath the porch, and pick up stones. They approach Jesus as if they are going to stone him. Some of Jesus' apostles step closer to protect him, but he puts his hand up to signal he is fine. No need for a fight or physical confrontation. Jesus focuses on the Pharisees and replies, "I have shown you many good works from my Father. For which one of these are you trying to stone me?" (John 10:32). Their answer is immediate and laden with immature indignation as they reply, "We are not stoning you for a good work, but for blasphemy. You, a man, are making yourself God" (John 10:33). We have to give these young Pharisees one thing: they do understand Jesus' message about his being God and that gives him some hope for them. They are young; maybe he can change their hearts. His look and tone of voice soften and indicate a desire to instruct and draw the younger Pharisees deeper into his mystery as he replies, "Can you say that the one whom the Father has consecrated and sent into the world blasphemes because I said 'I am the Son of God'? If I do not perform my Father's works, do not believe in me; but if I perform them, even if you do not believe me, believe the works, so that you may realize and understand that the Father is in me and I am in the Father" (John 10:36-39). Jesus speaks as if he is giving them an invitation; everyone in the crowd can hear the difference in his voice. He is no longer condemning these leaders but trying to convince them—but for most of these young Pharisees, it falls on deaf ears. Some of the older ones in the background call for Jesus to be arrested, but he turns his back on them and walks away. Just as it has been many times when the authorities or even his own townspeople in Nazareth have tried to arrest or stone him, he just disappears, leaving his persecutors to wonder where he has gone. Ultimately, reflecting on all these attempts on his life will reinforce in the apostles the fact that he laid down his life on his own terms, or more exactly, on the terms of his Father.

The rest of the time in Jerusalem passes without any more incidents. Jesus preaches in the city and many people admire him because they can see the leaders have backed down on their active attacks. The leaders carp about him behind his back but only observe and do not confront him to his face. They know he has bested them yet again. Oddly enough during the feast, the leaders get news from some Roman guards that Herod, whose conscience is still tortured from his murdering John the Baptist, has been hearing more and more about Jesus and would like to see if he is John the Baptist come back to life. The leaders suggest to the Roman officials that Jesus be arrested, but the Romans tell them they have no such orders.

The Pharisees then get an idea. They suggest to the others a plan of telling Jesus that Herod is looking to arrest or kill him, so he should leave the city. If he heeds the warning, it will get him out of the city and Judea, maybe cause him to go into hiding, and certainly give the leaders time to regroup. Feigning real concern, some of them approach Jesus, bow reverently, and tell him that for his own safety he should, "Go away, leave this area, because Herod wants to kill you" (Luke 13:31). Jesus decides not to attack the Pharisees for their cunning lies and with almost a mocking defiance in his voice replies, "Go and tell that fox, 'Behold, I cast out demons and I perform healing today and tomorrow and on the third day I accomplish my purpose. Yet I must continue on my way today, tomorrow, and the following day for it is impossible that a prophet should die outside of Jerusalem'" (Luke 13:33-34). He is cryptically indicating no one including Herod can kill him against his own will and that he will give over his life at his own choosing in the city of Jerusalem. No one understands, though, and the Pharisees delivering the message bow again, turn, and walk away. They can only hope he will change his mind and leave.

On the last day of the feast, Jesus and his followers return to their campsite and spend a quiet night. The next morning they break camp and he tells them he is going to continue to tour Judea. If his popularity with the people of Jerusalem was the goal, the feast would have to be considered a success. Many people have come to believe in him, but he knows their faith is weak and will turn on a dime. Moreover, he knows the leaders, try as he might, will not relent in their desire to have him killed. Reflecting on his special affection for these people and their numerous unfaithful responses over the centuries, Jesus walks away from the others to the top of Mt. Olivet and stands looking over the city. After a short while, Peter walks up to where Jesus is standing and, saying nothing, joins him in taking in the view of the city. Shortly, still staring at the city and without looking at Peter, Jesus laments, "Jerusalem, Jerusalem, you who kill the prophets and stone those sent to you, how many times have I yearned to gather your children together as a hen gathers her brood under her wings, but you were unwilling. Behold, your house will be abandoned. But I tell you, you will not see me until the time comes when you say 'Blessed is he who comes in the name of the Lord'" (Luke 13:34-35). For a long moment, Jesus stares down at the city. Peter takes exact notice and is touched deeply to hear and see his sorrow. Jesus turns to Peter, and with a sad smile tells him it is time to move forward.

CHAPTER FIFTY-SEVEN

Another Sabbath Healing: Jesus Heals the Man with Dropsy

As December fades into January, Jesus continues to move about Judea although, from what we hear from John's gospel, this time he is mostly in towns farther away from the city of Jerusalem, closer to the Jordan River (John 11:40). In one such town, he accepts an invitation to dine on the Sabbath with one of the leading Pharisees. This Pharisee's motives are not pure, as he is trying to gather evidence against Jesus. He plans on having one of the town locals who is dreadfully sick with dropsy sit in a heap at his home entrance. If Jesus heals the man, he will violate the Sabbath, and if he does nothing for the man, it will look as if he doesn't care or lacks the power. It is amazing that these Pharisees are so relentless on attacking Jesus on the Sabbath issue even though it doesn't resonate as importantly to most of the people. The people generally see the good that is done far outweighs any legalism; the Pharisees do not.

Jesus enters the house with a few of his apostles and mingles with the house guests. At first, other than a smile and a nod as he passes the ill man, Jesus seems not to pay any attention to him. Most of the guests are closely observing Jesus to see what he is going to do about this sick man. As the time comes to recline for dinner, Jesus takes his seat and observes how the men all clamor for places of honor at the table. He will address them later on that point, but for now, when all are seated and after his host proposes a toast, instead of responding back with the customary nicety, Jesus asks them all, "Is it lawful to cure on the Sabbath or not?" (Luke 14:3). Quickly they all realize he has turned the tables on them and is asking them the same question they are proposing to him. Some look down, some shrug their shoulders, but no one responds. Jesus then gets up from the table and walks over to the man with dropsy. He lays his hands on him and pronounces him cured. The effect is immediate; the excess fluid in his body disappears, and in a flash he looks normal. The man looks over his body in disbelief, touches his arms, legs, face, and smiles broadly at Jesus, thanking him profusely. Jesus takes him by the hands and lifts him to his feet. He looks into the man's eyes and then tells him to go back to his home. He watches the man run out of the house, and when he is out of sight, Jesus turns and walks back to his seat and reclines there. The room is silent, but he breaks the silence by saying, "Who among you, if your son or ox falls into a cistern, would not immediately pull him out on the Sabbath day?" (Luke 13:5). There is no response. Both Jesus' words and watching the miracle being performed silences even the most stubborn of them in the room. He looks around the room—still no response. But he has more to say.

Referring to everyone's clamoring for the seats of honor, he tells them to listen to what he has to say. "When you are invited by someone to a wedding banquet, do not recline at table in the place of honor. A more distinguished guest than you may have been invited by him, and the host who invited both of you may approach you and say, 'Give your place to this man,' and then you would proceed with embarrassment to take the lowest place. Rather, when you are invited, go and take the lowest place so that when the host comes he may say, 'My friend, move up to a higher position.' Then you will enjoy the esteem of your companions at the table. For everyone who exalts himself will be humbled, but the one who humbles himself will be exalted" (Luke 14:8-11). Turning himself to look directly at the Pharisee hosting the dinner, Jesus continues, "When you hold a lunch or dinner, do not invite your friends or your brothers or your relatives or your wealthy neighbors, in case they may invite you back and you have repayment. Rather, when you hold a banquet, invite the poor, the crippled, the lame, the blind; blessed indeed will you be because of their inability to repay you. For you will be repaid at the resurrection of the righteous" (Luke 13:12-14). The room remains still as the wisdom of Jesus' words touches the hearts of many of the guests. A gentle, wet, early January breeze blows through the room, and as it does so it seems to break the spell. One of the guests calls out, "Blessed is the one who will dine in the kingdom of God" (Luke 13:15). Jesus looks at the man and smiles. This will allow him to make one more point before he takes his leave.

He gets up from his seat and begins to walk around the room while all the others remain seated looking at him. Almost as if he is lecturing them, he says, "A man gave a great dinner to which he invited many. When the time for the dinner came, he dispatched his servant to say to those invited, 'Come, everything is now ready.' But one by one, they all began to excuse themselves. The first said to him, 'I have purchased a field and must go to examine it; I ask you, consider me excused.' And another said, 'I have just married a woman, and therefore cannot come.' The servant went and reported this to his master. Then the master of the house in a rage commanded his servant, 'Go out quickly into the streets and alleys of the town and bring in here the poor and the crippled, the blind and the lame.' The servant reported, 'Sir, your orders have been carried out and still there is more room.' The master then ordered the servant, 'Go out to the highways and hedgerows and make people come in that my home may be filled. For I tell you, none of those men who were invited will taste my dinner'" (Luke 13:16-24). On finishing these words, Jesus walks back to his place at the table. Everyone is still quiet, and all eyes are locked on him. He knows he has angered some of these people but has most of them pondering his words. He has held a mirror up to their faces, and most are uncomfortable with the view. Jesus has made his point so as he sits back down, he turns to his host and comments how good the food smells. The Pharisee is relieved to be able to change the conversation, thanks Jesus for his compliment, and orders his servants to bring the food.

Chapter Fifty-Eight

Jesus Continues Visiting Judean Towns

As we noted already, since curing the crippled woman well over a month ago, Jesus' discourses have changed focus. Although he is still on guard against the Pharisees and other leaders, he is not as challenging as he was after the October Feast of Tabernacles in his conversations with the ordinary people. Indeed, it seems Jesus is intent for the next month or so to instruct and inspire. He wants to tell many parables, hoping that something will stick with each of his listeners. These are his last months, so he particularly wants his apostles to learn and remember as much as they can absorb.

It happens that he is in one town on a Sabbath and speaks at the temple. After the service, as everyone is leaving the temple area and scurrying back to their homes in the rain, one of the more enthusiastic townspeople calls out to him on the temple steps. He cries out for all to hear how impressed he is with Jesus and how he will follow him to the very ends of the earth helping him establish the new kingdom. Jesus stops in his tracks. He walks over to the man, puts his hands on his shoulders, and returns the man's broad smile. Only a few people remain on the temple steps given the rain, but Jesus turns around and looks at them with his hands still on the man's shoulders. In a gentle voice, not as a threat but almost as if a caution, he says, "If anyone comes to me without hating his father and mother, wife and children, brothers and sisters, and even his own life, he cannot be my disciple" (Luke 14:26). The words are shocking, but his tone of voice mitigates their apparent harshness. Raising his hands, he continues, "Whoever does not carry his own cross and come after me cannot be my disciple" (Luke 14:27). Abandoning family and taking up crosses does not seem to be the best way to attract recruits, but Jesus wants them to know the cost of following him. "Which of you wishing to construct a tower does not first sit down and calculate the cost to see if there is enough for its completion? Otherwise, after laying the foundation and finding himself unable to finish the work, the onlookers should laugh at him and say, 'This one began to build but did not have the resources to finish.' Or what king marching into battle would not first sit down and decide whether with ten thousand troops he can successfully oppose another king advancing upon him with twenty thousand troops? But if not, while he is still far away, he will send a delegation to ask for peace terms" (Luke 14:28-32). Jesus appreciates this man's enthusiasm but wants him and all to know what it takes to be a real disciple of his. Looking at his apostles, Jesus then finishes his discourse with these words: "In the same way, every one of you who does not renounce all his possessions cannot be my disciple" (Luke 14:33). The rain is intensifying, Jesus and the others are getting wet, and so everyone runs off to their homes.

The rainy season is generally a quiet time in the Judean area, so the people have more free time. In another town, on a day when the sun shines brightly for a change, Jesus sees a group of people sitting outside and having a picnic of sorts. He walks over to them and engages in conversation. The group consists of a family that does not have a very good reputation in the town; some of the men are considered to be shady in their business practices, and a number of the young adults in the family are quite the party-goers. They are celebrating the birthday of one of the younger ones in the family and are having a great time. Jesus spends a good part of the afternoon with them, laughing, participating in their games, and partaking of their food. Some of the Pharisees in the town notice he is with these people, so later on, after the party is over, they approach him on this matter of socializing with sinners. It is a topic Jesus has addressed many times before; this time he decides to use a series of parables to make his point. The three parables he tells here are among the best remembered in all of scripture. Looking in the eyes of the Pharisees gathered there, he begins.

"What man among you having a hundred sheep and losing one of them would not leave the ninety-nine in the desert and go after the lost one until he finds it? And when he does find it, he sets it on his shoulders with great joy, and upon his arrival home, he calls together his friends and neighbors and says to them, 'Rejoice with me because I have found my lost sheep'" (Luke 15:4-6). It is an image both vivid and real for these people. Raising his voice only enough to let them all know that what he is about to say is the key point, he continues, "I tell you, in just the same way there will be more joy in heaven over one sinner who repents than over ninety-nine righteous people who have no need of repentance" (Luke 15:7). This upsets some of the Pharisees, but this image of tender concern touches the hearts of most of them, as it also does the hearts of the common people listening. He moves on to his second parable, this time looking at some of the women in the crowd.

"Or what woman having ten coins and losing one would not light a lamp and sweep the house searching carefully until she finds it? And when she does find it, she calls together her friends and says to them, 'Rejoice with me because I have found the coin that I lost.'"(Luke 18:8-9). As the women are all nodding their heads in agreement, Jesus closes the analogy. "In just the same way, I tell you, there will be rejoicing among the angels of God over one sinner who repents" (Luke 15:10). But these two parables are about something that has been lost. Jesus saves the most powerful story for the last one. He tells everyone to listen closely—as should we.

"A man had two sons, and the younger son said to this father, 'Father, give me the share of your estate that should come to me.' So the Father divided the property between them. After a few days, the younger son collected all his belongings and set off to a distant country where he squandered his inheritance on a life of dissipation. When he had freely spent everything, a severe famine struck that country, and he found himself in dire need. So he hired himself out to one of the local citizens who sent him to his farm to tend the swine. And he longed to eat his fill of the pods on which the swine fed, but nobody gave him any. Coming to his senses, he thought, 'How many of my father's hired workers have more than enough food to eat, but here am I, dying from hunger? I shall get up and go to my father and I shall say to him, "Father, I have sinned against heaven and against you; I no longer deserve to be called your son; treat me as you would treat one of your hired workers."' So he got up and went back to his father. While he was still a long way off, his father caught sight of him and was filled with compassion. He ran to his son, embraced him, and kissed him. His son said to him, 'Father, I have sinned against heaven and against you; I no longer deserve to be called your son.' But his father ordered his servants, 'Quickly, bring the finest robe and put it on him; put a ring on his finger and sandals on his feet. Take the fattened calf and slaughter it. Then let us celebrate with a feast, because this son of mine was dead and has come to life again; he was lost and has been found.' Then the celebration began. Now the older son had been out in the field, and, on his way back, as he neared the house, he heard the sound of music and dancing. He called one of the servants and asked what this might mean. The servant said to him, 'Your brother has returned and your father has slaughtered the fattened calf because he has him back safe and sound.' He became angry, and when he refused to enter the house, his father came out to him and pleaded with him. He said to his father in reply, 'Look, all these years I served you and not once did I disobey your orders; yet you never gave me even a young goat to feast on with my friends. But when your son returns who swallowed up your property with prostitutes, for him you slaughter the fattened calf.' He said to him, 'My son, you are here with me always; everything I have is yours. But now we must celebrate and rejoice, because your brother was dead and has come to life again; he was lost and has been found'" (Luke 15:11-31).

So much can be said about this last parable. There will be commentary after commentary written on it. For now, some in the crowd identify with the returning son, some with the elder son, and some with the father. This story has them all thinking. Jesus merely lowers his head and walks away, leaving them each to their own thoughts. It is late January—day 846 of the 909 days that changed our world.

In another town, Jesus is walking by the home of a very wealthy merchant and sees his steward transacting with the various suppliers. He has a number of critical Pharisees in tow along with his apostles and some other followers. He decides to use the work of the steward as an opportunity to teach about money. Stewards make money for themselves by taking a commission from everyone from whom their master buys and sells items. It is similar to a tax collector, except he does not work for the hated Romans and therefore it is not considered an odious job. Indeed, it is a good job because a steward can make good money for himself. Jesus stops as soon as they pass by this steward's tent and asks them to gather around him. When they have done so, he begins his parable. "A rich man had a steward who was reported to him for squandering his property. He summoned him and said, 'What is this I hear about you? Prepare a full account of your stewardship because you can no longer be my steward.' The steward said to himself, 'What shall I do now that my master is taking the position of steward away from me? I am not strong enough to dig, and I am ashamed to beg. I know what I shall do so that when I am removed from the stewardship they may welcome me into their homes'" (Luke 16:1-4). He has decided to cut his commissions to nothing (and even lower) to ingratiate himself to those with whom his master does business. "He called in his master's debtors one by one. To the first he said, 'How much do you owe my master?' He replied, 'One hundred measures of olive oil.' He said to him, 'Here is your promissory note. Sit down and quickly right one for fifty.' Then to another he said, 'And you, how much do you owe?' He replied, 'One hundred kors of wheat.' He said to him, 'Here is your promissory note; write one for eighty.'" (Luke 16:5-7). Jesus then pauses for a second to let the story sink in and concludes, "And the master commended that dishonest steward for acting prudently. For the children of this world are more prudent in dealing with their own generation than are the children of light" (Luke 16:8-9).

It is a cryptic parable, but Jesus is trying to instruct them on using wealth and money as a means to an end and not as an end in itself. There are numerous looks of confusion in the eyes of those in the crowd, so he raises his voice and repeats the words he used on the Sermon on the Mount in Galilee ten months ago. "No servant can serve two masters. He will either hate one and love the other or be devoted to one and despise the other. You cannot serve God and mammon [money]" (Luke 16:13). With these last words, some of the Pharisees in the crowd start to snicker. They believe money is a sign of good favor with God. Jesus doesn't let them get away with it, though, and pointing to them says sharply, "You justify yourselves in the sight of others, but God knows your hearts; for what is of human esteem is an abomination in the sight of God" (Luke 16:15). These words are meant to sting the Pharisees—and they do. But they also confuse many in the crowd who also see riches as a sign of God's favor, so he decides to tell yet another parable to impress upon them the importance of sharing their riches. Turning his gaze from the Pharisees he calms his voice and looks around the crowd and begins.

"There was a rich man who dressed in purple garments and fine linen and dined sumptuously each day. And lying at his door was a poor man named Lazarus covered with sores who would gladly have eaten his fill of the scraps that fell from the rich man's table. Dogs even used to come and lick his sores. When the poor man died, he was carried away by angels to the bosom of Abraham. The rich man also died and was buried, and from the netherworld, where he was in torment, he raised his eyes and saw Abraham far off and Lazarus at his side. And he cried out, 'Father Abraham, have pity on me. Send Lazarus to dip the tip of his finger in water and cool my tongue, for I am suffering torment in these flames.' Abraham replied, 'My child, remember that you received what was good during your lifetime, while Lazarus likewise received what was bad; but now he is comforted here, whereas you are tormented. Moreover, between us and you a great chasm is established to prevent anyone from crossing who might wish to go from our side to yours or from your side to ours.' He said, 'Then I beg you, father, send him to my father's house, for I have five brothers, so that he may warn them, lest they, too, come to this place of torment.' But Abraham replied, 'They have Moses and the prophets. Let them listen to them.' He said, 'Oh no, Father Abraham, but if someone from the dead goes to them, they will repent.' Then Abraham said, 'If they will not listen to Moses and the prophets, neither will they be persuaded if someone should rise from the dead.'" (Luke 16:19-31). Jesus stops. No one in the crowd makes a sound; only the noise of the regular street activity can be heard in the background. Little do any of them know how prophetic this parable really is, for in a little over two months, Jesus himself will be the one risen from the dead in whom many will still refuse to believe.

As January passes into February, the rainy season is coming to an end, and the thought of growing crops begins to fill the heads of many farmers. In another town, Jesus is approached by a man who announces his plan to give more of his crops this spring to the poor. It is clear to all in the crowd this man is fishing for a compliment and trying to ingratiate himself to Jesus in front of the others. Jesus smiles at the man, turns away from him, walks around, and says, "Who among you would say to your servant who has just come in from plowing or tending sheep in the field, 'Come here immediately and take your place at table?' Would he not rather say to him, 'Prepare something for me to eat. Put on your apron and wait on me while I eat and drink. You may eat and drink when I am finished'? Is he grateful to that servant because he did what was commanded? So should it be with you. When you have done all you have been commanded, say, 'We are unprofitable servants; we have done what we were obliged to do'" (Luke 17:7-10). The man lowers his eyes, embarrassed by Jesus' recognizing his selfish motivation. Jesus, however, walks over to the man, asks him to raise his eyes, and tells him to do as he plans with giving more of his crops to the poor. His slight smile conveys both his gratitude for the man's generosity as well as forgiveness for his proud comment. This event, moreover, has a powerful effect on one of the apostles. Later on that day, struck by how mixed his and the other apostles' motives are for following Jesus, he says with stunning insight, "Increase our faith" (Luke 17:5). He sees how weak and self-centered his faith is. Jesus is touched. It is just the kind of attitude he wants his apostles to have, so he smiles broadly at the one making the request and promises, "If you have faith the size of a mustard seed, you would say to this mulberry tree, 'Be uprooted and planted in the sea, and it would obey you'" (Luke 17:6). All of the apostles marvel at Jesus' words. Yes, that is the kind of faith they want to have!

CHAPTER FIFTY-NINE

A Big Game Changer: Raising of Lazarus

It is mid-February, and Jesus keeps on the move in the outer parts of Judea, taking pains to stay away from Jerusalem. He also crosses the Jordan River from time to time and preaches to the Pereans. He is almost never followed by the Jewish leaders once he crosses the river, so periodically he allows himself that respite. His apostles will also come to understand later that the larger reason for going to Perea is his desire to show his apostles that the kingdom of God is not promised only to the Jews.

Jesus is talking to a small crowd in Perea when two men breathlessly come charging down the road calling out his name. Jesus stops speaking, and all eyes turn to these two men. It is hard to hear what they are yelling, but as they get closer, it becomes clear they are saying something about Lazarus. Their haste and body language indicate the news is not good. As they reach Jesus, the crowd parts to let them enter the circle and stand in front of Jesus. They gasp out the words that Lazarus has taken deathly ill, telling him, "Master, the one you love is ill" (John 11:3). Martha and Mary have asked them to find Jesus, and it has taken a while to track him down. They tell him their fear that Lazarus may even be dead already. Jesus tells someone in the crowd to get them a drink of water while he has the two men sit down. Sitting down next to them, he tries to calm them, saying, "This illness is not to end in death, but is for the glory of God, that the Son of God may be glorified through it" (John 11:4). The messengers protest, saying Martha and Mary are very, very concerned and are hoping Jesus may be able to do something, but he calmly tells them it will be all right. The messengers ask him if he will come back to Bethany with them to see Lazarus, but much to their chagrin he says he will go there in a few days. The messengers are crestfallen, but he, after offering them food for the trip, sends them on their way back to Bethany, while "he remains for two days in the place he is" (John 11:6). Even some of his apostles are surprised at this, because they know how much Jesus loves that family, but they quickly assume Lazarus' illness is not as serious as reported. Perhaps Martha, as she can be this way, is simply over-worried.

After two days, enough time for his apostles to almost have forgotten about Lazarus, Jesus gets up in the morning and announces, "Let us go back to Judea" (John 11:7). Bethany is only about two miles outside of the city of Jerusalem, so one of the apostles, referring to the confrontation back in December at the Feast of the Dedication, points out, "Rabbi, the Jews were just trying to stone you, and you want to go back there?" (John 11:8). Jesus smiles at the question and responds, "Our friend Lazarus is asleep, but I am going to awaken him" (John 11:11). These words cause each of his apostles to wrinkle his brow trying to figure out why he would risk going back so close to the city to only awaken Lazarus. It doesn't make any sense, so one of them blurts out in a tone of voice that indicates his total confusion, "Master, if he is asleep he will be saved" (John 11:12). Jesus' smile disappears slowly; he becomes serious and says in a solemn tone, "Lazarus has died. And I am glad for you that I was not there, that you may believe. Let us go to him" (John 11:15). The apostles let out a collective gasp; none of them thought Lazarus could be dead, especially remembering his words to the messengers a few days ago. They all know, however, given Jesus' tone of voice, that they are going to Bethany, and they also know drawing so close to Jerusalem could be dangerous. With a bravado all of the other apostles notice, "Thomas, called Didymus (Twin), says to his fellow disciples, 'Let us also go to die with him'" (John 11:16). They will go with him now, and Thomas is correct—ultimately all but two will die for him.

Jesus crosses the river back into Judea and makes his way to Bethany, but almost seems to dilly-dally. He spends the first night somewhere between the Jordan and Bethany. The next morning they get up and leave for Bethany by mid-morning. Everyone is surprised at his leisurely pace. Some of the apostles think perhaps Jesus is having second thoughts about going to Bethany so he is just taking his time. In any event, they easily get to the outskirts of the town by the mid-afternoon. It is day 864 of the 909 days that changed the world, and this day will be a big one. News of Jesus' arrival precedes him, and someone enters Martha's house and whispers to her that he is on his way. She is sitting among friends and professional mourners. Their house is packed. Lazarus had been a successful and well-liked man in the Jerusalem area, and, even though he was noted as a friend of Jesus, he stilled enjoyed the esteem of the Jewish leaders and the commoners. On hearing the news of Jesus' approach, Martha gets up and leaves the house. No one follows her, though, as it is assumed she is just taking care of some details around the house. She wants to meet Jesus without having the entourage of mourners trailing behind her. Looking over her shoulder to make sure she isn't being followed, once outside and a few hundred paces from her house, she runs down the road towards him. She cries when she sees him in the distance but manages to dry her eyes before she reaches him. Her heart is so heavy, but he gives her renewed hope.

Jesus sees her approaching and begins to run towards her also. He embraces her when they meet and as he does so, her tears begin again as she buries her head into Jesus' chest. Jesus' heart aches knowing how hard this has been for her. Martha pulls back from him a little, holds his hands, looks him in the eyes, and fighting back her tears says, "Lord, if you had been there, my brother would not have died. But even now I know that whatever you ask of God, God will give you" (John 11:21-22). It is an amazing act of faith in the midst of such heartache and disappointment. Not for a second does she complain about his taking his time in returning to Bethany after he received the news from the messengers. No, she accepts what he has done and has full faith in him. Jesus, drinking from the grief in her eyes, tells her what will happen shortly: "Your brother will rise" (John 11:23). Martha, with the delicacy of refusing to assume anything, responds with even more faith. "I know he will rise in the resurrection on the last day" (John 11:24). Jesus smiles at her faith and softly says, "I am the resurrection and the life; whoever believes in me, even if he dies, will live, and everyone who lives and believes in me will never die. Do you believe this?" (John 11:25-26) Those standing by lean forward, straining to hear his words, but then they straighten back up by the power of Martha's voice as she responds, "Yes, Lord, I have come to believe you are the Messiah, the Son of God, the one who is coming into the world" (John 11:27). Her words hang in the air for a few seconds before anyone moves. Finally, Jesus breaks the silence by telling her he would like to see her sister Mary. Martha smiles, asks Jesus to wait, and turns to run back to the house.

Martha slows down as she gets closer to the house. Her goal is to get her sister without alerting all the others that they are going to see Jesus. Entering the house slowly and calmly she walks up to her sister and whispers in her ear that Jesus wants to see her. Mary lets out a loud gasp, gets up, and rushes out of the house. Seeing her leave and supposing she is going to the gravesite, everyone in the house gets up and follows her. Quickly they realize she is not going to the grave, as she turns in the opposite direction when she exits the house. Mary is running, and in no time she reaches Jesus. As she sees him, she begins to cry loudly, and stumbles more than runs as she gets close to him. Jesus holds his arms open and waits for her. Reaching Jesus, Mary falls at his knees, embraces them, and amidst her sobs chokes out, "Lord, if you had been there, my brother would not have died" (John 11:32). The emotion is too much for everyone and all in the crowd begin to weep with her. Martha, arriving to see her sister at Jesus' feet, begins to deeply cry. Jesus looks at Martha, down at Mary, and at the crowd gathered around him. "He becomes deeply troubled and perturbed and says, 'Where have you laid him?'" (John 11:34). Overcome by his love for this family and the terrible tragedy of death as a result of original sin, "Jesus weeps" (John 11:35). Jesus weeps so hard that "many of the Jews say, 'See how he loved him'" (John 11:36). God weeps. Imagine—God weeps. They all make their way to the gravesite. As they are walking along, some of the mourners, likely a few of the Pharisees who had come to pay their respects to the sisters, say among themselves, "Could not the one who opened the eyes of the blind man have done something so that this man would not have died?" (John 11:37). Jesus chooses not to respond, and as they approach the cave in which Lazarus is buried, Jesus begins to cry again. Jesus stops about twenty yards from the cave and orders some of the men to "take away the stone" (John 11:39) covering the entrance. Martha is startled at Jesus' request and verbalizes what everyone else is thinking: "Lord by now there will be a stench; he has been dead for four days" (John 11:39). Jesus turns his gaze from the cave to Martha and tells her, "Did I not tell you that if you believe you will see the glory of God?" (John 11:40). Martha lowers her eyes and nods in agreement. Jesus repeats his command to remove the stone. The apostles can hear in his voice that tone of authority and power and realize something tremendous is about to happen, so a few of them approach the stone and, with the help of other men, move it away. The crowd all gasps as the stone is rolled away, expecting a terrible smell. "Jesus raises his eyes to heaven and says, 'Father, I thank you for hearing me. I know that you always hear me, but because of the crowd here I have said this, that they may believe that you sent me'" (John 11:41-42). He cannot be any clearer about his origin. Lowering his eyes and looking at the open cave, Jesus cries out in a loud voice, "Lazarus, come out" (John 11:43). Everyone's eyes are on the cave opening, and in a moment they see some shadow from deep in the cave approach the entrance. Many step back, put their hands to their faces, and shudder as "the dead man comes out, tied hands and foot with burial bands, and his face wrapped in a cloth" (John 11:44). The silent, walking corpse stops, and Jesus says, "Untie him and let him go" (John 11), but for a second no one moves. Jesus says nothing, and the crowd stares at the wrapped body of Lazarus. Finally, one of the apostles moves forward and with his knife cuts the wrappings away from Lazarus. First the hands and legs are cut loose and then the apostle begins to unwrap the face covering. Silence reigns as the anticipation of who or what is under those wrappings overwhelms all. Never has anyone seen anything like this before. When the cloth surrounding his head is removed, everyone can see it is Lazarus who is looking with astonishment and confusion at Jesus. Lazarus approaches him and the two men embrace. Both Martha and Mary have fallen on their knees and are holding each other as Jesus leads Lazarus over to his sisters. The women stand up and the three of them, reunited, hug each other while the crowd looks on in utter amazement.

The news of this miracle spreads rapidly. Jesus' popularity soars as people hear how he wept for and then raised Lazarus from the dead. Many people, yet again, come to believe in him (although in truth for the wrong reasons) as the one who has been promised them. If he can raise people from the dead, what can he not do? The Pharisees and the other leaders quickly convene their judging assembly, the Sanhedrin, because they see the spike in his popularity. "What are we going to do? This man is performing many signs. If we leave him alone, all will believe in him and the Romans will come and take away both our land and our nation" (John 11:48-49). They are concerned about losing power and prestige but justify their jealousy behind misguided concerns. "But one of them, Caiaphas, who is high priest this year, says to them, 'You know nothing, nor do you consider that it is better for you that one man should die instead of the people, so that the whole nation shall not perish'" (John 11:49-50). Caiaphas' words serve as a lightning rod, and the Sanhedrin noisily votes and agrees to pursue Jesus' capture and execution. Although they have tried to arrange his arrest and even death in the past, this formal vote by the Sanhedrin adds an official stamp to their desires. Not all are in agreement with the vote, among them Nicodemus and a few other leaders of good will, but these men are silenced by the majority. A group of men are appointed to make plans on how to proceed with Jesus' capture and execution as the meeting ends. Nicodemus returns to his house but is driven to distraction by what he knows will be happening to Jesus, so he makes some prudent inquires about Jesus' whereabouts. Later that night, accompanied by one of his trusted friends, Nicodemus, much like he had done almost two and a half years ago when Jesus first arrived in Jerusalem, sneaks out of the town and goes to where Jesus is staying. Jesus receives him with a smile. Nicodemus says he is sorry, but his arrest and murder by the Jewish leaders is imminent. Nicodemus tells him he tried to stand up for him but was shouted down by the others. Jesus nods in agreement; he knows it is getting near the end. He thanks Nicodemus for coming to him and tells him he will accept his advice and move away from the city for a while. Although they know the leaders have been out to get Jesus, the apostles take this news badly. Can Jesus be captured and murdered, and if so, what does that mean for them? They have given themselves fully to him. Can it all be unraveling? One of them—we know who it is—begins to make plans about how he can abandon this ship before it goes down. Perhaps he can even figure out a way to profit if Jesus' demise is near.

Early the next morning, Jesus and his apostles get up and travel to the border of Samaria and Judea and take up residence in Ephraim. It is a quiet, unsophisticated kind of town, off the beaten path and higher up in the mountains, so it is a place where they will be able to stay for a little time before they are noticed. There are some breath-taking vistas from up there. Early in the morning, as Jesus goes off to pray, he is able to take in the view in peace. To the south, he can look down and see Jerusalem, where he will lay down his life in a little less than two months. He can also see Mt. Olivet where he recently camped while visiting Jerusalem and the city of Jericho conquered by Joshua so many centuries ago, the Jordan River and crossing where he was baptized by John almost two and a half years ago, and in the far distance Machaerus, where John was beheaded a little over a year ago. To the west, he can see Samaria, where he met the woman at the Well of Jacob and first so plainly revealed himself as the Son of God to that Samaritan almost one and a half years ago, and to the north, he can see the Jordan River valley run all the way up to the Sea of Galilee, where he walked and bade Peter to do the same during the glory days in Galilee. To the east, he can see Perea and parts of Decapolis, where he had met many non-Jews of good will. We can only imagine in the quiet of his prayer what thoughts he has as he reminisces about his ministry, knowing the end is near. Imagine—God contemplating the death of his human nature. It is too much for us to understand; nevertheless, after each morning of prayer, Jesus returns to his apostles and uses the time to encourage and instruct them. He must give them all the help he can, for he knows how challenging it will become for them.

CHAPTER SIXTY

Jesus Begins His Last Tour: The Curing of the Ten Lepers

J esus has spent the better part of the last five months in Judea. Raising Lazarus from the dead has increased his popularity, but his enemies are steeled in their desire to kill him. The Sanhedrin has passed a formal proposal to do so. Jesus knows the time is short, so after some time in Ephraim, he decides to make one last grand tour of Israel. It is early March—day 882 of the 909 days that changed our world. The rainy season is over, the landscapes are all turning a deeper green, and many people are working in the fields. Some early flowers are beginning to bud, and the birds sing more loudly; it is the beginning of the delightful spring season. Jesus leaves Judea by cutting west from Ephraim until he reaches the north/south road that goes from Galilee to Judea through Samaria. He makes a right on reaching the road and takes the road through Samaria. It is his plan to make one last tour of these lands—Samaria, Galilee, Perea, and Judea—before he allows himself to be crucified. This last trip will only take about three weeks, but it will be one punctuated with miracles and many enthusiastic crowds. As he makes his way through Samaria and passes the Well of Jacob, he is easily recognized by the townspeople of Sychar, who quickly run to tell the others about his presence. Jesus pauses and smiles as the people come running down the hill to see him. He greets them warmly, inquires about their families and crops, and heals their sick. He has a special greeting for the woman to whom he revealed himself over a year and a half ago at the well. As she approaches him, he smiles at her and encourages her to continue living a virtuous life and being faithful to God. The townspeople are so thrilled to see him that they press him to stay with them, and he agrees to do so. It is a wonderful evening for everyone, including Jesus, as he is here among these Samaritan friends. Jesus says nothing to warn them about his impending doom, but it weighs heavily on his mind as he knows many will be scandalized at his death.

The next morning, he and his apostles bid farewell to the good people of Sychar and continue along the road north to Galilee. By midday they are at the border of Samaria and Galilee and upon entering the Galilean territory approach a small town on the road. This is a village with only a few huts, but on its outskirts resides a colony of lepers who, by law, can never come into the town. Because of this border location, this leper colony is populated by Samaritans as well as by Jews. Sharing the common misery and loneliness of their illness has somehow dampened the prejudices of their healthy countrymen. They work together and try to help one another. The lepers from this colony take turns calling out for alms from those passing along the road. If they are lucky, the passersby will take pity on them and throw them some coins. As Jesus and his apostles come close to the town, some of the ten lepers whose shift it is to solicit alms see the crowd and recognize Jesus. They have heard many stories about him, and so they call out together in a loud voice, "Jesus, Master! Have pity on us" (Luke 17:13). Jesus stops and looks around those blocking his view in the direction of these voices. He steps out so he can have a clear look. The lepers are quiet, as even at this distance, they can feel the power of his gaze. Birds chirp in the background, and the noise of a few children playing in the town can be heard, but otherwise, all is quiet. Suddenly, still looking at the lepers, Jesus raises his voice and says, "Go show yourselves to the priests" (Luke 17:14), and then he turns his attention back to the people with whom he is speaking.

Instantly each of these ten lepers feels something happen to him. They turn to go to the temple, and as they make their way there, strange and wonderful effects take place. Those with crutches drop them as they no longer feel their need, and those with distorted noses, feet, and hands see their limbs returning to normal and their skin turning as clean as a newborn baby's. Indeed, by the time these ten make the short trip to the temple, running by the time they get there, they are cured, and it is evident to the priest who pronounces them so. These ten men are overwhelmed with joy. Some of them go running back into the town, some run off in the direction of where they lived before being confined to the leper colony, and some even return to the leper colony to announce their good news, but only one does something different. "One of them, realizing he has been healed, returns, glorifying God in a loud voice" (Luke 17:15), and as he approaches Jesus, this man, a Samaritan no less, falls at his feet and thanks him profusely for healing him. Jesus smiles down at the man while placing his hand on his head. Then, raising his eyes, looking at the Jewish crowd around him and shaking his head slightly, says, "Ten were cleansed were they not? Where are the other nine? Has none but this foreigner returned to give thanks to God?" (Luke 17:17). He lets those words hang in the air for a moment and then looks down at the Samaritan, takes his hands off his head, and tells him, "Stand up and go; your faith has saved you" (Luke 17:18). The Samaritan stands up as requested, looks at Jesus with eyes full of gratitude, and turns to go back to his old town and find his family. This man is doubly blessed. He and the others have received the blessing of physical healing, but he alone, because of his faith in Jesus, is told he is saved. Faith and gratitude are key ingredients for salvation.

CHAPTER SIXTY-ONE

Jesus Speaks of the New Kingdom

Jesus and his apostles are back in Galilee. We are only some two weeks away now from Jesus' death, but the talk of his being the Messiah and the leader of the new kingdom is feverishly picking up steam among the people. The anticipation is building that he is about to lead some great political uprising. In one Galilean town, Jesus and his companions are approached by a group of Pharisees who try to pin him down on when this new kingdom will come. They hope to have him pick a date they can use to denounce him when it doesn't come about. He sees right through their plans but chooses to make a key point about his kingdom, not so much to the Pharisees, but to his apostles and followers. He doesn't even look at the Pharisees in answering their question but turns his back on them and faces the others in the crowd. "The coming of the kingdom of God cannot be observed and no one will announce, 'Look, here it is,' or 'There it is'" (Luke 17:20-21). He then takes a long pause as he looks around the entire crowd. Everyone feels he is looking straight at them and what he is about to say will be important and directed at them. Jesus' voice gets louder as he finishes, "Behold, the kingdom of God is among you" (Luke 17:21).

His words baffle most of the people there. To those who are looking for him to be the leader of a new kingdom that will overthrow the hated Romans and restore the Jewish nation to its former heights, these words are troubling indeed. He seems to be saying there will be nothing to point at to indicate the kingdom has come, and if such is the case, then he must not be the one who will overthrow the Romans. Moreover, the translation of the word "among" can also mean "within." How can the kingdom of God, this new kingdom, be among or within them now? They are still under Roman rule. It makes no sense. Many of these people wander away shaking their heads. The Pharisees have not gotten the specific answer they want, but are pleased hearing Jesus' message about no visible sign of the new kingdom. They are even happier, though, seeing how Jesus' response has had a negative effect on a number of folks in the crowd. They pat themselves on the back for a job well done and walk away smiling.

Most walk away; only his apostles and some close disciples remain with Jesus. They, too, are confused, as they are also looking for some kind of political leader. They have come to believe Jesus is more than that, but nevertheless, they have held on to their belief that part of his new kingdom will include political changes. They are not going to walk away; they have been with him too long, and they love him too much. Jesus can see the confusion in their faces, but he decides to drive home, almost harshly, the point that the apostles must be attached to him and to him alone. He will not be instituting this great earthly political kingdom they are pining after, but when he does return at the end of the world, terrible signs will precede him. He gets a distant look in his eyes and says, "The days will come when you will long to see one of the days of the Son of Man, but you will not see it. There will be those who will say, 'Look, there he is,' or 'Look, here he is.' Do not go off; do not run in pursuit. For just as lightning flashes and lights up the sky from one side to the other, so will the Son of Man be in his day. But first he must suffer greatly and be rejected by this generation. As it was in the days of Noah, so it will be in the days of the Son of Man; they were eating and drinking, marrying and giving in marriage up to the day that Noah entered the ark, and the flood came and destroyed them all. Similarly, as it was in the days of Lot; they were eating, drinking, buying, selling, planting, building; on the day Lot left Sodom, fire and brimstone rained from the sky to destroy them all. So will it be on the day the Son of Man is revealed. On that day, a person who is on the housetop and whose belongings are in the house must not go down to get them, and likewise a person in the field must not return to what was left behind. Remember the wife of Lot. Whoever seeks to preserve his life will lose it, but whoever loses it will save it. I tell you, on that night there will be two people in one bed; one will be taken and the other left. And there will be two women grinding meal together; one will be taken and the other left" (Luke 17:22-36). As Jesus finishes these words, some of his disciples, not knowing what to say, ask him, "Where [will these people be taken] Lord?" (Luke 17:37). Jesus cryptically responds, "Where the body is, there also the vultures will gather" (Luke 17:37). We do not know how or when the end of this world will come, but it is clear, for some at least, the end will not be happy. For now, though, the confused apostles and disciples decide not to ask anymore questions.

CHAPTER SIXTY-TWO

Jesus Preaches on Prayer

In another town in Galilee, as Jesus is making his way back to the Sea of Galilee to begin his last pilgrimage to Jerusalem for his final Passover, he is approached by some people who tell him they have been praying for the new kingdom and are anxiously awaiting its arrival. In the crowd, as usual, some Pharisees hang in the background hoping to entrap Jesus. The Pharisees wonder if he will respond to this comment with a more exact revelation of when this kingdom will arrive. Instead, he uses this as an opportunity to teach about the importance of being persistent in prayer. He smiles at the man who makes the comment and tells him it is good to pray and to pray with perseverance. He lifts his right index finger up in the air indicating he has a story to tell them. "There was a judge in a certain town who neither feared God nor respected any human being. And a widow in that town used to come to him and say, 'Render a just decision for me against my adversary.' For a long time the judge was unwilling, but eventually he thought to himself, 'While it is true that I neither fear God nor respect any human being, because this widow keeps bothering me I shall deliver a just decision for her lest she finally come and strike me.'" (Luke 18:2-6). He stops and looks around the crowd. Everyone is quiet, expecting him to say more— and he does. "Pay attention to what the dishonest judge says. Will not God then secure the rights of his chosen ones who call out to him by day and night? Will he be slow to answer them? I tell you, he will see to it that justice is done for them speedily" (Luke 18:6-8). Those in the crowd nod in approval; God has heard their prayers, and Jesus seems to be promising the answer will come soon—speedily, as he puts it. But as those words hang in the air for a second or two, he follows them up with a strange comment that seems to muddy the waters. With a somewhat puzzled look on his face, Jesus asks, "But when the Son of Man comes, will he find faith on earth?" (Luke 18:8). Once again people ask themselves what he can mean by these words. Many already know he frequently refers to himself as the Son of Man, so why is he asking this question?

Jesus has more to say, though. He turns his attention to the Pharisees in the background and tells them he has a story about prayer and that they should listen to it well. Looking at them, he begins, "Two people went up to the temple area to pray; one was a Pharisee and the other was a tax collector. The Pharisee took up his position and spoke this prayer to himself: 'O God, I thank you that I am not like the rest of humanity—greedy, dishonest, adulterous—or even like this tax collector. I fast twice a week, and I pay tithes on my whole income.' But the tax collector stood off at a distance and would not even raise his eyes to heaven but beat his breast and prayed, 'O God, be merciful to me, a sinner.'" (Luke 18:10-13). Turning his gaze away from the Pharisees, he finishes by saying, "I tell you, the latter went home justified, not the former; for everyone who exalts himself will be humbled and the one who humbles himself will be exalted" (Luke 18:14). It is both a powerful lesson and a direct attack on the Pharisees in the crowd. The Pharisees have no response but the crowd is mostly subdued waiting to see if either Jesus or the Pharisees have more to say. Jesus looks once again at the Pharisees and, one by one, they turn and walk away. As they do, the crowd begins to murmur about how he was able to outmatch them. For most of them, the lessons about prayer he is trying to teach seem to get lost in the political battle that has just taken place. Jesus, however, is not concerned; he knows these words will stick in the minds of his closest disciples and someday they will understand their truth and wisdom. For now, he tells the crowd he must be on his way, as he will be leaving soon for the Paschal feast in Jerusalem.

This last tour of Galilee has been an interesting one. He has performed a number of unrecorded miracles along the way that have increased the enthusiasm and belief of many people that Jesus is the Messiah. His confrontations with the Pharisees have usually ended with his besting them, so this adds fuel to the fire. Troubling is the fact that he does not really act as if he is going to be the political Messiah for whom they are looking nor are his words full of the rhetoric they expect. Indeed, his words are frequently disquieting. There is great hope that Jesus is the Messiah, but it is hope planted in shallow soil. It will not stand the heat of the events of the next few weeks.

CHAPTER SIXTY-THREE

Jesus and the Little Children

I n a day or two, Jesus arrives on the west side of the Sea of Galilee at the city of Tiberias. As he has made his way through Galilee on this his final tour, lots of people have been following him. Many want to make the trip to Jerusalem with him, as they think this will be the time he introduces his new kingdom. They are curious and excited to see what will happen. In addition to these people, there are, of course, the apostles, disciples, his mother, and the other holy women who can't help but be excited themselves with all the rumors and talk going on. Jesus and his followers pause to form a caravan before they begin the Jordan River route to Jerusalem. It is going to be a huge caravan given all the people who want to travel with him. Indeed, some of the Pharisees, noting the size of the crowd, leave immediately in order to get to Jerusalem before Jesus to warn the leaders in Jerusalem about his soaring popularity and this general sense that something big is about to happen on this Paschal feast.

While waiting to finalize the caravan, people are pressing in on Jesus, but some bold mothers, many with infants in their arms, push to the front of the crowd. Some of the apostles see them doing this and tell the women to stand back and wait their turn. Jesus will have no part of that decision, however, so he calls out to the women to bring their children forward. His smile on seeing the children come to his side seems to brighten up the whole area. It is so clear to all watching how much he enjoys seeing these little ones. With both of his hands resting on a child's head, Jesus addresses the crowd surrounding him. "Let the children come to me and do not prevent them; for the kingdom of God belongs to such as these. Amen, I say to you, whoever does not accept the kingdom of God like a child will not enter it" (Luke 18:16-17). Jesus finishes and affectionately sends the children back to their mothers, who are all beaming with enthusiasm. Many in the crowd, however, look at one another and ask what he can mean by these words. Some guess he means his followers must follow his orders like a child follows the orders of his parents. Yes, that's it, and many of them nod their heads in approval as this interpretation works its way through the crowd while Jesus is dismissing the children. Yes, they think, when the time of the new kingdom comes, we will have to follow his orders like a child—or like an obedient soldier. Jesus will be the general, and we must act like his soldiers in this new kingdom of Israel. Some are not so sure and are about to ask Jesus for more clarification, but are prohibited from doing so as a prominent rich man approaches him. What happens next marks one of the more memorable exchanges in the gospels.

CHAPTER SIXTY-FOUR

The Rich Man

The crowd lets this man through because he is well known. He is rich and a successful businessman, and one who is highly regarded by all in the community. He is neither arrogant nor unjust like many of the successful businessmen in Tiberias. His personality, his fairness, and his generosity are such that all admire him. Approaching Jesus, he falls to his knees. The crowd is silent, straining to hear what will be said. The man asks, "Good teacher, what must I do to inherit eternal life?" (Mark 10:17). It is an interesting question on the heels of the crowd's focus on the earthly kingdom of God just a few minutes ago. Jesus sees into this good man's heart and tries to draw him closer. "Why do you call me good? No one is good but God alone" (Mark 10:18). He waits a moment to see if the man will make the jump from addressing Jesus as a "good teacher" to addressing him as something much more than that. The man does not, saying nothing, so Jesus continues, "You know the commandments: You shall not kill; you shall not commit adultery; you shall not steal; you shall not bear false witness; you shall not defraud; honor your father and mother" (Mark 10:19). Jesus knows, of course, this rich man has done a good job of keeping these commandments, but he wants to see if the rich man wants more—and he does. As if he knows there is more to it than just keeping those commandments, the rich man replies, "Teacher, all these things I have observed from my youth" (Mark 10:20).

This man has been following the commandments but somehow he senses he is being called to do more. Jesus then looks at him, and as St. Mark says in his gospel, "loves him" (Mark 10:21). A radiance flows from Jesus' eyes that is clearly visible to those watching this scene. The rich man can see it, and his face brightens with anticipation. Jesus is about to offer this rich man more, and so with an inviting voice says, "You are lacking in one thing. Go sell what you have and give it to the poor, and you will have treasure in heaven; then come, follow me" (Mark 10:21). The rich man's countenance immediately changes, "his face falls" (Mark 10:22), and for a long time he doesn't move. The intense internal struggle taking place becomes evident in his face. Finally, he slowly gets up looking at Jesus with sorrowful eyes. He says nothing, however, lowers his eyes, and turns away from Jesus. The crowd parts for him as he walks into it. He is "sad, for he has many possessions" (Mark 10:22). Jesus watches the man walk away with a look more of pity than disappointment.

When the crowd closes up again and the rich man is no longer in sight, Jesus looks around and says, "How hard it is for those who have wealth to enter the kingdom of God" (Mark 10:23). These words are so clear, yet, just as in the past when he has taught that poverty or riches do not mean someone is or is not a sinner, they totally befuddle the crowd. Among those confused are his own disciples. Seeing the incomprehension in everyone's face, Jesus continues, "Children, how hard it is to enter the kingdom of God! It is easier for a camel to pass through the eye of a needle than for one who is rich to enter the kingdom of God" (Mark 10:24-25). Most of the people in the crowd are speechless. Not more than five minutes ago they were thinking about obeying Jesus as a soldier when he brings his new kingdom of prosperity to Israel, and now they are hearing that being rich is a problem. One of Jesus' disciples, one who has been less focused on the material kingdom yet himself is distressed about the caution against wealth, calls out, "Then who can be saved?" (Mark 10:26). Jesus responds, "For human beings it is impossible, but not for God. All things are possible for God" (Mark 10:27). His words do little to overcome their bewilderment. Everyone is lost in their own thoughts trying to piece together their perception of what this kingdom of God will be about and what these words of Jesus mean. Their thoughts are interrupted by the cry from the men who are going to be the leaders of the caravan. They tell everyone to make their final preparations, for they will be leaving for Jerusalem shortly. The crowd disperses, each to his own family, to get ready for the pilgrimage.

Peter and the apostles, like the others, are pondering these last words of Jesus. As they make the final preparations for the trip, when Jesus is alone with his family and closest apostles, Peter stops Jesus. With an inquiring look on his face and in his voice, Peter, looking for some reassurance, says, "We have given up everything and followed you" (Mark 10:28). It is a statement of fact, and Jesus looks at him with a grateful smile of love. He puts both his hands on Peter's shoulders and then turns his gaze to the other apostles gathered there and says, "Amen, I say to you, there is no one who has given up house or brothers or sisters or mother or father or children or lands for my sake and for the sake of the gospel who will not receive a hundred times more now in this present age: houses, and brothers, and sisters, and mothers, and children, and lands, with persecutions, and eternal life in the age to come" (Mark 10:29-30). Then, referring to those who are worldly successful, he finishes by saying, "But many that are first will be last and the last will be first" (Mark 10:31). His smile is bright as he looks at this group of men who have given up everything to follow him. They all smile back, bolstered and encouraged by his words. Yes, they think to themselves, we have given up much, but we will receive much back both now in the new kingdom to come here on earth as well as the one to come afterwards. For a second, even Judas, whose faith has been steadily waning, begins to wonder if Jesus will prevail against the Pharisees and the other leaders. His faith takes a turn up from its generally downward path. Unfortunately, it won't last for long.

Chapter Sixty-Five

Last Pilgrimage to Jerusalem

It is mid-March and day 891 of the 909 days that changed the world. The caravan leaves Tiberias, makes its way down the western shore of the Sea of Galilee, crosses the Jordan where the sea empties into the river, and begins making its way down the eastern shore. The caravan is lively, as many are anticipating the possibility that Jesus will do something great at the Paschal feast. There are others in the caravan, however, who talk of the hatred of the Jewish leaders for Jesus and they speculate that the leaders will try to harm or silence him. In any event, he is the talk of the caravan. He walks ahead of his disciples and seems not to want to engage in conversation with them or anyone else. Some of his apostles begin to fear, as they know going back to Jerusalem brings great risks. Others are emboldened by the rising enthusiasm for him (Mark 10:32).

While they are at camp the first night and after everyone has retired to their own tents, Jesus is surrounded only by his apostles and some of his closer disciples. As Jesus has been apart all day, one of the disciples tells Jesus how favorably the caravan was talking about him. In a solemn, quiet, yet firm voice, as if he wants only them to hear this, he says, "Behold, we are going up to Jerusalem and the Son of Man will be handed over to the chief priests and the scribes, and they will condemn him to death and hand him over to the Gentiles, who will mock him, spit upon him, and put him to death, but after three days he will rise" (Mark 10:33-34). As lucid as these words are to us, none of the apostles, with perhaps the exception of one, understands what Jesus is saying (Luke 18:34). Most choose to think he cannot possibly be talking about his own death. Some think he might be using some kind of allegory. But the one exception? Judas, as this talk of death is too real to him—and he wants not part of it.

The next day, as the caravan continues along the eastern shore of the Jordan, Jesus is much more animated. It is a beautiful spring day, and the air is full of the smells of early spring. Jesus' spirits seem high and seeing him in such an apparent good mood causes the apostles to dream all the more about the upcoming new kingdom. Two of his apostles in particular—James and John—are becoming more excited about the new Israel on earth and decide to make sure they will have a prominent spot in it. It is amazing, at this late date, as much as they love Jesus, how much these men remain focused on their own worldly success and how little clue they have as to what is going to happen. These two disciples have the added encouragement of their mother, who is a supporter of Jesus and is herself convinced he is about to institute this great new kingdom. She encourages her sons to speak to him and indeed accompanies them when they approach him at the end of the second day's journey.

CHAPTER SIXTY-SIX

The Requests of James, John, and Blind Bartimeaus

In Mark's account of this episode, the two men speak directly to Jesus, but in Matthew's version, it is their mother who makes the original request. In any event, it is clear what their goal is. With just the apostles and a few others present, the two men ask Jesus, "Grant in your glory that we sit one on your right, the other at your left" (Mark 10:37). The other apostles hear these words and stop in their tracks, glaring at James and John. Jesus shakes his head a little from right to left with a tight smile on his lips as if to indicate his amazement. He says to the brothers, "You do not know what you are asking. Can you drink the cup that I drink or be baptized with the baptism with which I am baptized?" (Mark 10:38). Filled with bravado and emboldened by Jesus' response, which seems encouraging—as if an affirmative answer from them might mean their request will be granted—they both enthusiastically say, "Yes, we can" (Mark 10:39). Unfortunately for them, though, Jesus does not grant their request. "The cup that I drink, you will drink, and the baptism with which I am baptized you will be baptized; but to sit at my right or at my left is not mine to give but is for those for whom it has been prepared" (Mark 10:40). The look of hopeful anticipation drains from John and James' faces as well as from their mother's. The other apostles, still glaring at the two for such a bold and self-interested question, begin to mutter and complain. It is not a pretty sight as words and looks travel among them all. Jesus holds up his hands, summons them all to be quiet, and tells them to sit down. He sits down also, and they form a circle, the sun beginning to go down behind him to the west. Speaking slowly and clearly, indicating yet again how important these words are, he says, "You know that those who are recognized as rulers over the Gentiles lord it over them, and their great ones make their authority over them felt. But it shall not be so among you. Rather, whoever wishes to be great among you will be your servant; whoever wishes to be first among you will be the slave of all. For the Son of Man did not come to be served but to serve and to give his life as a ransom for many" (Mark 10: 42-45). After he finishes speaking, he looks around the circle, but he is greeted by mostly blank stares or lowered eyes. The apostles do not, or do not want, to really understand these words, but the words do have the desired effect of ending the bickering among the apostles, although there is some lingering resentment towards John and James. Jesus waits a second and then changes the conversation, and they talk about how beautiful the weather and what a great night for sleeping it will be.

The next morning is as glorious as the previous day, and the caravan is on its way bright and early. They cross the Jordan River in the morning hours and by early afternoon are in the city of Jericho. The caravan pauses in Jericho to secure supplies and rest a bit before pushing on towards Jerusalem. The closer the caravan gets to Jerusalem, the more excitement there is. Most want to keep Jesus in their sight, wondering when he will be making his move; therefore, as they leave the city of Jericho, a sizable crowd walks along with him and his disciples. As the caravan pushes its way out of the city, a blind man—Bartimaeus by name—is taking his usual place along the rode begging for alms. The Paschal feast is the biggest one, so he and other beggars line the road seeking assistance from the pilgrims.

Being used to the sounds of all the caravans coming and going to Jerusalem over many years, Bartimeaus is taken aback by the loudness of Jesus' approaching caravan. It is so much noisier than most groups of travelers, so he inquires as to the reason for all the commotion. One of the people in front of the caravan gives Bartimeaus a quick glance, and tells him that Jesus of Nazareth is in the caravan. Now Bartimeaus has heard much about this Jesus and feels inspired to call on him to heal his blindness. Looking with his blank eyes in the direction of the growing noise, he starts crying out in a loud and piercing voice, "Jesus, son of David, have pity on me!" (Mark 10:47). It is a request noteworthy as much for its affirmation of Jesus as the son of David as well as for its intensity. As people in the caravan pass him by, many tell Bartimeaus to be silent. However, he will have no part of being silent and shouts the louder and more piercingly, "Son of David, have pity on me!" (Mark 10:48).

Jesus, still some fifty yards away, hears his cries and stops. Everyone walking with him quiets down and the cry from the blind man now dominates all other sounds. Jesus tells a few of his apostles, "Call him" (Mark 10:49). As Jesus waits, they approach the blind man, still calling out for Jesus, and tell him, "Take courage and get up; he is calling you" (Mark 10:49). Bartimaeus jumps to his feet, throws off the dirty rag of a coat he keeps over himself, and eagerly asks them to lead him to Jesus. When they get in front of Jesus, the apostles step aside and Jesus asks the blind man, "What do you want me to do for you?" (Mark 10:51). In words that will echo down over the ages as a prayer to make as we try to find out how better to serve God and others, the blind man says, "Master, I want to see" (Mark 10:51). Jesus looks at the man and can see the faith behind those blind eyes. He smiles and says, "Go your way; your faith has saved you" (Mark 10:52). Instantly, the man can see and begins to thank Jesus; those that know the blind man throng around him to validate the miracle, and the crowd begins to praise God as they realize this man has been cured. The excitement about Jesus grows all the more. Bartimaeus asks him if he can accompany him on his way, and Jesus smiles and nods his head. Bartimaeus gladly "follows him on the way" (Mark 10:52). This miracle emboldens the crowd all the more. Yes, something big is about to happen in Jerusalem this Paschal feast. After all these centuries of waiting in hope, might they be the ones who will witness the coming of the new kingdom?

CHAPTER SIXTY-SEVEN

Zacchaeus

It is getting late in the day as Jesus and his adoring crowd leave Jericho. Walking home from work at the same time is a publican, one of the chief publicans who oversees the hiring of the Jews who collect the taxes for the Romans. His name is Zacchaeus. He is ahead of the big crowd, but from the noise level and his knowledge that Jesus is going to be passing through Jericho today, he figures it must be Jesus and his followers. Now, as we have already learned, Zacchaeus and his fellow publican tax collectors are despised by the Jewish people, yet Zacchaeus has heard stories of how Jesus has shown kindness towards those shunned by others. Indeed, he has heard a fellow publican, Levi—now called Matthew—is counted among his closest disciples. He has heard all the talk of miracles and of the upcoming kingdom, and he is intrigued. Moreover, Zacchaeus is a good man who listened to John the Baptist and later Jesus when they were baptizing at the Jordan. There was something about Jesus even then that caught his attention; he has never been able to shake it.

Zacchaeus wonders how he might see Jesus, for although Jesus will be passing right by his house, Zacchaeus is a small man and knows he will not be able to see over the crowd. Because he is a publican, he knows no one will make way so he can get closer to the front. Suddenly, he gets an idea. The sycamore trees in his yard hang over the wall that separates his house from the road. It is spring, so the leaves have thickened up quite a bit, and he decides to climb up the tree, hide among the leaves, and watch Jesus as he passes by. He excitedly races home, climbs up the tree, moves out on a limb that goes beyond his wall and over the road, and waits for Jesus. He can see down the road and much to his happiness confirms that

Jesus will be passing right under him. In about three minutes the first of the crowd with Jesus passes underneath him and no one notices Zacchaeus at all. He is all the more excited. Finally, Jesus himself comes into clear view. He is smiling and talking with the people on his left and right, sometimes spinning around to say something to those behind him, and sometimes calling out to those a few paces ahead of him. The noise level and excitement from the crowd are palpable. As Jesus gets directly underneath him, without any hint of warning whatsoever, Jesus stops. He looks straight up, right into Zacchaeus' eyes. Zacchaeus is dumbfounded and embarrassed. How does he know exactly where Zacchaeus is hiding? Everyone near Jesus also looks up, although many of them can't see Zacchaeus because of the leaf cover. Jesus calls up to Zacchaeus, "Zacchaeus, come down quickly, for today I must stay at your house" (Luke 19:5).

Zacchaeus cannot believe his ears. Jesus wants to stay with him, a publican—and a chief publican at that. It is too good to be true. With the speed of a man twenty years his junior, Zacchaeus reverses his course down the branch into his yard and rushes to the front gate to greet Jesus. As he sees Jesus smiling at him, cognizant of all his sins, but because Zacchaeus wants to show him that he desires to do well, he looks up at Jesus and blurts out, "Behold, half of my possessions, Lord, I shall give to the poor, and if I have extorted anything from anyone I shall repay it four times over" (Luke 19:8). It is the enthusiasm of a conversion moment. Jesus smiles at him and says, "Today salvation has come to this house" (Luke 19:9), and then turning to face the crowd continues, "because this man, too, is a descendant of Abraham. For the Son of Man has come to seek and to save what is lost" (Luke 19:9-10).

The mood of the crowd changes instantly. Whereas a few minutes ago there was tremendous enthusiasm for Jesus, now "they begin to grumble saying, 'He is going to stay at the house of a sinner'" (Luke 19:7). Although Jesus' favoring an outcast like Zacchaeus is not terribly surprising to the apostles and other close disciples, it turns off many of the newer followers. This is not what they expect from the leader of the "kingdom of God which (they believe) will appear immediately" (Luke 19:11). Jesus then holds up his hand to quiet everyone and tells them the following parable. "A nobleman went off to a distant country to obtain the kingship for himself and then return. He called ten of his servants and gave them ten gold coins and told them, 'Engage in trade with these until I return.' His fellow citizens, however, despised him and sent a delegation after him to announce, 'We do not want this man to be our king.' But when he returned after obtaining the kingship, he had the servants called to whom he had given the money, to learn what they had gained by trading. The first one came forward and said, 'Sir, your gold coin has earned ten additional ones.' He replied, 'Well done, good servant! You have been faithful in this very small matter; take charge of ten cities.' Then the second came and reported, 'Your gold coin, sir, has earned five more.' And to this servant, too, he said, 'You take charge of five cities.' Then the other servant came and said, 'Sir, here is your gold coin; I kept it stored in a handkerchief, for I was afraid of you, because you are a demanding person; you take up what you did not lay down and you harvest what you did not plant.' He said to him, 'With your own words I shall condemn you, you wicked servant. You knew that I was a demanding person, taking up what I did not lay down and harvesting what I did not plant; why did you not put my money in a bank? Then on return I would have collected it with interest.' And to those standing by he said, 'Take the coin from him and give it to the servant who has ten.' But they said to him, 'Sir, he has ten coins.' 'I tell you, to everyone who has, more will be given, but from the one who has not, even what he has will be taken away. Now for those enemies of mine who did not want me as their king, bring them here and slay them before me.'" (Luke 19:12-27).

It is a hard parable. What does he mean by this? Many interpret it as a prediction of how he will rule this new kingdom by slaying all those who oppose him. Others interpret it as his saying that people like Zacchaeus will be given more, and they don't like that message at all. There is more grumbling from the crowd, and as Jesus turns his attention back to Zacchaeus, many in the crowd move away to secure their own accommodations for the evening. The quickness with which this crowd has gone from enthusiasm to criticism foreshadows how they, in one week's time, will change from hailing him as a king on one day to calling for his crucifixion four days later.

CHAPTER SIXTY-EIGHT

Dinner at Bethany

Jesus and his closest apostles enjoy a delightful dinner at Zacchaeus' house and spend the night there. Getting up the next morning, they continue the journey to Jerusalem. Many of those who followed Jesus yesterday quickly join him again, but the crowd is noticeably smaller, as a number have been put off by his staying with Zacchaeus and his story about the talents. From the western outskirts of Jericho, where Zacchaeus lives, to the city of Bethany, which is just outside of Jerusalem, the distance is about twenty miles, which makes it a journey of less than a day. Leaving in the mid-morning from Zacchaeus' house, Jesus and his followers arrive in Bethany late in the afternoon "six days before the Passover" (John 12:1), which makes it Friday, one week before Jesus' death. It is day 900 of the 909 days that changed the world.

As the people of Bethany realize Jesus is approaching, the whole town is excited. He has not been here since he raised Lazarus from the dead about a month and a half ago. When Jesus arrives, the entire town greets him. There are, of course, special hugs for Lazarus and his sisters, Mary and Martha. One of the leaders of the town, Simon the Leper, a man who had been cured of leprosy at some unmentioned point during Jesus' ministry, invites him to a feast the following evening after the sun sets on the Sabbath. He tells Jesus that Lazarus and his sisters will be there as well as many others. He enthusiastically accepts, and, as it is Friday, the day before the Sabbath, and the sun is rapidly sinking, everyone returns to their homes, while Jesus stays with Lazarus and his sisters. The other apostles and followers are the welcome guests of the Bethany townspeople. It is a happy scene as the sun settles below the horizon in this little town only a few miles away from where Jesus will be crucified in a week.

The next morning the temple Sabbath service is jammed with people. Not only are the Bethany townspeople there and the crowd with Jesus, but a large number of people have come from Jerusalem. "A large crowd of the Jews finds out he is there and come, not only because of Jesus, but also to see Lazarus, whom he had raised from the dead" (John 12:9). Jesus speaks in the crowded temple, and, yet again, all are mesmerized. Afterwards, he is surrounded by people who are anxious to know if he is the Messiah. He patiently and affectionately greets and speaks to them all but does not make any specific mention of his being the Messiah. As the day progresses, those from Jerusalem make their way back to the city with many gushing over Jesus and marveling at seeing Lazarus. The chief priests in Jerusalem overhear all this enthusiasm and, already plotting to kill Jesus, "plot, too, to kill Lazarus because many of the Jews are turning away and believing in Jesus because of him" (John 12:10-11).

Meanwhile, back in Bethany, Jesus and his apostles attend the banquet given by Simon the Leper. It is a monumental feast, and much of it has been planned by Lazarus' sister Martha, who also delights in "serving" (John 12:2) the feast. The mood in the room is one of delight and great anticipation. Everyone is wondering what this Paschal feast will bring. As Martha's sister Mary watches and takes part, she wonders what she can do to show her affection and admiration for Jesus—and she hits on a great idea. Running back to her house, she gets an "alabaster jar of perfumed oil, costly genuine spikenard" (Mark 14:3) and quickly retraces her steps back to Simon's house. On re-entering the room she begins walking very deliberately up to Jesus with the jar in her hand. Many stop their conversation as she passes by, and by the time she reaches Jesus, the noise in the room has almost stopped. Holding the alabaster jar up, she breaks it open. The aroma quickly fills the room as she solemnly pours a little on Jesus' head as if anointing a king. Jesus, looking solemn himself, does not move as she pours it on him. Then she bends down and, in a gesture of unconditional service to her king, pours the rest of the oil on his feet, massages it in with her hands, and uses her hair to wipe his feet dry. Meanwhile, the room has become totally quiet. For Jesus' apostles, this is reminiscent of the incident in Magdala at the Pharisee's house well over a year ago, although, for all of them, the pouring of the oil on his head is unmistakably a symbol of his being a king—

and they all note he did nothing to stop her from doing so. But one of them—and an apostle of Jesus to boot—voices his disapproval: "Judas, one of his disciples and the one who would betray him, says, 'Why was this oil not sold for three hundred days' wages and given to the poor?'" (John 12:5). Judas' comment strikes a chord with some of the other disciples, who also begin to grumble about the "wasting" of this money. It is an odd moment, as some focus on the symbolism of Jesus' being the Messiah, and others complain about the cost of the oil. Jesus shakes his head at Judas' comment, does not specifically address the symbolism of his being anointed as king, but predicts his upcoming death, as he says, "Leave her alone. Why do you make trouble for her? She has done a good thing for me. The poor you will always have with you, and whenever you wish you can do good to them, but you will not always have me. She has done what she could. She has anticipated anointing my body for burial. Amen, I say to you, wherever the gospel is proclaimed to the whole world, what she has done will be told in memory of her" (Mark 14:6-9).

The reaction in the room is almost as varied as its number. For most, however, it is yet another frustratingly incomprehensible remark. If he is going to be a king, how can he be talking about his death already? Some are jealous of Mary and the fact that he said she would be remembered down through the ages. For Judas, Jesus' rebuke along with his wavering faith in Jesus' ability to overcome the Pharisees is the final straw that breaks the back of his belief in Jesus. From this moment on, he will look for a way to quietly yet effectively separate himself from Jesus and his movement. It is the saddest of all the consequences of this dinner, yet it goes unnoticed as Jesus invites all to continue with the dinner and the enjoyment of one another's company. The noise picks up again, and in no time the party is back in full swing. Only Judas and Jesus know that Judas' heart has now abandoned Jesus.

CHAPTER SIXTY-NINE

Palm Sunday

The next day, Sunday, Jesus is up early and is praying as he watches the sun rise in the east over the Jordan River. His prayer is intense as he struggles to unite his will with his Father's in the face of what is to transpire in the next few days. Calmed by his prayer and returning to Lazarus' house, he is greeted with the delicious aroma of the meal Martha and Mary are preparing for him. How much they love him! How much he loves them! During the meal, the other apostles make their way to the house to prepare the journey to Jerusalem. It is a gloriously brilliant spring day. The sun is shining brightly; the air is crisp and ripe with the smells of the blossoming flowers. Jesus' mood seems good this morning, and the combination of his mood and the beautiful spring day cause the apostles to be excited themselves that something great is about to happen. Meanwhile, a crowd of people arrive at Lazarus' house as they, too, want to make the journey with Jesus into Jerusalem.

As Jesus walks among the people, he says to two of his apostles in a loud enough voice for many to hear, "Go into the village opposite you and as you enter it, you will find a colt tethered on which no one has ever sat. Untie it and bring it here. And if anyone should ask you, 'Why are you untying it?' you will answer, 'The Master has need of it'" (Luke 19:30-31). These two disciples walk back down the road a bit to the small village of Bethphage and there find the colt just as Jesus had predicted. They look around, but there is no sight of the owner, so they shrug their shoulders and begin to untie the animal. As they do so, out from one of the tiny structures in this town comes charging a man as if he has been shot out of a canon, screaming, "Why are you untying the colt?" (Luke 19:33). The two apostles immediately stop untying the animal and holding their hands up as the owner reaches them, nervously answer, "The Master has need of it" (Luke 19:34). Instantly, a change takes place in the owner. His face, red from running and screaming at the same time, calms immediately. He looks at the two, unties the colt himself, and gives it to the two disciples telling them to take it to the Master. Dumbfounded by what has just happened, the two quietly take the colt and return back to Bethany.

Meanwhile, back at Lazarus' house the crowd has grown as all wait for Jesus to renew the journey to Jerusalem. Last night's anointing by Mary has people thinking he is about to declare himself the king, the Messiah, and they all want to witness his triumphant entry into Jerusalem. Jesus' serenity, the big crowd, a glorious day—yes, they think to themselves, surely he will declare himself the Messiah this Paschal feast. When the two disciples return with the colt, there is a call for Jesus to get up on the colt and ride it into Jerusalem. Some spread their coats on the animal and Jesus mounts. The cries of the crowd grow louder and louder, and they say, "Blessed is the king who comes in the name of the Lord. Peace in heaven and glory in the highest" (Luke 19:38). The scene is truly amazing. Some take their cloaks and place them on the ground where Jesus and the animal are passing. Others run ahead, cut down some palm branches, and place them along the path.

As Jesus exits the town on the colt, he takes the road which ascends up and over Mt. Olivet on the way to Jerusalem. It is sheer pandemonium as the people cover the road with palm branches and their own clothing, wave palm branches as Jesus passes by, and hail him as the king. Halfway up the slope to the top of the mountain, two Pharisees in the crowd approach Jesus as he passes by, walking along with him for a moment and saying, "Teacher, rebuke your disciples" (Luke 19:39). Jesus looks at them sharply, stretches his hand out as if to point out the intensity of all the enthusiasm, and instead of rebuking the crowd, rebukes the Pharisees. "I tell you, if they keep silent, the very stones will cry out" (Luke 19:40). The Pharisees stop, and as Jesus continues along on the colt leaving them behind, the cries of the crowd grow louder still as the chastised Pharisees disappear off the road and shrink back into the crowd.

Soon they are at the summit of Mt. Olivet, and as they reach it, with the sun behind them in the east, the city of Jerusalem comes gloriously into sight. From the top of this mountain the city looks impressive indeed, especially the temple in all its gold and splendor with the sunlight shining on it. The crowd grows louder still at the sight of Jerusalem, their anticipation fueled by the vista of the city. Jesus halts his colt and as he surveys the city, those near him can see tears in his eyes. Why is he crying? Jesus sits back on the colt, lowers his eyes, raises both arms out towards Jerusalem and quietly laments, "If this day you only knew what makes for peace—but now it is hidden from your eyes. For the days are coming upon you when your enemies will raise a palisade against you; they will circle you and hem you in on all sides. They will smash you to the ground and your children within you, and they will not leave one stone upon another within you because you did not recognize the time of your visitation" (Luke 19:42-44). It is a stunning prediction of what will, in fact, happen to the city in the year AD 70—some thirty-seven years after his death. For now, he lowers his arms and composes himself. This has all happened so quickly most do not notice. He begins the descent down the west side of Mt. Olivet with the noise level of the crowd never having subsided.

As the procession comes down the west side of Mt. Olivet, it passes the Garden of Gethsemane on the left where Jesus will be arrested in four days' time, crosses over the bridge that spans the Kidron stream, and enters the city through the Golden Gate. The noise level is so loud and the crowd so enthusiastic as he enters the city that everyone flocks to see him as he enters. In fact, the commotion attracts the attention of the Roman procurator in Jerusalem, Pontius Pilate, who orders his guards to the gate area to observe the goings on. The Romans, of course, have heard talk of this Jesus being a king and so they are on their toes. Yet meekly riding on a colt with no army behind him except this army of followers, Jesus' entry does not seem very king-like at all, and so the soldiers relax. Some loudly scoff at the silliness of a "king" riding on a little colt. Nevertheless, all eyes are fixed on Jesus as he enters the city gates. There are no enemies bold enough to approach him now, not with all this excitement. The Roman soldiers, too, are content to just watch.

Upon getting well within the courtyard of the Golden Gate, Jesus stops and dismounts. He begins to walk through the crowd, which parts in his path. He makes his way towards the temple. Many are convinced this will be the grand confrontation with the Jewish leaders, but on his arrival at the temple none of the leaders is visible on the temple steps. Jesus walks up the steps, enters the temple, and quickly reappears outside. He holds up his hands, waving at the crowd, and then walks back down the stairs into their midst. People ask him if he is now going to declare himself the king and Messiah but, oddly, they think, he does not respond to these questions. Rather, he turns his attention to individuals in the crowd and engages in private conversations. It is as if all of a sudden he does not want to be the center of all this attention. The absence of the Jewish leaders as well as Jesus' sudden change of attitude quickly dampens the people's enthusiasm. In a short period of time, they begin to disperse and go about the ordinary Paschal feast activities. There is still plenty of talk about Jesus, and most people still keep an eye on him just in case something happens, but the mood has changed. As the day goes by, most are disappointed, for they were so convinced he was going to do something grand today.

Jesus walks around in the city for most of the day, almost as if he is surveying it, and avoids any hint of an imminent revolt or declaration of messiah-ship. Even his apostles are disappointed. As the day begins to wind down, Jesus and his disciples make their way to leave the city by the same gate through which they entered. Some people are still following him, but no longer are there enthusiastic chants singing his praises. Jesus makes his way back up the west side of Mt. Olivet on his way back to Bethany. As he reaches the top, with dusk approaching, he turns around to look at the city again. He can see the lights of the city now, and for a moment, those who had seen him weep this morning think he will do so again. But he does not. He lets out a heartfelt sigh, and turns to make his way down the slope to Bethany.

CHAPTER SEVENTY

Monday in Jerusalem

The next morning Jesus and his apostles make their way from Bethany back to Jerusalem taking the same road up and over Mt. Olivet. As they are making their way up the east side of the slope, Jesus notices a fig tree off the side of the road up a short distance. As they approach the tree, he examines it, looking for some fruit to eat, even though the apostles (and, they assume, Jesus) all know it is not the time of year for the tree to produce fruit (Mark 11:12-13). Then, in a comment that startles the apostles with its apparent harshness, Jesus addresses the fig tree, saying, "May no one ever eat of your fruit again" (Mark 11:14). With no further ado, he walks back to the road and continues the trip up the slope.

His mood is different today. He seems much more focused than he was yesterday, as if he has a specific mission that requires concentration. There is little conversation as the group reaches the summit of Mt. Olivet and proceeds down the west side. People are camped all over the mountain, and many greet him along the way, some even hurrying to join him on his journey into the city. Today, though, he is not like a celebrity making his way onstage to an adoring crowd, but more like a stage crew member who has a difficult and important task ahead of him. Therefore, as Jesus, his apostles, and the others following him cross the Kidron brook and enter the city gates, there is not the din of commotion marking Jesus' arrival that yesterday had stopped all the normal Paschal commerce in the temple courtyard. Today, as he enters, it is business as usual—and it sparks the same reaction it did in him two Paschal feasts ago.

Jesus doesn't need or use a whip this time. With a look of total concentration in his eyes, "He overturns the tables of the moneychangers" (Matthew 21:12) and then walks over to those who are selling doves and turns over their chairs also. Enough merchants in the courtyard remember the scene from two years ago that the place cleans out quickly, as Jesus addresses them all saying, "My house shall be a house of prayer, but you are making it a den of thieves" (Matt 21:13). As the merchants scatter, he makes his way to the temple steps, where today there are some Pharisees who have come out of yesterday's hiding. The commotion has attracted the Roman guards again, and they move in to investigate. But before they can do so, a lame man with a pleading look on his face approaches and boldly stands in Jesus' path at the bottom of the temple stairs. Jesus stops and his face softens. He looks into this man's eyes, smiles, and instantaneously the man feels and knows he is healed. He drops his crutch and lets out a loud cry of joy, thanking Jesus.

Jesus then turns around and sees another lame man and cures him. Emboldened by what they see happening, "The blind and lame approach him in the temple area and he cures them" (Matt 21:14). The crowd gasps at these miracles, for never before has Jesus been so free with his healing power in the city of Jerusalem. There have been isolated cures here but never anything like this. Even the Roman soldiers take pause. How is he doing this? Can this be true or is this some kind of staged hoax? As Jesus performs these miracles, he seems to grow more joyful. His smile broadens as he reacts to the sheer, unabashed joy of those cured. Some of the children in the crowd, mimicking what they heard people chanting yesterday as Jesus first entered the city, "begin to cry out in the temple area, 'Hosanna to the Son of David'" (Matt 21:15). A few of the Pharisees, never ceasing to be out of touch, become indignant and object, "Do you hear what they are saying?" (Matt 21:16). Jesus promptly answers them quoting part of Psalm 8: "Yes, and have you never read the text, 'Out of the mouths of infants and nurslings you have brought forth praise?'" (Matt 21:16). He doesn't finish the rest of the psalm, but the Pharisees and all the other learned Jews in the crowd know the psalm continues with the promise of the Lord destroying his enemies. The inference to the Pharisees is that Jesus thinks they are the enemy to be destroyed. As they retreat back into the temple, they resolve all the more to get rid of him before he somehow has the chance to get rid of them.

The rest of Monday is a glorious day of healing the sick, mingling in and out of crowds of people, speaking with children in the courtyard, and even talking with some of the Roman soldiers as he passes them by. His popularity, which had waned yesterday as the day wore on, today is on the rise again as the sun moves towards the west. Jesus knows, however, that the Pharisees are plotting to capture and kill him and realizes staying inside the city too late might be dangerous. Besides, it is not quite the time to let them prevail, so he takes his leave of the city as the sun sets and once again crosses Mt. Olivet to spend the night in Bethany. Tomorrow will be a busy one and the last one in the city before his arrest.

CHAPTER SEVENTY-ONE

Tuesday: Morning of the Last Day at the Temple

U p and out again early the next morning, Jesus and his apostles
make their way back to Jerusalem once again taking the road up
the east side of Mt. Olivet. When they had returned to Bethany last
night the sun was down, so they were unable to see the fig tree Jesus
had cursed earlier in the day; besides, all of them had forgotten about
the incident in the excitement of what had transpired the rest of the
day. As they start out from Bethany, the apostles are all in a great
mood. Making their way up the side of the mountain, they all see the
fig tree. It is dead, its leaves brown with many having already fallen
off, the trunk with a blackish discoloration, the branches brittle. No
life at all remains.

Peter verbalizes what is in the minds of the other apostles. "Rabbi,
look! The tree that you cursed has withered" (Mark 11:21). Once
again, the question of why Jesus would do such a thing to a tree—out
of season no less—arises in each apostle's mind. Many remember the
parable he told not that long ago about the master who allowed his
workman to give an unproductive tree another year, feeding it with
even more fertilizer to help it grow. Here he has cursed an innocent
tree and it is dead. Only later will the apostles better understand that
Jesus is subtly making a point: Wealth and good fortune are not signs
of virtue; just as poverty and bad fortune are not signs of vice. Unfor-
tunate events (even an untimely death), which at first blush might
seem harsh and "unfair" treatments by God, are always opportuni-
ties to grow deeper in faith and love. Jesus' response emphasizes this
point. "Have faith in God. Amen, I say to you, whoever says to this
mountain, 'Be lifted up and thrown into the sea,' and does not doubt
in his heart but believes what he says will happen, it shall be done

for him. Therefore I tell you, all that you ask for in prayer, believe that you shall receive it, and it shall be yours" (Mark 11:22-24). In the face of what is going to transpire in three days' time and the trials the apostles will be subject to from then on, these are crucial words. After finishing, Jesus pauses a moment and then, as if to remind the apostles of another important tenet of his message, adds, "When you stand to pray, forgive anyone against whom you have a grievance, so that your heavenly Father may in turn forgive you your transgressions" (Mark 11:25).

As they continue the trip to Jerusalem over the summit of Mt. Olivet, Jesus seems to become more and more focused. Once again, many of the pilgrims camped on the mountainside join Jesus' caravan. Excitement grows as most, recalling yesterday's miracles, wonder what great things will happen today. It is only Jesus' focused attitude that keeps the noise level down. Coming down Mt. Olivet, Jesus and his followers cross the Kidron and enter the city through the Golden Gate. The Roman guards are in attendance in the background as Pilate has ordered them to keep an eye on things. The people of the city are all anxiously awaiting Jesus' return, and a huge cheer goes out as he enters the city gates. Jesus smiles at them and waves but quickly makes his way to the temple area. This will be a day of confrontation and parables—his last public appearance before being arrested. The Pharisees are waiting for him.

Jesus walks up the temple steps, accompanied by a few of his apostles, leaving a silent crowd behind him. He advances towards a group of Pharisees, chief priests, and other leaders also standing there. One of the chief priests, referring to yesterday's miracles, asks, "By what authority are you doing these things? Or who gave you the authority to do them?" (Mark 11:28). It is the same tired question Jesus has heard from them before. He quickly turns the tables on them. Looking at the one asking the question, yet turning his head around as he answers it so all in the crowd below can hear, he replies, "I shall ask you one question. Answer me, and I will tell you by what authority I do these things. Was John's baptism of heavenly or of human origin?" (Mark 11:29-30). This question puts the chief priests and leaders into a tight spot. They turn their backs on him and the crowd as they huddle together to discuss their response. They know if they say heavenly origin, Jesus will ask why they didn't believe him, yet if they say human origin, the crowd will be upset, since most believe John was a prophet. After discussing it, the chief priest who asked the question turns back towards Jesus, and the crowd hushes to hear his answer. "We do not know" (Mark 11:33), he cowardly replies. Amidst the cries of protest from the crowd at the chief priest's non-response, Jesus bellows out, "Neither shall I tell you by what authority I do these things" (Mark 11:33).

This is his last pre-arrest meeting with his enemies, so he presses the point with them, knowing it will not have any effect on most now, but hoping that someday, when it is all over, for some of these men it will. He looks at the group of leaders to indicate he is addressing them, yet again turns his head from time to time towards the crowd so they can also hear him. "What is your opinion? A man had two sons. He came to the first and said, 'Son, go out and work in the vineyard today.' He said in reply, 'I will not,' but afterwards he changed his mind and went. The man came to the other son and gave the same order. He said in reply, 'Yes, sir,' but did not go. Which of the two did his father's will?" (Matt 21:28-31). It is apparently an easy question, so one of the younger Pharisees immediately says it is the first one, although many of the older leaders realize this parable is meant to be critical of them and begin to shake their heads from side to side as if to say "no." But Jesus makes his point. "Amen, I say to you, tax collectors and prostitutes are entering the kingdom of God before you. When John came to you in the way of righteousness, you did not believe him; but tax collectors and prostitutes did. Yet even when you saw that, you did not change your minds and believe him" (Matt 21:31-32). It is a clear condemnation; in the face of overwhelming evidence, these men are holding on to their own preconceived notions. Their lips may say "yes" to the law of God, but their hearts and actions speak a resounding "no." Jesus will finish this session with the leaders by telling them one last parable that will be obvious to all.

"Hear another parable. There was a landowner who planted a vineyard, put a hedge around it, dug a wine press in it, and built a tower. Then he leased it to tenants and went on a journey. When vintage time drew near, he sent his servants to the tenants to obtain his produce. But the tenants seized the servants and one they beat, another they killed, and a third they stoned. Again he sent other servants, more numerous than the first ones, but they treated them in the same way. Finally, he sent his son to them, thinking, 'They will respect my son.' But when the tenants saw the son, they said to one another, 'This is the heir. Come let us kill him and acquire his inheritance.' They seized him, threw him out of the vineyard, and killed him. What will the owner of the vineyard do to those tenants when he comes?" (Matt 21:33-40). Again, before the older ones had time to stifle the answer, some of the younger leaders shout out, "He will put those wretched men to a wretched death and lease his vineyard to other tenants who will give him the produce at the proper times" (Matt 21:41). It is another amazing moment; the condemnation of the Jewish leaders comes from their own mouths. Jesus knows they are planning to kill him and has them pass judgment on themselves for doing so.

He finishes by making a prophecy based on Psalm 118:22-23 with which these men are very familiar. "Did you never read in the scriptures: 'The stone that the builders rejected has become the cornerstone; by the Lord has this been done, and it is wonderful in our eyes'? Therefore I say to you, the kingdom of God will be taken away from you and given to a people that will produce its fruit. The one who falls on this stone will be dashed to pieces; and it will crush anyone on whom it falls" (Matt 21:42-44). There is fire in his eyes as he delivers these final words, but his countenance quickly changes to one of sadness. He longs for these leaders to see the error of their ways but also sees clearly that their hearts are closed. Indeed, their bitterness and anger only intensifies as "the chief priests and Pharisees hear these parables, (for) they know he is speaking about them. Although they are attempting to arrest him, they fear the crowds for they regarded him as a prophet'" (Matt 21:45-46). Looking at the crowd, the Jewish leaders know there is nothing to do at the moment, and it is better to retreat and plan their next move. They turn their backs on Jesus and the crowd and disappear into the temple.

After Jesus watches the Jewish leaders depart, he turns to the crowd and tells them another parable. They all can see that he has beaten back the leaders. Some think this will be the time he declares himself the Messiah. Even the Roman soldiers are anxiously awaiting what he will say next. Everyone leans forward to hear him better. He won't exactly declare himself king, but the story he is about to tell will imply he is one, reiterate that the Jewish leaders are not to be followed, and prophesy good things to the less fortunate. His voice is strong and his face serious yet not stern—this is a story of hope. "The kingdom of heaven may be likened to a king who gave a wedding feast for his son. He dispatched his servants to summon the invited guests to the feast, but they refused to come. A second time he sent other servants saying, 'Tell those invited: Behold, I have prepared my banquet, my calves and fattened cattle are killed, and everything is ready: come to the feast.' Some ignored the invitation and went away, one to his farm, another to his business. The rest laid hold of his servants, mistreated them, and killed them" (Matt 22:2-6). He pauses here for a moment and looks about. Most in the crowd get the point. Jesus is the king and the Pharisees and leaders are the invited guests. It is so far similar to the parable about the vineyard he has just told the Pharisees. But there is more, and so, after this brief pause as the crowd looks intently at him, he continues, "The king was enraged and sent his troops, destroyed those murderers, and burnt the city" (Matt 22:7). Yes, the apostles and many in the crowd hear these words and think to themselves this is a clear signal his reign is about to take place. But Jesus wants them all to know that his kingdom is for everyone and continues, "Then he (the king) said to his servants, 'The feast is ready, but those who were invited were not worthy to come. Go out, therefore, into the main roads and invite to the feast whomever you find.' The servants went out into the streets and gathered all they found, bad and good alike, and the hall was filled with guests" (Matt 22:8-10).

Jesus' voice is at its strongest and clearest as he finishes these words. His kingdom is open to all, but despite that generosity, there will always be people who will choose not to do their part. He lowers his voice, taking on a sadder tone as he finishes the parable. "But when the king came in to meet the guests, he saw a man there not dressed in a wedding garment. He said to him, 'My friend, how is it that you came in here without a wedding garment?' But he was reduced to silence. Then the king said to his attendants, 'Bind his hands and feet, and cast him into the darkness outside, where there will be wailing and grinding of teeth.' Many are invited, but few are chosen" (Matt 22:11-14). Although wedding garments would frequently be provided by a host at a wedding, it still seems a harsh ending and leaves almost everyone in the crowd, including his apostles, wondering. Only later would the apostles come to realize Jesus' lesson is that the kingdom of heaven is open to all but requires an active acceptance. Meanwhile, the Pharisees and Jewish leaders are inside the temple plotting their next move.

CHAPTER SEVENTY-TWO

Tuesday: Early Afternoon of the Last Day at the Temple

The Jewish leaders feverishly try to come up with another angle by which to get Jesus. One of them, commenting on the noticeable presence of the Roman soldiers in the courtyard, comes up with an idea. "Suppose," he says, "we try to trap the Nazarean into saying something in violation of Roman law? If we can get him to do so, with all the Roman soldiers around, we will have witnesses against him and then he can be charged with treason—for which the penalty is death." It is an idea they all embrace, and, to make sure Jesus doesn't see the trap coming, the leaders decide to send some disciples of the Pharisees as well as some Herodians. In this way, their faces or dress will not give them away. It will be a sneak attack, of sorts.

Having finished his parable about the wedding feast, Jesus mingles with the crowd. Everyone pushed to be near him, but he patiently greets and speaks to all. He and his apostles are offered food and other items by vendors who compete with one another to prove who can be more generous to this future Messiah. Jesus accepts some of the food offered to him, but refuses any other gifts. It is the early afternoon by the time the Jewish leaders are ready to set their trap.

Shadowing the crowd and waiting until he is well within earshot of a group of Roman soldiers, the small group of "junior" Pharisees and some relatively unknown Herodians work their way up near the front of the crowd. From there they call out, "Teacher, we know that you are a truthful man and that you teach the way of God according to the truth. And you are not concerned with anyone's opinion, for you do not regard a person's status. Tell us, then, what is your opinion?" (Matt 22:15-17) In their glee at their cleverness, they have to fight not to smile as they continue, "Is it lawful to pay the census tax to Caesar or not?" (Matt 22:17) There it is, they think; they've got him. If he says "yes," the people will be disappointed in him, for they expect him to lead them against this wretched Roman rule. If he says "no," it will be treason; with the Roman witnesses, it will mean certain punishment.

The crowd comes to a complete silence waiting to hear Jesus' reaction; even the Roman soldiers' ears perk up to hear what he will say. But Jesus knows the malice in the hearts of those asking the question and is not moved by their flattery. Pausing for a second, he slowly walks towards those asking the question, and the crowd parts for him. Standing in front of these men, Jesus looks sharply at them and says, "Why are you testing me, you hypocrites? Show me the coin that pays the census tax" (Matt 22:18-19). Uncomfortable under Jesus' stare but still confident, they produce a Roman coin and give it to him. Jesus turns it over in his hand, looking at both sides intently. After a pregnant silence, he holds up the coin and asks the inquisitors, "Whose image is this and whose inscription? They reply, 'Caesar's.' And at that Jesus [looking them straight in the eyes] says, 'Then repay to Caesar what belongs to Caesar and to God what belongs to God'" (Matt 22:20-22). It is a masterful answer. Most in the crowd smile, the Roman soldiers lean back and relax some, and the disingenuous inquisitors smile nervously, knowing they have been thwarted, and bow and sink back into the crowd.

Observing Jesus handling the Pharisees and the Herodians, a different group of Jewish leaders—the Sadducees—decide to make another surreptitious attack. The Sadducees, although proponents of the Law of Moses, do not believe in the resurrection of the dead as do the Pharisees and other Jewish leaders. Like the other leaders, however, their power is threatened by Jesus, so they decide to trip him up by proposing an unlikely and absurd problem. After a short time has passed from Jesus' previous confrontation, a group of them approach him. They are dressed in their finery and the crowd makes way for them. Approaching Jesus, one of them begins, "Teacher, Moses said, 'If a man dies without children, his brother shall marry his wife and raise up descendants for his brother.' Now there were seven brothers among us. The first married and died and, having no descendants, left his wife to his brother. The same happened through the second and third, through all seven. Finally, the woman died.

Now at the resurrection, of the seven, whose wife will she be? For they all had been married to her" (Matt 22:24-28). In Deuteronomy 15:5-10, which these men have quoted, Moses only speaks of two brothers, but they have expanded the number to make it seem all the more unsolvable. Some even have a hint of a smirk on their faces as their spokesman finishes his question. Let's see how he gets out of this one, they think to themselves. It is amazing to see how patient Jesus is with these men whom he knows have no good will towards him. He does not get angry at their motives but uses their question to expound an important truth on the theology of the body, which some two thousand years later will be more fully explained by Pope John Paul II. Jesus looks calmly at them and replies, "You are misled because you do not know the scriptures or the power of God. At the resurrection they neither marry nor are given in marriage but are like the angels in heaven" (Matt 22:29-30). And then addressing the Sadducees' lack of belief in the resurrection of the dead, he continues, "And concerning the resurrection of the dead, have you not read what was said to you by God: 'I am the God of Abraham, the God of Isaac, and the God of Jacob'? He is not the God of the dead but of the living" (Matt 22:31-32).

The Sadducees have no answer; he has humiliated them. They, too, politely nod and disappear back into the crowd, their faces calm but their hearts seething with anger and hatred for this man who is usurping their authority and making them look bad in front of the common people.

The entire establishment is not against Jesus, however. In addition to some Pharisees like Nicodemus, some Scribes are open to Jesus' words. For these men, it is not about their personal pride but about seeking the truth. On seeing how Jesus has just handled his enemies, one of these Scribes asks him, "Which is the first of all the commandments?" (Mark 12:28). This is virtually the same question another man had asked some four months ago, which became the opportunity for Jesus to preach the parable of the Good Samaritan. Today, though, rather than asking the questioner to propose an answer, he will use the occasion to sum up the essence of his teachings for the last time. Standing up tall, nodding his head up and down as if this is exactly the thing he wants to talk about, Jesus holds his hands up and quiets the crowd. When all eyes are on him, he commands,

"The first is this: 'Hear O Israel! The Lord our God is Lord alone. You shall love the Lord your God with all your heart, with all your soul, with all your mind, and with all your strength.' The second is this: 'You shall love your neighbor as yourself.' There is no greater commandment than these" (Mark 12:29-31). Jesus' words hang in the air. No one speaks for a long time—and Jesus just waits. Finally, the Scribe who asked the question, filled with the insight he has just received, cries out, "Well said, teacher. You are right in saying, 'He is One and there is no other than he.' And 'to love him with all your heart, with all your understanding, with all your strength, and to love your neighbor as yourself is worth more than all burnt offerings and sacrifices'" (Mark 12:32-33). Yes, loving God and others is so much more than just empty rituals. Jesus is thrilled at this Scribe's response, for he sees the truth clearly. The only thing lacking in him now is the realization that Jesus is God. He looks at this man, his eyes ablaze with love, puts his hands on his shoulders and says, "You are not far from the kingdom of God" (Mark 12:34). The Scribe is lost in Jesus' gaze, the crowd is quiet, and "no one dares to ask him anymore questions" (Mark 12:34).

CHAPTER SEVENTY-THREE

Tuesday: Late Afternoon of the Last Day at the Temple

It is getting late in the day. Having worked his way deeply into the courtyard as the day has proceeded, Jesus now begins to walk back towards the Golden Gate. In doing so, he passes the temple, and, as he approaches the temple steps, a number of Pharisees are standing at the top. Jesus, in hopes of converting a few, decides to speak frankly. Looking up at them, he calls out a question: "What is your opinion about the Messiah? Whose son is he?" (Matt 22:42). The Pharisees look back at him with cold and severe eyes, but knowing that Jesus is from Nazareth and therefore thinking he has no connection to David, some of the elder ones realize this is a good time to remind this adoring crowd that the real Messiah is supposed to come from the line of David. One of them boldly calls out, "David's" (Matt 22:42). Jesus, nodding his head in agreement, calls back, "How then does David, inspired by the Holy Spirit, call him 'lord,' saying: 'The Lord said to my lord, 'Sit at my right hand until I place your enemies under feet'? If David calls him 'lord,' how can he be his son?" (Matt 22:43-45). Of course, Jesus is a descendant of David; it is just that no one knows it, but he is trying to get the Pharisees, and indeed the entire crowd, to call into question their traditional interpretation of the Messiah. It is lost on everyone now. The Pharisees have no response and, knowing this discussion is likely to end in another embarrassment, just stare back at him. Looking at the Pharisees for a long moment, he turns and faces the crowd. He holds his hands up to quiet everyone and then lays down his final words in condemnation against the Jewish leaders. Let us listen as members of the crowd, with Jesus up a few steps on the temple stairs and the Jewish leaders at the top, as he lays down the gauntlet one last time. As he gives this long speech, his voice gets louder and louder, firmer and firmer. We listen to these words carefully, sensing the building expectation of the crowd that Jesus will finally declare himself the Messiah.

"The Scribes and the Pharisees have taken their seat on the chair of Moses. Therefore, do and observe all things whatsoever they tell you, but do not follow their example. For they preach but they do not practice. They tie up heavy burdens and lay them on people's shoulders, but they will not lift a finger to move them. All their works are performed to be seen. They widen their phylacteries and lengthen their tassels. They love places of honor in synagogues, greetings in the marketplace, and the salutation 'Rabbi.' As for you, do not be called 'Rabbi.' You have but one teacher, and you are all brothers. Call no one on earth your father; you have but one Father in heaven. Do not be called 'Master'; you have but one Master, the Messiah. The greatest among you must be your servant. Whoever exalts himself will be humbled; but whoever humbles himself will be exalted.

"Woe to you, scribes and Pharisees, you hypocrites! You lock the kingdom of heaven before human beings. You do not enter yourselves, nor do you allow entrance to those trying to enter.

"Woe to you, scribes and Pharisees, you hypocrites! You traverse sea and land to make one convert, and when that happens you make him a child of Gehenna twice as much as yourselves.

"Woe to you, blind guides, who say, 'If one swears by the temple, it means nothing, but if one swears by the gold of the temple, one is obligated.' Blind fools, which is greater, the gold, or the temple that made the gold sacred? And you say, 'If one swears by the altar, it means nothing, but if one swears by the gift on the altar, one is obligated.' You blind ones, which is greater, the gift, or the altar that makes the gift sacred? One who swears by the altar swears by it and all that is upon it; one who swears by the temple swears by it and by him who dwells in it; one who swears by heaven swears by the throne of God and by Him who is seated on it.

"Woe to you, scribes and Pharisees, you hypocrites! You pay tithes of mint and dill and cummin, and have neglected the weightier things of the law: judgment and mercy and fidelity. But these you should have done without neglecting the others. Blind guides, you strain out the gnat and swallow the camel.

"Woe to you, scribes and Pharisees, you hypocrites! You cleanse the outside of the cup and dish, but inside they are full of plunder and self-indulgence. Blind Pharisee—cleanse first the inside of the cup, so that outside also may be clean.

"Woe to you, scribes and Pharisees, you hypocrites! You are like whitewashed tombs, which appear beautiful on the outside, but inside are full of dead men's bones and every kind of filth. Even so, on the outside you appear righteous, but inside you are filled with hypocrisy and evildoing.

"Woe to you, scribes and Pharisees, you hypocrites! You build the tombs of the prophets and adorn the memorials of the righteous and you say, 'If we had lived in the days of our ancestors, we would not have joined them in shedding the prophets' blood.' Thus you bear witness against yourselves that you are the children of those who murdered the prophets; now fill up what your ancestors measured out. You serpents, you brood of vipers, how can you flee from the judgment of Gehenna? Therefore, behold, I send to you prophets and wise men and scribes; some of them you will kill and crucify, some of them you will scourge in your synagogues and pursue from town to town, so that there may come upon you all the righteous blood shed upon the earth, from the righteous blood of Abel to the blood of Zechariah, the son of Barachiah, whom you murdered between the sanctuary and the altar. Amen, I say to you, all these things will come upon this generation" (Matt 23:1-36).

It is a ringing, public denunciation of the Jewish leaders. The crowd is amazed to hear such a public tongue-lashing of their leaders. Never has anything like this happened before. Even the Roman soldiers in the crowd are stunned to hear these bold and stinging words. They are amazed all the more as there is no response from the leaders on top of the temple steps. Is this Jesus about to take control of the Jewish people? Will his next words be ones proclaiming himself the new leader, the Messiah? The anticipation is palpable—but Jesus lowers his eyes, shaking his head from side to side. When he speaks again, his voice is full of remorse and sorrow. Everyone strains to hear him as he continues, "Jerusalem, Jerusalem, you who kill the prophets and stone those sent to you, how many times I yearned to gather your children together, as a hen gathers her young under her wings, but you were unwilling! Behold, your house will be abandoned, desolate. I tell you, you will not see me again until you say, 'Blessed is he who comes in the name of the Lord'" (Matt 23:37-39). He finishes and looks down at the ground. These words and his body language have the instantaneous effect of taking the air out of the crowd. These cannot be the words or the emotions of the Messiah, can they? They all stand around speechless as Jesus, without looking back at the temple or the Pharisees, turns his face towards the Golden Gate and slowly walks away, the crowd parting for him with few, save his apostles, following him.

As he approaches the Golden Gate but not yet outside, he sits down on a bench. Opposite him are some large chests with trumpet-like openings for people to donate money to the poor. As these are the high holy days, many people stop and put money into the chests as they enter or leave the city. Some put in large sums of coins and look around to make sure they have been noticed. Some pass by without putting anything in. Most quietly make a private and unnoticed donation. Jesus is quiet and seems lost in his thoughts as he looks on as people pass by. His apostles, seeing his clear change of mood, are mulling around him, all of them lost in their own thoughts. There are a few others standing around and some who recognize Jesus and greet him as they pass in or out of the gate, but for the most part it is almost as if he is merely one of the pilgrims resting on a bench.

As he watches the donations go into the chests, he notices an old and frail woman who stops there. She is a poor widow, not dressed very well, and seems to be talking to herself. Jesus nods his head at his apostles to watch what the woman is doing. She reaches into her little sack and begins to hunt around at the bottom of it. After a few seconds, she pulls out "two small coins worth a few cents" (Mark 12:42). Holding them in one hand, she combs through the bag one more time with her free hand, apparently looking for more. Unsuccessful with the attempt to find more coins, she holds one now in each hand and pauses for a moment, seemingly contemplating whether this is really what she wants to do. Then, with a look of determination, she puts both coins in the poor box, lets out a sigh, and walks out of the Golden Gate on her way home. Jesus calls his disciples together and says, "Amen, I say to you, this poor widow put in more than all the other contributions to the treasury. For they have all contributed from their surplus wealth, but she, from her poverty, has contributed all she had, her whole livelihood" (Mark 12:43-44). They are sobering and challenging words. Little does this poor widow know what a good example she has given for all mankind.

CHAPTER SEVENTY-FOUR

Tuesday: Jesus Final Words of the Day in the City

It is late in the afternoon now, and Jesus seems tired and ready to leave. There is a group of Jews from Greece just entering the city. It has been a long trip for them, but they have heard much about Jesus and inquire as to where he may be. A few leaving the city point him out, so they make their way over towards him, where he is talking to his apostles and disciples about the widow. Being men of cultured manners, these Greek Jews do not want to barge into the middle of the gathering, so they ask one of the men to introduce them to Jesus. As it turns out, the man they ask is Philip, one of the twelve, indeed one of the first followers of Jesus way back from the day he met him along the Jordan River and brought Nathaniel, now known as Bartholomew, to meet Jesus. Philip is a bit taken aback by their dress, and although he can tell from their accent they are likely not from Judea, he fears they are yet more Pharisees looking to harass Jesus. He quickly decides to ask someone else their opinion. Seeing Andrew standing near, he touches him on the shoulder and converses with him quietly about these men. In a short time, Andrew and Philip agree to introduce these men to Jesus, who has finished his discourse about the widow and is now quietly sitting down on the bench again. As Andrew and Philip approach Jesus and tell him about these men, he stands up but seems to look right through them. It is clear his mind is deeply engaged in some conundrum. He begins to speak in a solemn tone. He looks at no one in particular but over their heads, as if he is speaking to the entire world. "The hour has come for the Son of Man to be glorified. Amen, Amen, I say to you, unless a grain of wheat falls to the ground and dies, it remains just a grain of wheat; but if it dies, it produces much fruit. Whoever loves his life, loses it, and whoever hates his life in this world will preserve it for eternal life. Whoever serves me must follow me, and where I am, there also will my servant be. The Father will honor whoever serves me" (John 12:23-26). He has said words like this before, but his intensity and sincerity seem all the more impressive now. Suddenly his face takes on a look of great concern.

"I am troubled now. Yet what should I say? 'Father, save me from this hour'? But it is for this purpose that I came to this hour. Father, glorify your name" (John 12:27-28). The apostles will only come to understand much later how Jesus is struggling with what is about to happen to him. His entire human nature is cringing at the thought of what awaits him in a short three days. All of a sudden there is a sound from the sky. Some hear words, and most hear what they think is strange-sounding thunder, made all the stranger by the lack of clouds. The words heard by the apostles and by Jesus are, "I have glorified it and will glorify it again" (John 12:28). Jesus seems to take great comfort in these words, and his face softens. He brings his gaze down to eye level and pans the small crowd, stopping for a brief second on the eyes of each apostle. He continues, "This voice did not come for my sake but for yours. Now is the time of judgment on this world; now the ruler of this world will be driven out. And when I am lifted up from the earth, I will draw everyone to myself" (John 12:30-32).

These last words miff the small number who hear them. Many believe the Messiah will live forever, so if Jesus is the Messiah how can he (the Son of Man, as he calls himself) ever be lifted up, or crucified? Only common criminals get lifted up, and even if the Messiah is not going to live forever, crucifixion could not be the way the real Messiah would die. But he doesn't directly answer their question. Instead he responds, "The light will be among you only a little while. Walk while you have the light, so that darkness may not overcome you. Whoever walks in the dark does not know where he is going. While you have light, believe in the light, so that you may become children of the light" (John 12:35-36). Of course, we know now he is referring to himself as the light, but it is all too cryptic to the small gathering of people there, so with the exception of his apostles, most begin to walk away shaking their heads. Although he has moments of great power, this Jesus doesn't seem to act consistently like the

Messiah. The Greek Jews who came to meet him don't know what to think but Jesus suddenly smiles at them, inquires about their trip, and welcomes them to the Paschal feast. After conversing with Jesus, they, too, walk away discussing the strange noise that came from the sky, but more importantly, how much interest Jesus seemed to have in each of them. So with only his apostles with him, he gets up and slowly walks out the Golden Gate. It is the last time he will leave the city as a free man. Next time, he will be carrying his own instrument of death on his shoulders.

CHAPTER SEVENTY-FIVE

Jesus' Last Words Outside the City

Jesus and his followers make their way across the Kidron, pass the Garden of Gethsemane on the right, and make their way up the west side of Mt. Olivet. The sun is low in the horizon now, and as they get to the top, Jesus stops and motions to the apostles to sit and rest a while. They all give him space; he clearly is deeply disturbed and it makes all of them nervous—all, that is, except one: Judas. Having observed the entire goings on the last three days, he is now totally convinced Jesus is not going to prevail over the Jewish leaders. Whoever he may be, Jesus is not the Messiah. Judas decides he will get out now while the getting out is good. Jesus' mood convinces Judas all the more.

Jesus stares at the sun setting over the city. It is a beautiful sight, but the vista does nothing to lighten his mood. He calls over some of the apostles and, while looking at the city in fading sunlight, says, "You see all these things, do you not? Amen, I say to you, there will not be left here a stone upon another stone that will not be thrown down" (Matt 24:2). These are extremely depressing words for the apostles to hear—so much so that the two sets of brothers, Peter and Andrew and James and John, move closer to him and ask, "Tell us, when will this happen, and what sign will there be of your coming, and of the end of the age?" (Matt 24:3). On hearing this question, Jesus turns his gaze from the city to look at the four apostles. A faint smile lightens his face; these are four men who have been faithful to him from the very beginning. They are about to enter into a challenging few days that will change the course of their lives in a way they have never imagined. He loves them deeply and wishes they didn't have to go through what is in front of them, just as he wishes in his humanity that he didn't have to go through what awaits him. Let us listen closely to his words as recorded in Matthew.

"See that no one deceives you. For many will come in my name, saying, 'I am the Messiah.' And they will deceive many. You will hear of wars and reports of wars; see that you are not alarmed, for these things must happen, but it will not yet be the end. Nation will rise up against nation. And kingdom against kingdom; there will be famines and earthquakes from place to place. All these are the beginning of the labor pains. They will hand you over to persecution, and they will kill you. You will be hated by all nations because of my name. And then many will be led into sin; they will betray and hate one another. Many false prophets will arise and deceive many; and because of the increase in evildoing, the love of many will grow cold. But the one who perseveres until the end will be saved. And this gospel of the kingdom will be preached throughout the world as a witness to all nations, and then the end will come.

"When you see the desolating abomination spoken of through Daniel the prophet standing in the holy place, then those in Judea must flee to the mountains, a person on the housetop must not go down to get things out of his house; a person in the field must not return to get his cloak. Woe to pregnant women and nursing mothers in those days. Pray that your flight might not be in winter or on the Sabbath, for at that time there will be great tribulation, such as has not been since the beginning of the world until now, nor ever will be. And if those days had not been shortened, no one would be saved; but for the sake of the elect, they will be shortened. If anyone says to you, 'Look, here is the Messiah!' or 'There he is!' do not believe it. False messiahs and false prophets will arise and they will perform signs and wonders so great as to deceive, if that were possible, even the elect. Behold, I have told it to you beforehand. So if they say to you, 'He is in the desert,' do not go out there; if they say to you, 'He is in the inner rooms,' do not believe it. For just as lightning comes from the east and is seen as far as the west, so will the coming of the Son of Man be. Wherever the corpse is, there the vultures will gather.

"Immediately after the tribulation of those days, the sun will be darkened and the moon will not give its light, and the stars will fall from the sky, and the powers of the heavens will be shaken. And then the sign of the Son of Man will appear in heaven, and all the tribes of the earth will mourn, and they will see the Son of Man coming upon the clouds of heaven with power and great glory. And he will send out his angels with a trumpet blast, and they will gather the elect from the four winds, from one end of the heavens to the other.

"Learn a lesson from the fig tree. When its branch becomes tender and sprouts leaves, you know that summer is near. In the same way, when you see all these things, know that he is near, at the gates. Amen, I say to you, this generation will not pass away until all these things have taken place. Heaven and earth will pass away, but my words will not pass away.

"But of that day and hour no one knows, neither the angels in heaven, nor the Son, but the Father alone. For as it was in the days of Noah, so it will be at the coming of the Son of Man. In those days before the flood, they were eating and drinking, marrying and giving in marriage, up to the day that Noah entered the ark. They did not know until the flood came and carried them all away. So will it be also at the coming of the Son of Man. Two men will be out in the field; one will be taken and the other left. Two women will be grinding at the mill; one will be taken and one will be left. Therefore, stay awake! For you do not know on which day your Lord will come. Be sure of this: if the master of the house had known the hour of night when the thief was coming, he would have stayed awake and not let his house be broken into. So, too, you must be prepared, for at an hour you do not expect, the Son of Man will come" (Matt 24:5-44). These harsh and foreboding words of Jesus are perplexing, and it is hard for us even today to understand what they mean. When will the end of time come? How will it come? One thing does seem certain from these words in the days of the early church: the end of the world was expected to happen sometime in the near future. Two thousand years later, we still wait, and we can only wonder if two thousand years from now, others will still be waiting.

Jesus has not finished his discourse, but his voice becomes less stern as he continues, "Who, then, is the faithful and prudent servant whom the master has put in charge of his household to distribute to them their food at the proper time? Blessed is that servant who the master on his arrival finds doing so. Amen, I say to you, he will put him in charge of all his property" (Matt 24:45-47). Once again, though, his voice hardens as he says, "But if that wicked servant says to himself, 'My master is long delayed,' and begins to beat his fellow servants and eat and drink with drunkards, the servant's master will come on an unexpected day and at an unknown hour and will punish him severely and assign him a place with the hypocrites, where there will be wailing and gnashing of teeth" (Matt 24:48-51). Jesus stops for a moment and looks intensely at each of the four. His smile then gradually returns and he calls together the other apostles. As they gather around him, with the sunset fading over the city behind his shoulder, he teaches them.

"The kingdom of heaven will be like ten virgins who took their lamps and went out to meet the bridegroom. Five of them were foolish and five were wise. The foolish ones, when taking their lamps, brought no oil with their lamps. Since the bridegroom was long delayed, they all became drowsy and fell asleep. At midnight, there was a cry, 'Behold, the bridegroom! Come out to meet him!' Then all those virgins got up and trimmed their lamps. The foolish ones said to the wise, 'Give us some of your oil, for our lamps are going out.' But the wise ones replied, 'No, for there may not be enough for us and you. Go instead to the merchants and buy some for yourselves.' While they went off to buy it, the bridegroom came and those who were ready went into the wedding feast with him; then the door was locked. Afterwards, the other virgins came and said, 'Lord, Lord, open the door for us!' But he said in reply, 'Amen, I say to you, I do not know you.' Therefore, stay awake, for you know neither the day nor the hour.

"It will be as when a man who was going on a journey called in his servants and entrusted his possessions to them. To one, he gave five talents; to another, two; to a third, one—each according to his ability. Then he went away. Immediately the one who received the five talents went and traded with them and made another five. Likewise, the one who received two made another two. But the man who received one went off and dug a hole in the ground and buried his master's money. After a long time the master of those servants came back and settled accounts with them. The one who had received five talents came forward bringing the additional five. He said, 'Master, you gave me five talents. See, I have made five more.' His master said to him, 'Well done, my faithful servant. Since you were faithful in small matters, I will give you great responsibilities. Come; share your master's joy.' Then the one who had received two talents also came forward and said, 'Master, you gave me two talents. See, I have made two more.' His master said to him, 'Well done, my good and faithful servant. Since you were faithful in small matters, I will give you great responsibilities. Come; share in your master's joy.' Then the one who had received the one talent came forward and said, 'Master, I knew you were a demanding person, harvesting where you did not plant and gathering where you did not scatter, so out of fear, I hid your talent in the ground. Here it is back.' His master said to him in reply, 'You wicked, lazy servant. So you knew that I harvest where I did not plant and gather where I did not scatter? Should you not then have put my money in the bank so that I could have gotten it back with interest on my return? Now then! Take the talent from him and give it to the one with ten. For to everyone who has, more will be given and he will grow rich; but from the one who has not, even what he has will be taken away. And throw this useless servant into the darkness outside, where there will be wailing and gnashing of teeth.'

"When the Son of Man comes in his glory, and all the angels with him, he will sit upon his glorious throne, and all the nations will be assembled before him. And he will separate them one from another, as a shepherd separates the sheep from the goats. He will place the sheep on his right and the goats on his left. Then the king will say to those on his right, 'Come, you who are blessed by my Father. Inherit the kingdom prepared for you from the foundation of the world. For I was hungry and you gave me food, I was thirsty and you gave me drink, a stranger and you welcomed me, naked and you clothed me, ill and you cared for me, in prison and you visited me.' Then the righteous will answer him and say, 'Lord, when did we see you hungry and feed you, or thirsty and give you drink? When did we see you a stranger and welcome you, or naked and clothe you? When did we see you ill or in prison and visit you?' And the king will say to them in reply, 'Amen, I say to you, whatever you did for one of these least brothers of mine, you did for me.' Then he will say to those on his left, 'Depart from me, you accursed, into the eternal fire prepared for the devil and his angels. For I was hungry and you gave me no food, I was thirsty and you gave me no drink, a stranger and you gave me no welcome, naked and you gave me no clothing, ill and in prison, and you did not care for me.' Then they will answer and say,

'Lord, when did we see you hungry or thirsty or a stranger or naked or ill or in prison and not minister to your needs?' He will answer them, 'Amen, I say to you, what you did not do for one of these least ones, you did not do for me.' And these will go off to eternal punishment, but the righteous to eternal life" (Matt 25:1-46).

Jesus stops, and a long period of silence follows. These lessons on faithfulness, making good use of talents, and treating everyone as the images of God are barely comprehended by the apostles now, but they are burned into their hearts and minds. They will have ample time to reflect on them in the following days and years. After a few minutes, which seem like an eternity of silence, Jesus looks once more over the city of Jerusalem below them and almost whispering says, "You know that in two days' time it will be Passover and the Son of Man will be handed over to be crucified" (Matt 26:2). These words are so stark, yet no one, perhaps with the exception of Judas, can believe they are literally true. They ask no questions; they seem a deflated and confused bunch of men standing on top of a mountain while the final light from the western sky illuminates the great city of Jerusalem.

Jesus sighs, smiles sorrowfully at all of them—yes, even at Judas. They quietly make their way down the east side of Mt. Olivet. Entering Bethany, they each prepare to go to the townsperson who is hosting them. Jesus will, of course, be spending the night at Lazarus' house, but before they all separate for the night, he tells them tomorrow (Wednesday) they will not be going back into the city but will do so on Thursday evening, the Passover. He puts his hands on each of them, apostle by apostle, looks into their eyes, and the love he communicates instantly raises their spirits. One by one, they leave. Judas is among the last of the apostles remaining there and he refuses to look into his eyes when Jesus wishes him a good night. Peter and Andrew are the last two. Jesus smiles at them, and they smile back; yes, this will all work out fine.

As Jesus is left alone and turns to go to Lazarus' house, we can only imagine the thoughts going through his head. Suddenly he drops to his knees and begins to pray. He will spend most of tonight and the whole day tomorrow in prayer; he feels the need and desire to unite himself to the will of his Father. As we count the days in modern times, it is three days until his death and five days before his resurrection. It is day 904 of the 909 days that changed the world. We will leave it for others to chronicle the last few days. For now, we will leave him here, on his knees, united in prayer with his Father.

Chronology of the Gospels

Chapter	Title	Day	Year / Month	Notable Events / Parables	Matthew	Mark	Luke	John
1	John the Baptist	1	1 Mid-October	John recognizes Jesus	3:13-17	1:9-11	3:21-22	n/a
2	Temptation in the Desert			Pharisees confront John about who he is	4:1-11	1:12-13	4:1-13	1:19-34
3	The First Disciples	45	1 Early December	John, Andrew, Peter, Phillip, and Nathaniel meet Jesus	n/a	n/a	n/a	1:35-43
4	Wedding Feast at Cana	54		First Miracle	n/a	n/a	n/a	2:1-12
5	The First Paschal Visit to Jerusalem	153	2 Mid-March	Jesus drives the merchants from the temple for the first time; Nicodemus meets Jesus at night	n/a	n/a	n/a	2:13-3:21
6	Jesus in Judea; Cure of the Beggar at the Pool; John Arrested	270	2 Mid-July	Jesus remains in Judea baptizing for some four months	4:12	1:14	n/a	3:22-26; 5:1-47
7	Jesus Meets a Woman in Samaria			Jesus reveals himself as the Messiah	n/a	n/a	n/a	4:1-42
8	Second Miracle at Cana			Roman official from Capernaum asks Jesus to cure his dying son	n/a	n/a	n/a	4:43-54
9	Jesus Returns Home to Nazareth			Townspeople seek to kill Jesus after his address in the temple	n/a	n/a	4:16-30	n/a

Chapter	Title	Day	Year Month	Notable Events / Parables	Matthew	Mark	Luke	John
10	Jesus Settles in Capernaum	306	2 Mid-August	Capernaum becomes Jesus' new home	4:13-16	n/a	4:31	n/a
11	Jesus Calls the First Four; A Big Day of Miracles	423	2 Mid-December	Jesus calls Peter, Andrew, James, and John; he heals Peter's mother-in-law and numerous others	4:18-22; 8:14-17	1:16-34	4:31-41	n/a
12	Jesus Takes His First Tour of Galilee			The morning after all these miracles, Jesus is found in prayer in the foothills; he leaves on a tour and notably cures a leper	4:23; 8:1-4	1:35-45	4:42-44; 5:12-16	n/a
13	Jesus Returns to Capernaum	450	3 Mid-January	Peter makes a huge catch of fish with Jesus in his boat; some men lower their palsied neighbor through the roof to reach Jesus	9:1-8	2:1-12	5:1-11; 5:17-26	n/a
14	Jesus Chooses Another Unlikely Disciple			Jesus chooses Levi (Matthew) and confronts the Pharisees at Levi's dinner party	9:9-13	2:13-17	5:27-32	n/a
15	Jesus Teaches About Fasting and Breaks the Sabbath Rules	504	3 Late February	On the Sabbath, Jesus' disciples pick grain and the Pharisees present a man with a withered hand to Jesus	9:14-17; 12:1-14	2:18-3:6	5:33-6:11	n/a
16	Jesus Chooses His Apostles			Jesus names his twelve apostles	10:1-4	3:7-19	6:12-19	n/a
17	Sermon on the Mount	522	3 Mid-March	The Beatitudes	5:2-7:27	10:2-12	6:20-49; 11:1-13	n/a

Chapter	Title	Day	Year / Month	Notable Events / Parables	Matthew	Mark	Luke	John
18	The Centurion's Servant	531	3 / Late March	"Lord, say the word and my servant will be healed"	8:5-13	n/a	7:1-10	n/a
19	The Widow's Son			Jesus raises her son from the dead	n/a	n/a	7:11-17	n/a
20	The Messengers from John the Baptist			Jesus praises John the Baptist	11:2-19	n/a	7:18-35	n/a
21	Jesus Meets the Woman of Magdala			She washes Jesus' feet with her tears, dries them with her hair, and anoints his feet with oil	n/a	n/a	7:36-50	n/a
22	Jesus' Female Followers			Jesus' faithful female followers	n/a	n/a	8:1-3	n/a
23	An Eventful Day in Capernaum	549	3 / Mid-April	Pharisees accuse Jesus of using the power of Beelzebub; Jesus asks, "Who is my mother…"; Jesus begins to speak in parables and tells the kingdom of God parables	12:22-13:53	3:20-4:34	8:4-21; 11:14-23; 13:18-21	n/a
24	Jesus Calms the Sea			Jesus tells a Scribe, "Foxes have their dens…"	8:18-27	4:34-41	8:22-25	n/a
25	The Healing of the Gerasene Demonic			Demonic spirits (Legion) enter swine and jump off a cliff; townspeople ask Jesus to leave them	8:28-34	5:1-10	8:26-39	n/a

Chapter	Title	Day	Year / Month	Notable Events / Parables	Matthew	Mark	Luke	John
26	Another Busy Day in Capernaum			Jesus cures the woman who is bleeding and raises Jairus' daughter from the dead	9:18-26	5:21-43	8:40-56	n/a
27	Second Rejection in Nazareth; Last Tour of Galilee; Mission of the Apostles			Jesus sends out his apostles two by two	13:54-58; 9:35-10:42	6:1-13	9:1-6	n/a
28	Death of John the Baptist			Herodias' dance	14:1-12	6:14-29	9:7-9	n/a
29	Feeding of the Five Thousand	567	3 Early May	Apostles return from their mission; Jesus tries to take his apostles for a break but they are followed by the crowds	14:13-21	6:30-44	9:10-17	6:1-14
30	Jesus Walks on Water			Peter tries to walk on the water	14:22-33	6:45-52	n/a	6:15-21
31	Morning of Miracles; Afternoon of Rejection; Bread of Life Teaching			Jesus teaches about the Holy Eucharist and many leave him	14:34-36	6:53-56	n/a	6:22-71
32	Jesus Confronts the Pharisees	603	3 Early June	Jesus chastises the Pharisees for being more concerned about externals than internals	15:1-20	7:1-23	n/a	n/a
33	Jesus Travels to the Tyre and Sidon Region			Jesus cures the Syro-Phoenician woman's daughter	15:21-28	7:24-30	n/a	n/a
34	Miracles in Decapolis; The Feeding of the Four Thousand	675	3 Mid-August	Jesus cures the deaf man and it seems to take more effort	15:29-38	7:24-8:9	n/a	n/a

Chapter	Title	Day	Year Month	Notable Events / Parables	Matthew	Mark	Luke	John
35	Jesus Confronts the Pharisees in Dalmanutha			Jesus tells the Pharisees they will be given no sign except that of Jonah	15:39-16:12	8:10-21	n/a	n/a
36	The Blind Man at Bethsaida			This miracle also seems to require more effort by Jesus	n/a	8:22-26	n/a	n/a
37	The Confession of Peter			"You are the Christ...," says Peter, and Jesus says the church will be built on Peter	16:13-20	8:27-39	9:18-20	n/a
38	The First Prophecy of the Passion			Jesus tells Peter, "Get behind me Satan"	16:21-28	8:30-9:1	9:21-27	n/a
39	The Transfiguration	693	3 Early September	Jesus shows his glory to Peter, James, and John	17:1-13	9:2-13	9:28-36	n/a
40	The Demonic Boy			The boy's father confesses, "I believe, help my unbelief"	17:14-21	9:14-29	9:37-43	n/a
41	Jesus Takes a Mini-Tour of Galilee			Second prophecy of the Passion; apostles argue about who will be the greatest among them; Jesus pays the temple tax from a fish's mouth; parables of lost sheep; wicked servant who would not forgive his fellow servant	17:22-18:35	9:30-50	9:43-50	n/a
42	Journey to the Feast of Tabernacles	729	3 Early October	Jesus not welcomed in Samaritan towns; revisits his friends in Sycar, but two refuse his invitation to follow him	n/a	n/a	n/a	7:1-13

Chapter	Title	Day	Year Month	Notable Events / Parables	Matthew	Mark	Luke	John
43	Jesus Arrives at the Feast of Tabernacles	738	3 Mid-October	Jesus tells the Pharisees he comes from above	n/a	n/a	9:51-56	7:14-36
44	Jesus at the Feast of Tabernacles			Guards can't arrest him because "no one speaks like him"	n/a	n/a	n/a	7:37-53
45	The Woman Caught in Adultery			Teaching on divorce and forgiveness	19:1-12	10:1-12	n/a	8:1-11
46	Last Hours of the Feast of Tabernacles			Jesus says he is the "I AM" and many move to stone him, but he disappears	n/a	n/a	n/a	8:12-59
47	The Man Born Blind	747	3 Late October	Jesus cures a blind man who challenges the Pharisees when they question him; the blind man's parents are afraid when summoned by the Pharisees	n/a	n/a	n/a	9:1-41
48	The Parable of the Good Shepherd; The Mission of the Seventy-Two			Jesus condemns some cities for their lack of faith and sends out 72 other disciples with his 12 apostles	11:20-24	n/a	10:1-16	10:1-21
49	The Return of the Seventy-Two			"Come to me all you who are labored and burdened"	11:25-30	n/a	10:17-24	n/a
50	Parable of the Good Samaritan	765	3 Mid-November	Jesus responds to a question about who is my neighbor	n/a	n/a	10:25-37	n/a
51	Jesus Dines with Martha and Mary	774	3 Late November	Mary sits at Jesus' feet while Martha makes the final preparations for the meal	n/a	n/a	10:38-42	n/a

Chapter	Title	Day	Year Month	Notable Events / Parables	Matthew	Mark	Luke	John
52	Another Turning Point: Jesus Dines with a Judean Pharisee			Challenges the Pharisees at the dinner party; severity of blaspheming against the Holy Spirit	n/a	n/a	11:37-54	n/a
53	Jesus Continues His Tour of Judea			Parables of building a bigger barn, the birds of the air, the servant who is on watch; Jesus explains the parables to Peter and the others	n/a	n/a	12:1-48	n/a
54	More Harsh Warnings from Jesus in Judea	810	3 Late December	Jesus says he has come to set a "daughter against her mother"; Jesus talks about some current events; parable of the fig tree	n/a	n/a	12:49-13:9	n/a
55	Jesus Cures a Crippled Woman on the Sabbath			More kingdom of God parables	n/a	n/a	13:10-17	n/a
56	The Feast of the Dedication			Pharisees try to stone Jesus for blasphemy; Jesus laments how he would gather Jerusalem under his wing	n/a	n/a	13:22-35	10:22-39
57	Another Sabbath Healing; Jesus Heals the Man with Dropsy			Jesus tells the Pharisees not to seek the seat of honor at a dinner party	n/a	n/a	14:1-24	n/a
58	Jesus Continues Visiting Judean Towns	846	4 Late January	Parables of the one lost sheep, the woman who loses a valuable coin, the prodigal son, the poor man and Lazarus	n/a	n/a	14:25-17:10	n/a

Chapter	Title	Day	Year Month	Notable Events / Parables	Matthew	Mark	Luke	John
59	A Big Game Changer: Raising of Lazarus	864	4 Mid-February	Caiaphas tells the other Pharisees, "It is better one man dies…"; Jesus leaves for Ephraim	n/a	n/a	n/a	11:1-54
60	Jesus Begins His Last Tour; Curing of the Ten Lepers	882	4 Early March	Jesus goes from Ephraim through Samaria back into Galilee for the last time	n/a	n/a	17:11-19	n/a
61	Jesus Speaks of the New Kingdom			Jesus provides a glimpse of the end of the world	24:23-41	13:21-23	17:20-37	n/a
62	Jesus Teaches on Prayer			Widow and the dishonest judge; Pharisee/tax collector praying in the temple	n/a	n/a	18:1-14	n/a
63	Jesus and the Little Children			"Whoever does not accept the kingdom of God like a child…"	19:13-15	10:13-16	18:15-17	n/a
64	The Rich Man			He goes away sad because he has many possessions	19:16-20:16	10:17-31	18:18-30	n/a
65	Final Pilgrimage to Jerusalem	891	4 Mid-March	Third prophecy of the Passion	20:17-19	10:32-34	18:31-34	11:55-57
66	The Requests of James, John, and Blind Bartimaeus			"Master, I want to see"	20:20-34	10:35-52	18:35-43	n/a
67	Zacchaeus			Parable of the talents	n/a	n/a	19:1-28	n/a

Chapter	Title	Day	Year Month	Notable Events / Parables	Matthew	Mark	Luke	John
68	Dinner at Bethany	900	4 Late March	Judas asks why the ointment was not sold instead of poured on Jesus' feet	26:6-13	14:3-9	n/a	12:1-11
69	Palm Sunday			Is this the day Jesus will declare himself the Messiah?	21: 1-11	11:1-11	19:29-44	12:12-19
70	Monday in Jerusalem			Second cleansing of the temple	21:12-19	11:12-19	19:45-48 21:37-38	
71	Tuesday: Morning of the Last Day at the Temple			Parables of the two sons, the vineyard owner, and the king who gave a wedding feast	21:20-22:14	11:20-12:12	20:1-19	n/a
72	Tuesday: Early Afternoon of the Last Day at the Temple			Render to Caesar; woman married to seven brothers; the first of all Commandments	22:15-40	12:13-34	20:20-40	n/a
73	Tuesday: Later Afternoon of the Last Day at the Temple			Messiah is David's son?; "Woe to you, Scribes and Pharisees" speech; lament over Jerusalem; poor widow gives her only coins	22:41-23:39	12:35-44	20:41-21:4	n/a
74	Tuesday: Jesus' Final Words of the Day in the City			Jesus meets the Greek Jews; voice in the thunder	n/a	n/a	n/a	12:20-36
75	Jesus' Last Words Outside the City			End of the world discourse; wise and foolish virgins; another parable of talents; separating goats from the sheep at the Last Judgment	24:1-25:26	13:1-37	21:5-36	n/a

About the Author

Robert J. Dunne III, grew up in Bergen County, NJ. He went to Saint Joseph Regional High School in Montvale, NJ; Columbia University in NY for his B.A. degree; and the University of Chicago for his M.B.A. degree.

Bob spent most of his professional career working on Wall Street where he became a Managing Director at Salomon Brothers Inc. He left Wall Street to start a children's learning center in Lawrence, NJ. Since selling that business, he has been active in giving investment advice and volunteering for many charitable associations. He has been married to Paula since October 20, 1984, and counts that day as the best in his life. Bob and his wife are blessed with three children: Christina Marion Dunne; Robert J. Dunne IV; and Nicole Emily Dunne, all of whom, along with his wife, he numbers as his greatest blessings.

This is the first book written by Robert J. Dunne III. It is the fruit of many years of personal prayer, study, and reflection.

About Leonine Publishers

Leonine Publishers LLC makes fine Catholic literature available to Catholics throughout the English-speaking world. Leonine Publishers offers an innovative "hybrid" approach to book publication that helps authors as well as readers. Please visit our web site at www.leoninepublishers.com to learn more about us. Browse our online bookstore to find more solid Catholic titles to uplift, challenge, and inspire.

Our patron and namesake is Pope Leo XIII, a prudent, yet uncompromising pope during the stormy years at the close of the 19th century. Please join us as we ask his intercession for our family of readers and authors.

Do you have a book inside you? Visit our web site today. Leonine Publishers accepts manuscripts from Catholic authors like you. If your book is selected for publication, you will have an active part in the production process. This book is an example of our growing selection of literature for the busy Catholic reader of the 21st century.

www.leoninepublishers.com

CPSIA information can be obtained
at www.ICGtesting.com
Printed in the USA
FFOW02n1932280514
5556FF